Mrs. T. R. K. DAVEY
THE OLD RECTORY
COLD ASHTON
Nr. CHIPPENHAM
WILTS. SN14 8JU
TEL: MARSHFIELD 310

HE whom this scroll commemorates was numbered among those who, at the call of King and Country, left all that was dear to them, endured hardness, faced danger, and finally passed out of the sight of men by the path of duty and self-sacrifice, giving up their own lives that others might live in freedom. Let those who come after see to it that his name be not forgotten.

Capt. the Revd. Charles Edmund Doudney
Army Chaplains Department

'The beloved Chaplain Doudney, of 16th Infantry Brigade, had been killed at Ypres, October 16th 1915'. (Tubby Clayton, p.6, TALES OF TALBOT HOUSE).

THE BEST OF
GOOD FELLOWS

The Diaries and Memoirs of
The Rev. Charles Edmund Doudney,
M.A.,C.F. (1871-1915)

Compiled by Jonathan Horne.

Foreword by Major Tonie Holt.

IN MEMORY OF MY GRANDFATHER

'LEST WE FORGET'

© Jonathan Horne Publications 1995

All rights reserved.
No part of this publication may be reproduced,
stored in a retrieval system or transmitted, in any form
or by means, electronic, mechanical, photocopying, recording
or otherwise, without the prior permission of the publisher.

ISBN 0 9512140 8 X

First Published in 1995

JHP

Maps by Steve Freeman
Designed and produced by
David Hewitt Graphics

Contents

Foreword by Major Tonie Holt   7

Preface   9

Introduction   12

Chapter 1   Life in the Australian Outback   25
Chapter 2   A Parish in Bath   63
Chapter 3   Europe in Turmoil   85
Chapter 4   Base Hospital, Rouen   107
Chapter 5   Called to the Front   123
Chapter 6   The War Continues   137
Chapter 7   Home on Sick Leave   151
Chapter 8   Return to the Front   159
Chapter 9   The Final Days   171

Obituaries and Letters of Sympathy   181

Index   193

Maps   South Australia   28
            Europe - 1914   84
            Ypres - Poperinghe   128

I am indebted to the Imperial War Museum for allowing their photographs to be used in this book. Front cover and pages 132, 133, 136, 139, 141, 142, 148, 156, 161.

'Dead in Flanders'
dedicated to the Rev. C. E. Doudney

We laid him where his fallen comrades lie,
Behind the far-flung trenches ceaseless roar.
Brave heart, great heart, pierced by the bolts that fly,
From the cruel forge of War.

Priest of the creed of peace, yet so strong to dare,
He came to heal and hearten men that smite,
For all things holy and for all things fair,
The hell-born creed of might.

And here, where truth at last can conquer lies,
And more than mortals dreams' the Spirit gives,
God bade him offer love's last sacrifice,
Life that in dying lives.

So leave him, while the autumn shadows lower,
And darker still the war clouds hurry by,
And the warrior-saint who faced his hour,
Of travail worthily.

Count him not dead, nor quenched the fiery spark
Of the Spirit which thus with duty kept its tryst,
The swift shell struck- the pang- the mist- the dark!
And then- the Face of Christ!

Flanders October 1915.   Canon F.B. Macnutt.

Canon Macnutt, who ministered to the Rev. C.E. Doudney in his last hours, served with the Expeditionary Force in Flanders as Chaplain to the Forces, Residentiary Canon of Southwark Cathedral and Vicar of St. Matthew's, Surbiton.

Foreword

The padre has been part of the British Army for over 600 years. During the two World Wars of this century he was part of the Establishment fabric that shaped the military hierarchy. The ordinary soldier had little time for organised religion and for many in peace-time the padre was just another officer - one who worked on Sundays and was responsible for the hated church parades. But in war-time the padre frequently lost his Establishment image, and by sharing the discomforts of the front line soldier formed a true communion with those he tended.

There were just over 100 padres with the Army in 1914 and nearly 3,500 four years later. Perhaps the best known of them all was 'Woodbine Willy', Geoffrey Anketell Studdert Kennedy, whose plain speaking, simple poetry and Woodbine-distributing visits to the front line, endeared him to the ordinary soldier if not to the generals.

Another 'soldiers' friend' was Tubby Clayton, who opened Talbot House in Poperinghe as a 'Soldiers Rest' in memory of Gilbert Talbot, youngest son of the Bishop of Winchester, who was killed in the Ypres Salient in July 1915. Tubby, like Woodbine Willy, went on to become as well known in peace as he had been in war, while the movement he began, Toc H, is today an international Christian organisation.

This story is about another padre, Captain the Reverend Charles Edmund Doudney. It has been put together by his grandson, Jonathan Horne, from diaries, letters and accounts sent by Doudney to his local Bath papers. Doudney was a committed parish priest who loved his parishioners and they him, and who, through his writings, determined to maintain his links with home even while at the front line.

He was ordained deacon at the age of 23 and in 1896 began a ten-year stint in Australia as a missionary, including some time as a chaplain to the Commonwealth troops in South Australia. In 1906 he and his wife Zoe returned to England and were installed in the vicarage at St Luke's, South Lyncombe, Bath, where 'Charlie', as he was popularly known, embarked upon a busy life of fêtes, garden parties, fund raising and innovative ideas that filled his church.

In November 1914, in response to the possiblilty of invasion by Germans, the city of Bath formed a corps known as the Athlete's Volunteer Force and Charlie commanded one of the platoons. Two months later he was a Captain and in March 1915 he preached to over 500 men at the corps' first church parade at St Luke's. The following month, in response to a request from the Chaplain-General, Bishop Taylor-Smith, he left for France as a temporary Army Chaplain. He was 44 years old.

Doudney served mainly in the Ypres Salient or just behind it. During the early stages of the war chaplains were attached to medical units only and were more occupied with burials and visiting the dangerously ill in hospital than in holding services, returning at the end of a day to their own HQ. Doudney worked with 18th Field Ambulance (18th Brigade of 6th Division) in an advanced Dressing Station set up in the hop store in Valmertinghe. That hop store still exists today and can easily be recognised from the photograph in this book. But he didn't just stay in Vlamertinghe, he went out and about to the front line.

His accounts of moving around the battlefield have the same truthful immediacy as the poetry of Studdert Kennedy. In particular his discription of conducting burials in wet trenches is reminiscent of Studdert Kennedy's poem 'His Mate' and the search for the 'sodden dead'. Those visits to the forward areas would most certainly have been made by Doudney because he wanted to make them, not because he had been ordered to do so, and his description of visiting the Potyze Château area where the 18th Ambulance had an Aid Post, can be followed on the ground even now, since both the Chateau and its attendant wood are the sites of the Commonwealth War Cemeteries.

Just as back at home Doudney worked to establish a community of parishioners, so at the Salient he strived to encourage a community of soldiers through visiting the front line units and holding services. A piano was for him an essential part of his calling, the focus for hymns and prayer, and he 'looted' (his words) one from Ypres in June 1915. Charlie and the other Chaplains of the Sixth Division had frequent policy meetings at which, amongst other things, was discussed the setting up of a rest house for soldiers of all ranks. This idea was taken up by Charlie's replacement and became known as Talbot House.

On Wednesday 13 October 1915, while out on a burial party, Charlie was mortally wounded. At first it was thought that he might pull through, but on Saturday evening Charlie died.

Charlie's replacement was Tubby Clayton, and it cannot be too far fetched to imagine that he was inspired by Charlie's ministry. In his book 'Tales of Talbot House' he refers to Charlie as 'beloved Chaplain Doudney of 16th Infantry Brigade' and certainly Tubby recognised the worth of the padre whose wife had over 200 letters of condolence.

Major Tonie Holt.

Preface

For many years, my mother, Joy Poulden Horne (née Doudney), wanted to visit her father's grave in Belgium. Knowing almost nothing about my grandfather other than that he had been a padre killed during the First World War, I was prompted to do a little research. Looking through old family papers, I found an album containing newspaper cuttings which had been kept by Mrs. Edith Gollmick, one of my grandfather's sisters. The cuttings were mainly accounts written by Grandfather of his experiences at the front. It seemed that he had been sending reports back home for publication in the local papers. The entries were so fascinating that I had difficulty in putting down the album. As these cuttings contained only part of the story, many hours were spent digging into the archives of Bath Reference Library. During this research, it became evident that he was no ordinary man. I also discovered that Grandfather had undertaken missionary work in South Australia as a young man, but alas the information was sketchy and I had only a few old letters and notes to go on. And then as luck would have it a bundle of papers tied together with red, white and blue ribbon, carefully preserved by my grandmother, Zoe, came to light at my aunt's house. If I had not been working on this manuscript at the time, I would not have realised their significance or connected them with Grandfather as they were written anonymously. Close scrutiny and comparison with private letters confirmed my grandfather's authorship and revealed vivid and sensitive stories of life in the South Australian outback during the 1890s.

The Rev. Charles Edmund Doudney was known as 'Charlie' by many of his contemporaries and this is how he is referred to in this text. As far as possible I have used quotations drawn from archives, newspaper cuttings, letters, other documents and the few people who still remembered him. The mass of material that has been unearthed has made decisions on what to leave out the most difficult aspect of this publication.

I am sincerely grateful to my mother and Aunt Désirée for their help, support and encouragement in this project; also to cousins Arthur and Sybil Doudney, Ivy Gollmick and Luther's son Edward Poulden for their assistance with family history. I would like to thank in particular Mr. R.C. Kedge, who has allowed me to dip into his booklet, 'The First Hundred Years of St. Luke's Church', and Mr. Willis at the Imperial War Museum for his patience and helpfulness in chasing shadows and coming up with much useful information.

A special mention must go to Leslie Grigsby for her assistance in the presentation and editing of the script and also to Dot Jellinek. I am also indebted to Louise Clement, Jayne Dearman, Jill Gosling, Charlotte Haw, Stephen Campbell, John Jeffcott, Beatrice Peraire, Gayle Simpson, Debbie Sugg, Anna Wilson and to all those others who have helped and contributed towards the production of this book.

Jonathan Horne, 1995.

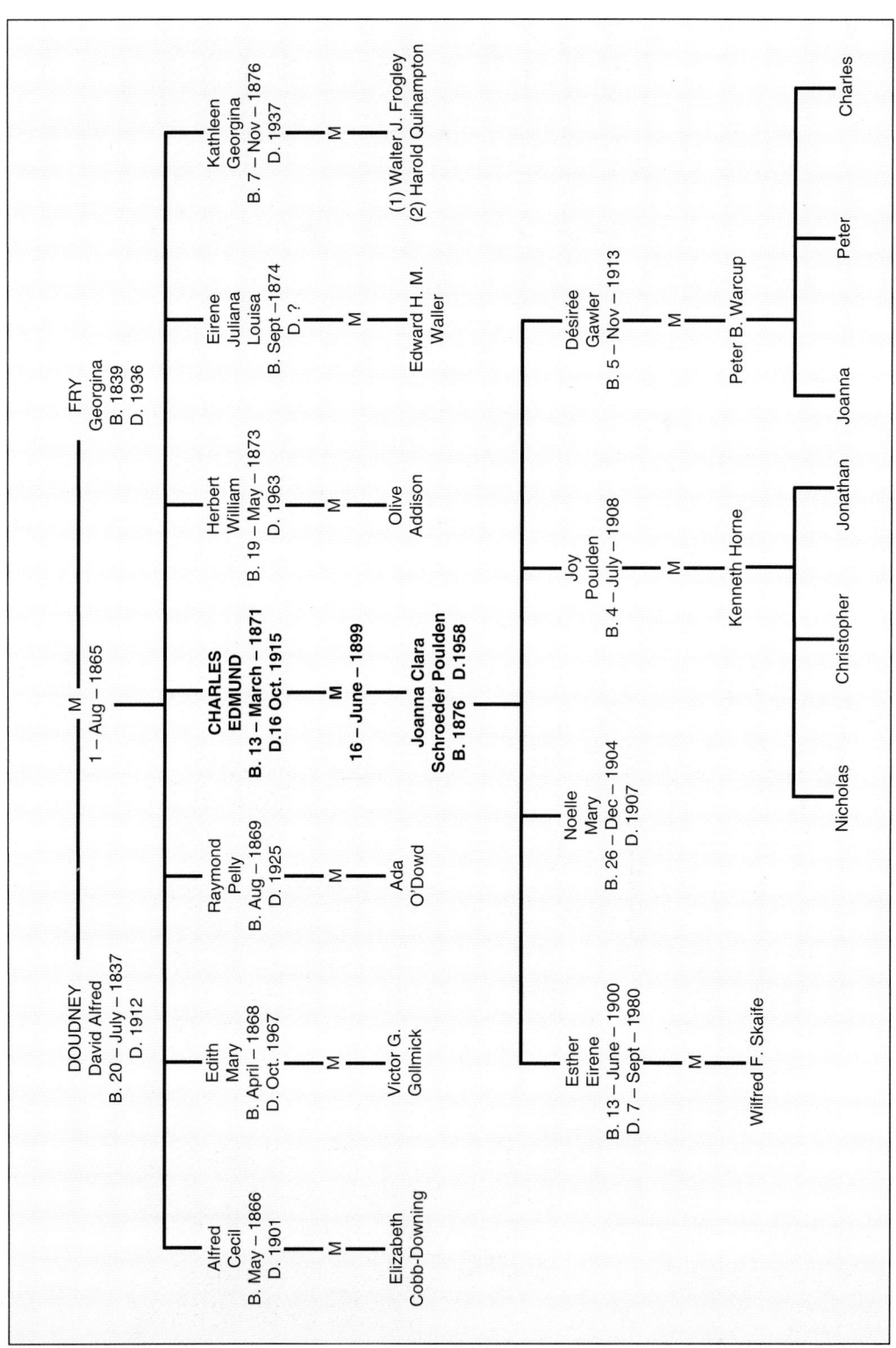

THE DOUDNEY FAMILY around 1895

From left to right: Kathleen, Eirene, Herbert, Charlie, Raymond, Edith, Cecil, Mother, D.A.D.

INTRODUCTION

THE DOUDNEYS

By tradition, it has been said that the Doudneys were descended from the Marquis d'Oudney, who came to England with the Huguenots in the 16th century. It does seem likely that the name is of French extraction, but unfortunately the story has not been substantiated.

Relying on more concrete evidence, this dialogue begins with a brief account of Charles Edmund Doudney's grandfather, the Rev. David Alfred Doudney, D.D., whose memoirs were published in a book compiled in 1894 by his eldest son, David Alfred (Charles's father), and his eldest daughter, Mrs. H.O. Adams.

David Alfred Doudney (1811 - 1893).

David Alfred Doudney was born at Portsea on 8th March 1811, the son of John Doudney and Sarah Lane. He was brought up in a God-fearing household, the Bible always being a close companion. His father kept a strict watch on the children, to preserve them from 'sin and vice', but John had one failing, his violent temper. Once young David said 'I shan't' to some request made by his older brother. His father overheard the words and gave him the severest chastisement he ever received, first with a cord and then with a cane. Even so, David thanked God for his severe upbringing, seeing it as a 'needful training', and continued to love and respect his father.

In 1824, at thirteen, David left home and went to Southampton to learn printing, a trade his father recommended and to which David adapted well. He moved to London in 1832, and in the same year married Jane Draper, the daughter of a Southampton minister. They were happy together and by 1840 had four children. David now had his own printing business, and at about this time learnt that the religious periodical, 'Gospel Magazine', which had been produced since 1766, was up for sale. He decided to purchase the copyright, making himself editor, and ran the paper for the next 53 years.

The years 1840 and 1841 were full of tragedy for the family and commenced with the loss of their third child, a boy of 14 months. During that summer and winter, his wife Jane gradually declined in health, and there were grave fears that she might not survive. In March 1841, their remaining three children became exceedingly ill with whooping cough and within a few weeks the eldest and youngest had died, leaving young David Alfred as the sole surviving child. Soon afterwards, Jane died of consumption. David Alfred senior was grief-stricken and turned to the Lord for support. However, he was to marry twice more, and had a further eleven children, only six of whom survived to maturity.

He decided to give up his printing business and after deep consideration entered the ministry. Residing in Ireland during the terrible famine, he was ordained at Waterford Catherdral in 1847. After ten years he returned home and was appointed to the new parish of St Luke's, Bedminster, Bristol. He remained there for some 32 years and became well-known throughout the city as a great orator. He retired to Southsea where he died in April 1893.

David Alfred Doudney (1837 -1912).

Meanwhile his eldest son, David Alfred (second born and last survivor of his first family), having obtained a degree at Dublin University, was ordained by the Bishop of Carlisle on 22nd December 1861, and nominated to the curacy of Stanwix, 'a most lovely and picturesque suburb of Carlisle.'

David moved to the new ecclesiastical district of St James's, Carlisle, which had a new church and school. On 1st August 1865 he married Georgina Fry, the grand-daughter of Elizabeth Fry, the famous prison reformer, and the young couple took up residence in the fine new vicarage. In 1866 their first child was born, Alfred Cecil. According to tradition, whilst Georgina was in bed convalescing she saw through the window her husband climb the church spire and watched with trepidation as he placed the last stone of the new church in place.

David Alfred was a very much loved man, who never spoke a bad word about anybody. In all, David and Georgina had seven children, the fourth being Charles, who was born on 13th March, 1871.

In 1880 the Rev. D. Doudney, M.A. (although a Doctor of Divinity, he only put M.A. after his name as he thought himself inferior to his father) was appointed to the rectory of Ore, and so the family moved south to Hastings, where they were to remain until 1897.

Charles Edmund Doudney (1871 - 1915).

Charles Edmund Doudney was educated at Hastings Grammar School, going on to Corpus Christi College, Cambridge and Ridley Hall. Whilst at Cambridge he took a keen interest in rowing and shooting, being captain of his college eight and rowing the Head of the River. From 1890-1894 he served as a member of the Cambridge Volunteers. He achieved a B.A. in 1892 and an M.A. in 1896. In 1894, at the age of 23, he was ordained Deacon and became curate at St John's the Evangelist, Penge, South London, assisting the vicar, the Rev. W. Smyly. In 1895 Charlie was ordained priest by the Bishop of Rochester.

Left: The Vicarage at Stanwix - Carlisle in the early 1870s.

Right: The Rev. David Doudney and Georgina (née Fry) with their young family photographed in about 1872.
Left to right: Mother, Herbert, Edith (seated at front), Raymond, D.A.D., Charlie, Cecil.

Left: Charlie aged 5.

Left: The Rev. David Alfred Doudney D.D., 1811-1893.

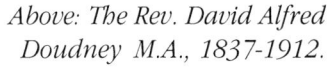

Above: The Rev. David Alfred Doudney M.A., 1837-1912.

Left: The Rev. Charles Edmund Doudney M.A., C.F., 1871-1915.

May 1892. Charlie seated second left, captained the Corpus Boat. (E.H.M. Waller seated right, later married Charlie's sister Eirene and became Bishop of Madras.)

Helmet Badge - Cambridge Volunteers.

From left to right: Mr. Plaint, Rev. W. Smyly (Vicar of St. John's the Enangelist Penge), and the new Curate Charlie.

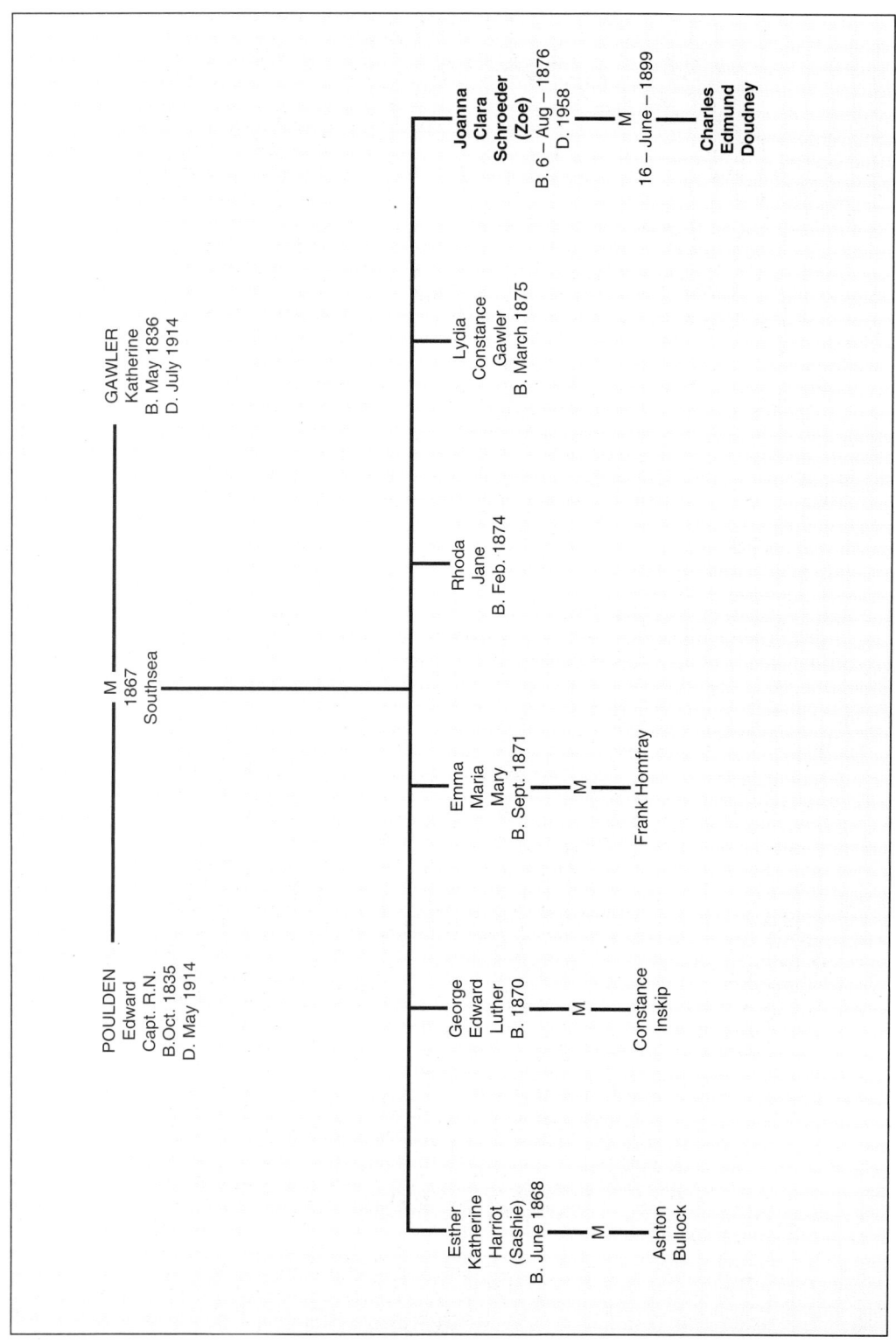

THE POULDEN FAMILY c.1895

Back row (standing) - left to right: Lydia (Arty), Luther (Ullo) later Captain Royal Engineers, Mary, Joanna (Zoe), Rhoda (Popsy), Ashton Bullock (Sasbie's husband).

Front row (seated) - left to right: Frank Homfray (Mary's husband), Mother (Katherine), Father (Capt. Edward Poulden R.N.), Esther (Sasbie).

THE POULDENS

Captain Edward Poulden R.N. (1835 - 1914)

Captain Edward Poulden R.N. was the grandson of Rear Admiral Richard Poulden, and the son of the Rev. James Poulden, rector of Fylton, near Bristol. In 1832 James married Harriet Schroeder, who was ten years his senior. She was 45 when she gave birth to Edward on 8th October 1835, and died six days later.

Edward entered the navy on 6th September 1849. He served in India, China, the West Indies, the White Sea (during the Crimean War) and the Pacific. He was later attached to the Channel Squadron and was on the gunnery staff of H.M.S. Excellent.

H.M.T.S. Formidable, off Portishead, Bristol (Inset: Captain Edward Poulden R.N. and Katherine).

On 24th May 1867, Edward married Katherine Gawler, the youngest daughter of Lt. Col. George Gawler (Second Governor of South Australia) and Maria Cox of Derby. In 1868 they had their first child, Esther (Sashie), and at about this time Edward was appointed Commander, having been in charge of the gunboat 'Stork'. In 1869 Edward was promoted to Captain Superintendant and given command of H.M.T.S. Formidable, which for a number of years had been moored at Sheerness in Kent, having been used as a guardship. In 1869 the Admiralty yeilded to the request of the philanthropic people of Bristol, and handed over the Formidable to a committee of gentlemen, who undertook the task of converting her into an Industrial School Ship accommodating about 350 boys. The Captain, accompanied by his family was responsible for the ship being towed from Sheerness to Portishead. The Formidable, known as the 'Industrial Training Ship for Homeless and Destitute Boys', became recognised as one of the leading benevolent institutions connected with Bristol, and became a familiar sight in the Bristol Channel until she was finally broken up in 1906.

Joanna Clara Schroeder Poulden (Zoe) (1876 - 1958).

Captain Edward Poulden and Katherine had six children, Zoe being the youngest, born at Malvern on 6th August 1876. She and her four sisters and one brother were brought up on board H.M.T.S. Formidable. In 1894, the Captain retired and the family moved to 16 Harvey Road, Blackheath.

◆ ◆ ◆ ◆ ◆

It was when Zoe went to stay with her eldest sister Sashie, who was now married to Ashton Bullock, a publisher, and living in Penge, that she was first introduced to Charles Edmund Doudney, the new curate of St. John the Evangelist. The Bullocks would organise little get-togethers at which they would often sing around the piano, Zoe being an excellent pianist. Charlie and Zoe's friendship grew and was much encouraged by Sashie, who was also deeply fond of Charlie. On one occasion Ashton hired a yatcht with a crew and the four of them had a wonderful day sailing from Felixstowe. *(Photographs, pages 22-23).*

It was at about this time that Charlie had another romance and actually became engaged, until the lady in question broke it off. This must have been unsettling and was probably the reason why - at the request of Dr. Harmer, his old tutor at Cambridge and now Bishop of Adelaide - Charlie decided to do missionary work in South Australia.

In preparation for the hardships of the Australian outback, Charlie took the trouble to 'walk' a London hospital (probably Bart's). Here he learnt the rudiments of everyday medicine, which proved to be an invaluable experience for the problems he would encounter. He also learnt about birth control - a subject little talked about at the time - and something on which his forbears had no notion.

Off Felixstowe.

(From left to right) Charlie, Zoe, Ashton and Sashie.

Zoe & Charlie.

Charlie.

Zoe & Sashie.

Charlie going home.

Orroroo Mission, 175 miles North of Adelaide, South Australia. Charlie's accommodation is marked.

1. Life in The Australian Outback

June 1896

It seemed as though Zoe's hopes of romance were over as Charlie set sail for South Australia to become the incumbent of Ororoo Mission, 175 miles north of Adelaide.

The Church Times, 22nd October 1915, hints at the hardships Charlie endured as a missionary in the outback.

> There came strolling one Holy Thursday into the Cathedral church of Adelaide a lay-looking Englishman who was in charge of an up-country mission. Young clerics wondered why the latest arrival from home chose this week for deserting his flock under Mount Remarkable. They twitted him with lazy ignorance. Not until years later did we find out that he was in cruellest pain from boils and blains; for it was heavy drought time, and he had small pay and less food and gunny bags for his bed, while for eight months he served a district as big as a shire, and the bush fold, whom he loved, worshipped him in return.

Not all of his experiences were painful, and it is obvious that Charlie was fascinated by the new world around him. The quality of his descriptive skills shows this in the following series of quotations from his writings.

The Bath Chronicle (publisher of a number of Charlie's adventures) includes, on 29th November 1915, an interesting and animated accent of the hardships of South Australia at the end of the last century.

> Life in the Australian bush has been so often described, that one would hesitate to add a word on the subject, were it not for the fact that most of what has been written has had reference to parts of the Island Continent, which are capable of bearing a fair if a scattered population. But practically the greater part of the country, of which I am about to write, is uninhabited save by a few nomad black tribes. An area, roughly speaking of 1,500 by 1,000 miles, representing the interior, has an average rainfall of from six to ten inches, and save for mines and far scattered sheep and cattle stations is unfitted to carry any population. Stretching right through the country, from north to south, and embracing much of the desert, is the State miscalled South Australia. As a rule, the dividing line between the desert and the fertile land is very distinctly marked, too often disregarded by adventurous farmers, tempted by some exceptional season, when the bordering wilderness has suddenly blossomed as the rose, to try his luck in wheat there - always with disastrous results. It was right on this borderland that I was settled

1 - Life in the Australian Outback

for some years. The place itself was civilized enough at the head of the railway and the head of the Spencer Gulf, the longest inlet in Australia. The town Port Augusta* nestled comfortably in sand hills, which moved from time to time when the hurricanes came in from the north-west, and the sun's rays, concentrated by the high ranges on either side of the gulf, made the water of the latter intensely salt by rapid evaporation, and the air tropically humid.

From hence we could gaze over the 'Never Never' land as it is called and see the long lines of camels swaying in, laden with wool from far off oases, and the imagination pictured it with all manner of romance. Looking anywhere to the north or north-west there was a great area of earth of 1,000 miles between us and the next town. One day I plunged over the line, and came back some weeks later a wiser man if thinner and drier. There had been a gold mine discovered some 300 miles up (Tarcoola), and to that had flocked the usual crowd of good and bad (very bad) fortune seekers. There were five hundred of them there without a shepherd, and as they were presumably in my parish I sought them out. I am not going to describe the manners and customs of the miners and their camp followers, the drunken loafers that always swarm round those places, but I fancy that some notes of the road may be interesting ... I travelled in a vehicle called a 'coach', though it's only resemblance to one consisted in the 'V.R. Royal Mail' painted in big letters on the sides. For the rest it was a four-wheeled wagon, on which two broad seats had been fixed both facing forwards. There was just room for eight persons, and on the occasion of which I am writing there were nine, including a woman and child. Four and, at times, five horses, or mules, were used, and changes were made at each well, making stages varying between 15 and 40 miles. A word about the driving. It is as fine an exhibition of rough skill as one would wish to see. The men simply do not care what horses are put in at the change stations. All they ask for is a strong harness ... After that all you are to do is not lose hold of your seat and avoid branches. There in front are the rough colts plunging and ramping and then breaking into a tearing gallop, maddened by the clash of the trace chains at their sides, and the driver will as likely as not turn round and ask you for a match.

It took five days and nights of travelling to reach the field, and we were pretty lucky in getting three nights under cover, or, rather, parts of nights, because we drove generally well into the night and started very early. The first day was monotonous in the extreme, and we reached our resting place long after dark ...

The next day we had sand for 40 miles - sand so loose and light that it was all that the horses could do to drag the coach at a straining walk, and alas, we, the passengers, who had paid to ride, had also to walk for many weary miles.

* Charlie became Rector of St. Augustines, Port Augusta in 1898.

Life in the Australian Outback - 1

The temperature was 110 degrees in the shade, and by midday, when we reached our stopping place - a well - we were dry. It is strange how vivid one's imagination gets when thirst sets in. And the pictures on one's brain all take the form of sparkling silver goblets - frosted silver - and brimming with ice cold water. We ran to the well, and, looking down, saw the cool glimmer far below, but the drawing apparatus was broken beyond repair. It was a patent affair for a horse to draw up a huge bucket and far too heavy for us to pull up. We tried various methods to reach the nectar, but to no purpose. And the water still gleamed, and our tongues seemed to swell and our lips became hard with a sticky deposit on them. Close by the child was crying softly in the trap and the heat shimmered over the sand. Someone suggested that we should join up all the harness and reins in a rope and let down a 'billy' can, and we were about to try that when another party came up, and our united strength sufficed to haul up the big bucket, and we drank our fill and also watered the horses.

If any map of these regions be consulted lakes numerous and of immense size will be noticed ... These lakes, however, are weird and uncanny in the extreme. Save in wet seasons they hold no water, but consist of vast expanses of salt, perfectly flat, of course, and dazzling white. The salt forms a crust some inches in thickness, beneath which is black mud. It is just strong enough in places to bear a trap, and when traversing them one experiences all the sensations of trying new ice, rendered the more exciting by the sight (in one place) of the upper portions of the skulls of two horses which had broken through. Some 'lakes' are altogether unsafe, and many are the yarns told of bold shepherds who had ventured over them in the search for wandering sheep ...

The third day was sultry, and it was easy to see that a storm was brewing, and sure enough on reaching the plain we could see, rising rapidly to the N.W., a reddish cloud. Watching it carefully, one could see that it was moving rapidly, and rolling as it went. Within half an hour the whole heaven was covered with one immense mass of dust. It was just a mighty wall, quite clearly defined, reaching up into the sky. The coping was fiery red, below purple, and at the bottom black as night. The front of the wall was not still, but was all in motion, rolling, curling exactly like the black smoke from a big chimney. Suddenly the top passed the sun and all was gloom. The driver got down and took the mules out and tied them securely to some stunted trees, and we waited. A low roar broke the stillness, and not a breath of wind moved a leaf. As the wall drew nearer it just swallowed up everything. Half a mile, 100 yards, and then seeming to fall from above like a mountain, it was over us. It was a tearing raging hurricane; gravel was swept up and carried along by it. (In a certain township - Ororoo - in 1897 every window on the windward side was broken by gravel in a similar gale.) Worst of all, it brought with it the darkness of night - pitch black darkness. We sheltered behind the trap until it was past. It might have been three minutes, not more certainly, but you would not have recognised one of the party. Our faces were wet with perspiration before, now they were covered with

1 - Life in the Australian Outback

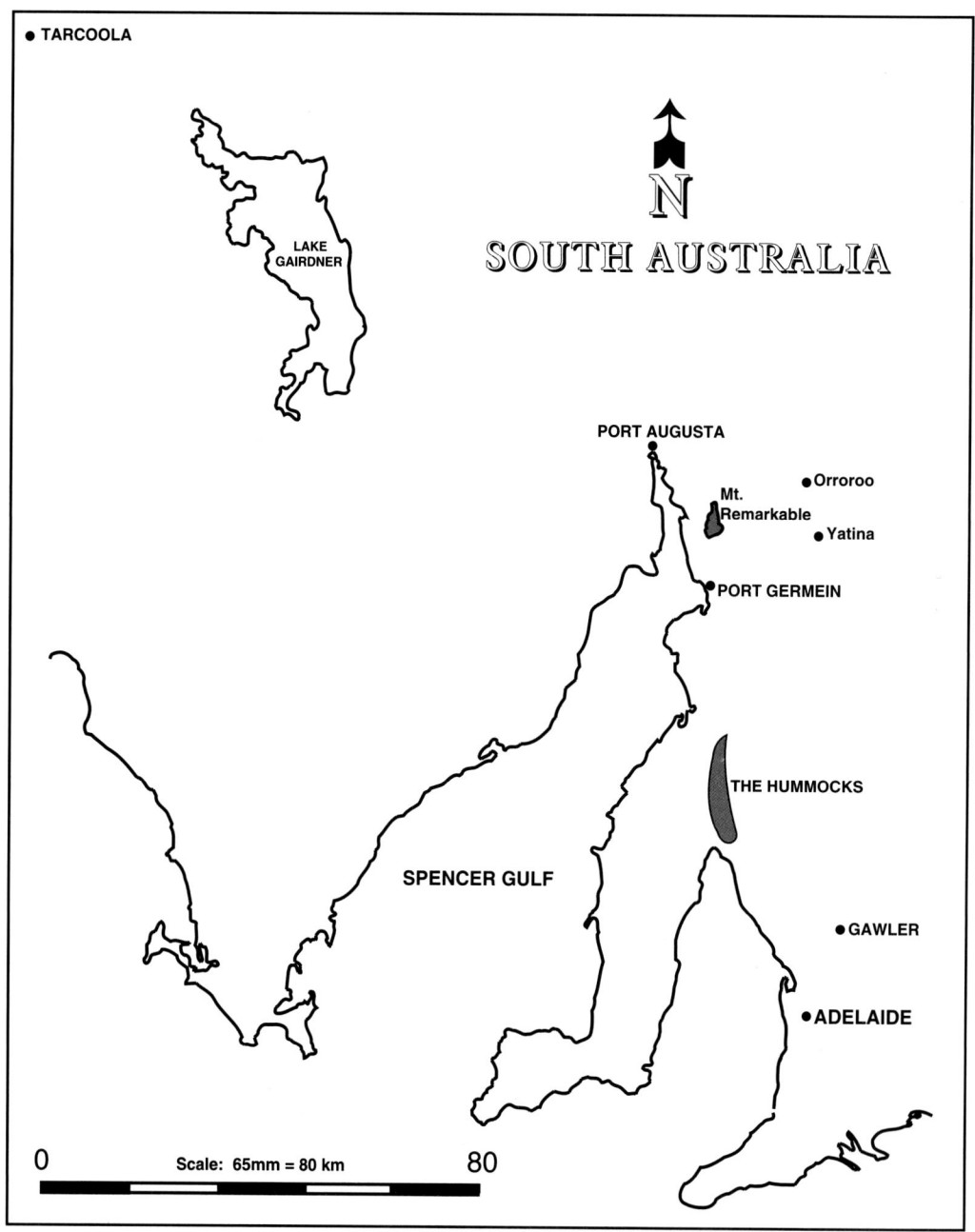

a coating of red dust! We stopped to change horses at a water hole, and as the next stage was a waterless 40 miles we essayed to fill our billycans with water. Horses were standing in the water, which was thick and rather green, but as it would be boiled it would not hurt. The man looked at me and said nothing but 'you wait', I did, and before that 40 miles past that green mud was nectar ...

That night was spent at a station-house. The kitchen where we had our evening meal was divided by a partition into two rooms. We went in and sat down at the rough board. But the old cook, a patriarchal-looking old man, had discovered my profession, and with great ceremony ushered me into the inner room, where the same mutton, tea and bread were laid on a table cloth. Feeling as though I could never look my fellow passengers in the face again, but being altogether in awe of this majestic chef, I ate my supper in loneliness and misery ...

From this point we had no incident of importance, and the country was monotonous in the extreme - one great expanse of stunted bush, the only excitement consisted in the occasional sight of emus or kangaroos and blacks.

The camping was delightful. No mosquitoes, no damp or rain ... no bath required to wake you up, the more advantage because you couldn't have one if you offered the price of rubies for it. At times of course, a billy full may be spared for ablutions, and it is wonderful what you can do with a quart of water when put to it. On the field the regulation system was: take a bucket of water - costing 2d, price fixed by Government, but you had to wait your turn at the condenser for even one - put aside enough for drinking, wash your body, then towels and handkerchiefs, then shirt, etc., and finally socks. Then put aside the water for some unfortunate horse or mule who is too far gone to object.

And so quite satisfied with coach travelling, and not longing for more we sighted the field, and saw in all directions the tents of the miners, some made of bags, some of calico, some of brushwood, and two magnificent tin houses of one room each. Here I so journeyed some days and heard strange language and stranger scenes, and learned something of what men can be and say and do when all restraints of civilization are taken away. And among other things I learnt that even in these circumstances some of the finest of human virtues live and thrive. You see the worst, perhaps, but you also see the best, for there's not much hidden in a mining camp.

⋄ ⋄ ⋄ ⋄ ⋄

1 - Life in the Australian Outback

The following series of stories entitled 'Yarns from the Bush' were first published in *The Treasury* - probably a Church magazine. Charlie's widow, Zoe, saved the papers and tied them together with a red, white and blue ribbon. On the front she scribbled a note : "These 'adventures' were all C.E.D.'s. I think the 'composition' was helped a little by the Rev. Arthur West, who was also out in South Australia (though not in the same district)." Fictitious names have been used in the stories; and likewise some of the place names, which are not recognizable on today's maps.

We had had heavyish drizzle for a day or two, which is unusual, because there it generally either rains or it doesn't - generally doesn't. That meant heavy roads, so I took my strongest horses and on a Saturday afternoon pulled out from Warrimo to The Hummocks. It was thirty miles away and I was billed there for first service on Sunday. Start was a bit later than I liked, to be quite happy, for the track was none of the easiest. Out of the township, up on to the big plain, mountain-ringed, where the road stretched away into the darkening distance, stretched on and on till the post and wire fences met in one line, with limitless expanse of low-growing scrub and barren looking bush on this side and that. That day you wanted all the eyes you had for the track. You wanted all your judgment to save your toiling horses. A foot deep into the sticky, muggling clay your buggy wheels sank, till the narrow tyres were clogged to the size of cartwheels. It was all my strong bush-bred team could do to pull the machine at foot's pace. Stony patches of solid oasis, a saving corduroy of light bush, and other fortuitous help, for them you must make for and welcome ... The long road seems endless, till the ascent comes to the hills, long looked for, and with it the good stone foothold. Through the windings of the shorter shoulders we turn into the sheep-station paddocks.

Paddock! No! not your three acres and a cow, among the trees and near the house, where the pony crops clover; nor the saddling enclosure at Ascot; that's not our Australian notion of a paddock. We think of 7000 acres of grassland fenced with miles of wire. You go through one gate, and then wander to the other outlet, which is a possible ten miles away, skirting the gums and the water courses ... down into the rocky beds of dry rivers, scrambling up ravines, pushing through mallee, till at last through the gathering dusk gleam the station lights. Half a score sheep-dogs babel a welcome as the ponies swerve into the big courtyard. The house is really about seventeen one-storied buildings, once occupied by the families of the men raising sheep. Times were better then. Those were palmy days on stations for squatters, before any land was enclosed or cut up into blocks for 'closer settlement'; the days before the 'cockie' was a burden, and desire failed. There had been plenty of high life here in old times - kangaroo hunts, four-in-hand picnics, evening dress and all the paraphernalia of luxury. *Tempora mutantur.* This was gone. The manager and his family with a few hands could do all the work except at shearing times. The rambling buildings - 'Government House' and bachelors' quarters and little chapel (now used as an office) - were mouldering to ruin in decay.

The manager hastened to meet me, insisted, as his courteous wont, on taking my horses ... After a cosy meal and a long yarn over the fire, I was taken to the bachelors' room, a cavernous dormitory, once the sleeping place for a dozen guests and men working on the station. Now the chief inhabitants were in the thatched roof - snakes and bats ... The big log fire, however, made up for much, though it did occur to me that the heat might bring down some of the roof dwellers.

Sunday morning meant a great cleaning-up of children, a putting-on of Sunday frocks, and a packing of the whole party into the family wagonette. You ought to have known that omnibus. It was the finest illustration of the conversion of energy I have ever met. It was prehistoric ... No effort had ever been made to effect the most obvious repairs, and no trace of the original paint was anywhere visible ... To it were now harnessed three strong, half-broken beasts, unicorn fashion, and into it were packed about twice as many passengers as it would ever have been licensed to carry. Full of faith that 'things as they are' will remain so, we rattled down the steep cutting, around the creek, and made our four miles to church. It was Matins and a Celebration of the Holy Communion for a congregation drawn from the usual couple of stores, one forge, one bank, and three inns of the little township. Then back to midday dinner - mutton hams and fresh mutton - which the station people snatched all standing, because the next point of the timetable is Yarrowie at 3.30, some thirty miles to the North. The track is all plain sailing by daylight, but sometimes you had to take it by night without a moon. Then look out. At one place the road ran across a creek through a very deep cutting, clinging as it were to the side of the slope, unfenced anywhere. The only guide for the jumping-off spot from the level to the sheer decline, a couple of five-foot gum posts. Miss them and you are lost ...

1 - Life in the Australian Outback

Yarrowie provides a strong Church hive of poor struggling 'cockie' farmers. The little worship shed is crowded. Strange to say the men are in a huge majority. Here for the first time I had to wear a veil during service, not because of the angels, but to avoid swallowing flies. It seemed as though some millions of brown-bellied buzzers spent their time in trying to get down my throat. About one per cent succeeded and that was enough. Then I understood the meaning of the notice on the board outside, 'Please shake yourself and run in'.

Tea would have been welcome to change the taste, but there is no time. Yatina, ten miles away, is waiting for Evensong. And what a relief it is, after driving over dangerous and heavy roads for twelve solid hours, to turn in at the Post Office, to see the good-humoured Postmaster opening the gate ready to unharness my horses; while his wife has a roaring fire inside to sit by, and great jorums of hot tea for you to drink.

Evening service was over. I had travelled over sixty miles in the last twenty-eight hours and preached three times. Man and beast were both done up. I was looking forward to a delightful evening with my post-office friends, when a man on horseback rode up with a message. A woman lay dying and had asked for the Holy Communion. Could I go? Well! it was not the priest who must be considered, but his horses. They were useless after their sixty mile drag through the mud, until they had had a night's rest. Besides, you would have to saddle back, for no buggy could cross the range to Poyser's house by the nearest way. It was his wife who was dying and he had allowed her to send for me! This was the chance I had been waiting for, and I would not miss it for worlds. Now I need a horse to take me to Poyser's.

A difficult, painful man was Poyser, very full of his own importance, very sure of his own judgment, and, as usually happens to such gentlemen, fairly constant in getting his own way ... He has enough learning to overbear the commonalty and to take the lead in public matters; he is sufficiently responsive to modernist feeling to show small respect for the representative of the Church, and to profess smiling contempt for those who still cling 'to the back number superstitions of the dark ages'...

Poyser('s) ... fellow-citizens ... hated him, and feared him; he hated the parson who didn't fear him one note; and he worshipped his wife, who bore him no children, but cost him hundreds of pounds for the doctor's bills, and scarcely lingered on this side of the grave ... He wouldn't, of course, have a parson to come near ... (but for his wife). 'Let the Methodies and 'Piscopalians mind their own silly business'. He was a common-sense man.

What horses were there that night? We routed round the township. The angels helped us, and we found in the storekeeper's stable the best horse for such a job that could have been had for miles, and he was fresh ... So by nine o'clock

Life in the Australian Outback - 1

I was in the saddle, making for the pass eastwards. It was now pitch dark, heavy icy rain was falling. The only thing I could see was the dim outline of the eager dun head in front of me; the only thing that I regretted, that I was too tired and wet and miserable to enjoy his magnificent canter. You can sleep at a canter, and I slept half the time, waking to find myself being carried up and up the rough course of a creek, scrambling sometimes in its dry bed, now along its canted sides; and then over the bleak and weird pass-top, awesome in its loneliness ...

Now my directions are clear. Cross the pass, strike a tiny settlement, turn due north, and ride till you get to the farm. With luck I managed to strike the village long after midnight, but did not like to wake anyone, for all the houses were of course in dense darkness. So I turned to the left, out on to the infinitely dreary 'Never-Never' country, the endless plain which stretches right into Australia's uncharted heart, where there is scarce an inhabitant ...

Remember the distance I had done since Saturday afternoon, and the necessary fatigue of the Church services, and the unnerving anxiety to be in time at the last call, and you will understand something of my desperation and distress at the fear of having lost my way. There was so much at stake: not only the reputation of the Church, as embodied in me, not only the supreme need of soothing Mrs. Poyser's last hour, but the cardinal chance of winning Poyser's soul from the grasp of the devil. If I could succeed he might be open to the means of grace, and through him how many smaller fry would be influenced! The whole thing hung on my 'bushmanship'. Was I going to prove that I could not find my way in the dark? Was I going to be beaten by ordinary fatigue?

Thanks be! At three in the morning, before even a star or gleam of dawn appeared, I struck a shepherd's hut. My delight! Yes, I banged and banged, and slammed and called at the door till a red-headed Irishman put out his head and swore roundly. I think it was whiskey neat which made his sleep so hard and talk so big. That didn't matter. He gave me my bearings and off I galloped, leaving him still blaspheming. It was easy going from the hut to the farm. And then I found the bush-doctor in possession. He wanted to press me into the service at once as anaesthetist for an operation. But not until I had satisfied Mrs. Poyser's cravings and given her the food which alone can satisfy, would I help him ...

Poyser sat there, numbed and hopeless in his sobs. It was no time then to approach him. It was enough that he was grateful, and that she was at peace before passing beyond into the dawn, off and out and away through the long morning from the rough bush farmhouse to the House of the King.

Seeking my horse - he had been fed and was somewhat rested I rode back over the range to Yatina, getting there, something the worse for wear, just before dusk, and enormously thankful for what I had been allowed to do ...

1 - Life in the Australian Outback

Yatina is on the narrow-gauge tramway that goes by the name of 'railway' in these parts ... The station is a couple of miles from the township, and to reach it one has to cross the inevitable creek. The mail coach did this daily, meeting the daily train. While I had been sleeping the windows of heaven had been open, and there had been a great rain. It came down in bucketfuls, and the creek was in flood. But no one thought it would be impassable. So we started off from the Post Office, one other passenger besides myself, and that one Poyser. He was hurrying to make arrangements for his wife's funeral. I sat by the driver, with all the mail-bags at my feet. Almost all the creeks in the north of South Australia have this peculiarity. Their banks are higher than the surrounding country. This formation it was which prevented us from seeing the state of the creek until we topped the bank. Then we saw below us a raging, swirling torrent of red-brown water sweeping over the roadway and plunging into a big hole, twelve feet below the built-up causeway. The river was about one hundred feet wide, as we found out afterwards, more than five feet deep, and it was racing so that no living horse could have kept its feet for a second in the full strength of mid-stream.

I don't know why we ever went in, for none of us for one moment expected to get through. I suppose that no one cared to be the first to show any fear. Certainly Poyser would rather have died than have allowed me to think that what I could do was beyond him. The dirty water was over the bottom of the track in a moment, and I grabbed the mail-bags to keep them dry. An instant later the horses were gone, the whole turn-out tumbling over the fall into a perfect whirlpool below. The coach itself was hurled against an immense gum-tree that grew in the bed of the creek and smashed into matchwood. The horses went clear to one side, and the shock broke traces and pole - which probably saved their lives. We three stood upon the seat as we swept over the brink and leapt clear of the gum-tree. At least Poyser and I cleared it, but the driver did not, and goes lame by consequence all his days. Then followed our fight for life. It was desperate and long-doubtful and the hardest I have ever been through. The encumbrance of a heavy overcoat, which there was no time to throw away, and the weight of heavy boots were a terrible handicap for swimming. The current was so strong that it carried you a dozen yards downstream for every foot you made towards land. Worst of all, the appalling suck of the whirlpool kept pulling you under. Why it was I can't tell, but strive as you might, you could only keep head above water to get breath now and again. And the water so dense black with mud that you could not see whether you were near the surface or at the bottom. Everywhere underneath it was black darkness. After struggling for what seemed hours of horrible nightmare. I reached the bank. Even then it was sometime before I could get a hold and crawl up, to lie panting but safe.

But the other two! I scanned the turbid river. Now I would catch sight of a bit of a coat-tail, now, and further on, a hand appeared. Your proper hero would have plunged in again at once, of course! I didn't. Just then there was nothing I wanted less than another bathe. So, instead, and it was much the easiest thing to do,

I ran down the bank alongside the floating occasional apparitions of struggling mankind. And as I ran it interests me to remember that I found myself humming Gerard Cobb's setting of 'Ford o'Cabul River', a song I had not heard for years.

There was a place where the land jutted out into mid-stream; so, getting ahead of the procession, I climbed out into the branches of a small tree that at the end of the point overhung the water. At least, it generally did but now was almost completely submerged. A hand came past, and was grabbed. Its body was pulled after it, the owner propped up in the tree. Strangely enough, he was more or less conscious, and able to give feeble help in fishing out Poyser when he came providentially within reach. He, however, was deadly unconscious; so we had to pump him out, and bring him round, as we could, by degrees. Then we lay down, all three on the bank exhausted, and tried to recollect things.

In ten minutes the whole township was around us. It turned out that several had watched the crossing from a distance, and having seen the coach pass down the bank, but not come up the other side, they drew the all too obvious conclusion. Very wisely, they sought us, not at the crossing, but a quarter-mile downstream.

So ended this particular three days' jaunt. There is a wire hawser across that passage now. And Poyser? Well, there are some happenings that do not fail to be told to all and sundry. The death of his wife, his own almost miraculous escape from drowning by the hand of one who he had most despised - a man must be more than human, or less, who does not learn something from such teachings.

◊ ◊ ◊ ◊ ◊

Charlie's earlier experiences in a London hospital proved invaluable in the following story.

Not often nowadays does a man get the chance of doing doctor's work as an amateur. And more rarely still does one do it under the authority and aegis of the profession itself. But in the Bush all things are possible. It goes without saying that you must be able to turn your hand to anything and everything ...

... It was this way, Slatterthwaite, the local man and a great ally of mine, who worked a district nearly as big as my parish - that is to say, about as much country as Kent and Sussex rolled into one - went off for a holiday. Goodness knows, he needed it, and I commended his wisdom in leaving no address while he wandered round the big towns of the Australian coast. He had engaged no locum, because no one would come ... So this time it was deemed sufficient to ask the neighbouring doctor to look after the practice, and come over two days a week for certain hours' surgery. The doctor's house was next door to my rooms, so that I saw a good deal of the locum on his visiting days, and liked him well. One day he complained of illness, and went back to his home looking decidedly bad. Indeed, it was no great surprise to me when I heard that he was laid up in bed with nasty complications. Two surgery days passed and no doctor appeared. Patients came and waited and asked questions, then went. For a week nothing special happened in the way of accidents. Then came a short pencil-note by post:

'My dear (Charlie), - I'm bad. Have tried to get ... '(naming two doctors each of them fifty miles away)' up even for a day for Slatterthwaite's practice. No good! They can't come. Will you help? Make use of anything in the surgery. Do lend a hand, there's a good chap.
- Yours, ...'

I'm afraid I laughed. But soon the real seriousness of the thing dawned on me. Next day was surgery day, and presently the local doctor's boy came round ... and he was to give the key of the surgery to me. I puzzled over the matter a goodish bit. It's no laughing matter suddenly to assume this kind of responsibility without any proper qualification. No doubt it was a tight place for the profession, and it was possible that I might be of some use to my absent friend - or even to his patients. On the other hand it was possible that I might make an egregious ass of myself and ruin somebody's life. In the end I decided on a compromise. I ordered the boy to stand guard at the door and tell all-comers that the doctor was ill, but that if they very much wanted treatment they must apply at the Parson's, next door. That, I thought, would shift the responsibility on to them. They would consult me at their peril. If they found me in the surgery it would look too much as though I really did know and could advise.

My practice began earlier than I had expected. A telegram came in the evening: 'Mid wifery case Alpina farm; accident at Schwan's Barcowie. Can you attend either?' These two places were in exactly opposite directions, so (fortunately, perhaps) I couldn't attend both, and I chose the accident. I knew my Barcowie people. But what was the nature of the accident? Round and round that surgery I wandered, collecting into a bag about three times as much material as a professional would have taken. Dressings, oiled silk, carbolic, iodoform, chloroform, a case of instruments, needles, ligatures, cotton wool in packets, a case of hypodermic syringes, and much more. Then I slung the bag over my shoulder and rode out into the night. I knew the farm and the people slightly, so there was no difficulty about getting there, though it was past midnight when I dismounted and knocked at the farmhouse door ... At moments like this you live very intensely, and are probably braced up twenty percent higher than ordinary strength. The house was brightly lighted. Everybody was up and anxious. I tried to assume the cheery doctor's best bedside manner, rather brusque:

'Well! What's happened?' 'John's thrown, sir.' 'Hurt badly?' 'That's just what we don't know. He's in great pain and a little off his head.' 'Well, let's see him', I said.

John was laying on a home-made stretcher-bed - four posts driven into the clay floor, the sacking stretched tightly across. He certainly was messed up above a bit, and I won't describe his appearance. The colt, it seems, had not only thrown him but kicked him, and there didn't appear to be much of his body that wasn't damaged. However, on closer inspection I found that torn clothes and blood and mud made appearances far worse that the case really was. Then to work. I thought I'd begin at the top end of him and work downwards. So I cleaned up his head, and washed, bandaged, and stitched a big scalp wound. Then we cut his clothes off, and I went over him inch by inch, as I had often seen real doctors do. No ribs broken, no real injury to the body, but ah! Here we are - leg gone. Femur clean broken, crepitus quite plain. So now what's to do? I took old Schwan aside and told him the case. The leg must be set and there are two alternatives. Either send him down to ... hospital next day, eighteen miles by road and seventy by train; or set it now, and risk my inefficiency giving him a game leg for the rest of his life.

'We'll ask him,' said the father.

By this time the patient was in his right mind. He had only been knocked silly by the kick on the head, and there was no fracture there. But the pain in his leg was now acute on the least movement, and he couldn't face the journey. As a matter of fact, I do not believe that in his then condition he would have survived.

So I got the father to write a request for me to set the leg. That was for protection against possible claims of damages for lameness. A Liston splint was soon made and the operation was over quickly, but I believe I suffered as much as the poor fellow. There was a lot of shrinkage, and the pulling-out of the limb meant much expenditure of nerve on my part - I dare not use chloroform. Sweat poured down us both - in his case from physical pain, in mine from nervous exhaustion. But it came off. The patient got immense relief at once, and except that he has a very slight limp, John Schwan is now as active as ever and has lived to break in many colts since that time. So ended my first operation, happily and well.

I was back home by five a.m. and after about a couple of hours' troubled sleep was not in the best imaginable mood for facing further possibilities of amateur doctoring. I sat pretending to work up a sermon, but really my thoughts would adhere far more closely to diseases of the body than of the soul. A knock at the door! Is it cancer or colic? Knife or medicine? No! Neither - it was a yearling whose tooth wouldn't come through ...

'Please will you come and see farver; he's sick' - from a small head in at the door. Good: that will take me off surgery for a piece, anyway. 'Farver' was in a bad way, dysentery. That I had no trouble about. You don't live long in the Bush without obtaining at first hand some expert knowledge on this head ... Diet was what I trusted to mainly, and my treatment was quite successful. The nursing was more than primitive, for in a day or two the small head reappeared with: 'Please, may farver have some apples?'

The next apparition was startling. A boy whom I knew but hardly recognised, entered abruptly with his mouth wide opened in a yawn of stupendous dimensions.

'Hullo, Willie,' I said; 'what's the row?' No answer - but an agonised pointing to his mouth. 'Something stuck in your throat, old chap?' Shake of the head. 'Well, shut your big mouth and tell me what's up,' I said. A howl.

Vague ideas of lockjaw floated over my brain, and all I could remember of that disease was its technical name of tetanus, which wasn't much help for the moment.

Then an inspiration - the jaw's stuck open! With the idea came remembrance of the treatment. A couple of corks, and pressure. Click! - up came the errant jaw. A yell followed by smiles.

And so the day wore on. Perhaps a dozen cases came in; several dental, and I wouldn't tackle them. They must grin and bear the toothache. A little chap was brought in with a broken collar-bone. This was set without much trouble. Only a few days later he tumbled off a wall on to it again, and the job was all to do afresh. As a matter of fact, the most of the cases were straightforward and easy, with quite an obvious diagnosis. During the whole week there was scarcely one which a good nurse could not have managed.

Over the homely matter of measles I nearly came a bad cropper. Towards evening of the first day a woman came in with a story of a child in a 'rash', and would I come at once? It was some distance, about fifteen or sixteen miles ... I promised to look in next day.

That evening I pulled down the reference books and crammed up all I could about diseases with 'rashes', and each one seemed on paper more easy to recognise that the last. But next morning I couldn't have detected small-pox from shingles by the signs. They ushered me into the room of the sick child with all proper ceremony, and I went through the orthodox ritual: examined tongue and pulse, took the temperature, and had a good look at the rash, standing as solemn as a judge. The mother looked at me inquiringly for the verdict - hung, so to speak, on my lips. I reflected that she probably knew about fifty times as much of the treatment of this particular trouble as I did - if we could only put a name to it. So I sat down and gazed at the child, and round and round in my frantic brain whirled a confused rabble of the descriptions of exanthema I had got up. All kinds of possibilities - scarlet fever, chicken pox, cow-pox, heat-rash, plague, and what not. Should I make a shot - tell them I would send some physic and leave the question open? When suddenly - oh, luck! - my strained senses caught the word 'measles' whispered by somebody in the room. Good gracious! Measles! Why, in the name of commonsense, had not the obvious occurred to me? ... I got up slowly and said, as if following a train of thought:

'Yes, a clear case of measles. Not bad, but you must take care. Warmth and bed and slops; and I'll send out some medicine.'

⋄ ⋄ ⋄ ⋄ ⋄

In this story, Charlie mentions 'Martin, that round-faced cousin of mine.' He may be speaking of his younger brother Herbert who joined him in the outback and took over the Ororoo Mission when Charlie moved to Port Augusta, in 1898. However, Herbert was of large stature and does not fit the physical description well. Perhaps the 'cousin' referred to was the Rev. Arthur West!

Do you know at all what it is like to descend suddenly upon a collection of farmers' houses, in an out-of-the-way corner of the universe, when you are a 'new chum' and a parson, and they are inclined to suspect you on both counts? You have to drive up quite unconcernedly to people who are utterly shy of strangers and depend upon them for 'tucker' and lodgment, quite apart from all ecclesiastical aspirations. It makes you shy to find them timid - and then they have no time for a man who cannot make his own way. There are two things which can save the situation in times like this - the sense of humour and the sporting instinct. God help the man who has neither! He may as well pack and make tracks. The opening gambit was an invitation to put up with an old couple who had been in the district nearly half a century and had reared a big family. Fisher their name was and, as appeared later, every second family for miles around was related to them by blood or marriage... Behold me, then, camping at the Fisher farmhouse, the horses turned into the paddock and the buggy drawn under the shade of an enormous plane tree. My cousin had come on this jaunt along with me, and he was the kind of fresh-looking, fat-faced boy whom everyone takes great pleasure in ragging.

First, they asked us whether we would care to shoot. We would - and then came a long day of striding through the waving yellow corn, because hares were becoming a pest ... the bag may have been anything under two hundred. That broke the ice, for they found we could shoot: and bethought them to try us with rifles up the Hog's Back and had a most glorious and exhausting day in the

1 - Life in the Australian Outback

ranges; but what took away all remnants of restraint was the way the 'new chum' sat the thoroughbred filly which never yet had felt bridle or harness.

And finally, came the water fight. It was not at all an orthodox way of getting a church built, yet it was one of the ultimate causes of getting together that crowded congregation in their own church, and so led the way to possibilities of Confirmation for all those sporting farmers and their families. But it is not a tale for drawing-room meetings, and would certainly have shocked the members of any decent parish. But it was a good fight and well sustained, arising in quite a simple way. The habits of these good-hearted farmer folk are primitive in the extreme. Many rise at the most unearthly hours and have milked half a score of cows apiece before six o'clock. But their guests and this you may regard as the acme of good breeding - they did not expect to appear for breakfast until quite reasonable hours. So it happened on a certain day when we were staying with the Fishers that I and my cousin lay abed long after the whole farm community had been at work. Windows, of course, were wide open, giving on to the tiled verandah which surrounds all the one-storeyed houses. Blazing sunlight flooded the air, golden and triumphant. What sprites of mischief danced in those molten beams?

His name was Martin, that round-faced, blue-eyed cousin of mine, and his bed lay right under the open window. Unassailable good nature was his, and he had a capacity for drawing out the latent humour of all men. That was why George, the youngest Fisher, passing along the verandah to water the horses, with a full stable bucket in his hand, was tempted to splash a few drops over the sleeper's face. Possibly the douche was more liberal than he intended. Anyhow, it woke Martin outright. In a flash he was out of bed, had seized the bedroom ewer and emptied it on his enemy before he could get out of range. Back came the rest of the bucket's contents, and this time it was I, sleeping and innocently unconscious, who got the full benefit. Yes! I woke too, and then it began in proper earnest. Anglican dignity of Orders went by the board. We scrambled into flannels and went in search of vengeance. We found a bucket, and we found George. He entrenched himself behind a reaping-machine, and was drowned out of his shelter shed. Then the others of the clan began to saunter up and, getting a share of the flying water, were soon drawn into the fight. Pails and mops and water-cans and ladles and hose squirted and slushed and splashed torrents of tepid water in all directions over half a score male and female Fishers. Oh! it was a naumachia: and as the tide of battle at length steadied by dint of laughter and exertion we stood still and the sun must have stood still - to watch an Homeric duel between Martin the Grand and the eldest paterfamilias of the Fishers. His sons and daughters stood and rocked with delight as they saw their staid and revered father locked in the tight embrace of a fat young new chum. They wrestled and tripped and gripped and twisted, and there was the green duck pond waiting to receive them. Martin was about half the size of his man, and could by no means free himself from the hug of those bear-like brown arms, but with cunning grip and trip he managed to heave him over the verge, and both went under with a mighty splash. That cured their wrath against each other; but when they crawled out, looking like swamped Excise men and saw me doubled up with laughter, they made as one man for me! As I went for the nearest shelter it seemed like a race in a nightmare. My legs were as lead with laughing. And their boots squelched and spurted water as they pursued me, making for a high gate which, just in time, I reached and barred against them.

You can believe that after the breakfast, whereat all the incidents of the fight were discussed amid roars of laughter, there was never any more shyness on either side ...

It was schoolboyish and disgraceful, no doubt; but somehow it knitted us all together, and when it came to the really great issues these men were as children in their eagerness to learn and do. Ye gods! is there anything like teaching men who want to learn?

This enthusiasm was infectious ... and it gradually dawned upon some of the leaders that a church must be built. But you can't make anything go unless you have what is called a 'social'. This means anything from a tea-fight to a Cinderella dance, with intervals for a concert and speech making and sandwiches... But the bazaar that we organised to raise the wind - such a bazaar and fête and sale and countryside corroboree! It merits complete treatment by itself.'

Intending to advertise the Bazaar, Charlie looked for help from the local newspaper in the hope that he could get some posters printed. The Editor was a red-bearded, fresh-faced Irishman, shaggy and dirty.

... He called himself O'Connor, of course, and when he spoke you knew he could not have been called anything else. Six feet odd of length, was cased in a suit which had been once white duck, but now was black and white in patches. When I first met him he was sitting on the deal table of his newspaper office, yarning out story after story to a half dozen idlers, sprawled on the floor. They smoked, and he smoked, only it looked as if he wanted all the matches in the parish to keep his pipe alight while he talked. It was the day his weekly issue ought to have come out, but the sub-editor was away, shooting black cockatoos and mountain duck, and the only person who seemed to be at all anxious about the issue was the little printer's devil, aged thirteen, who kept popping his head into the office every six minutes asking for 'more copy'; apparently about only half of the matter wanted had been sent up. O'Connor never stopped telling the story he was in the midst of, or answered the boy in any way, except by throwing a wooden ruler or an inkpot at him, and the cleverness with which that boy avoided out of his presence, like David from before Saul's javelin, was Biblical - quite.

1 - Life in the Australian Outback

Would he print me posters for the bazaar, why, of course he would, at once, they should take precedence of everything in the world, even the next issue. They should be glorious and gaudy, in purple and pink, and wondrous type. They should illuminate the district, they should mark an epoch; and so he went on; but all he did towards it was to tell the printer devil to attend to the gentleman. He continued the symposium. After waiting near an hour, I found that nothing was being done, or was going to be done, unless I went in and helped the compositor myself. So we set to work with a hand-press and some wooden type of various ages, and brought out sheets of which I have always been proud. Then, when two hours' dirty sweating and moiling had done the trick, in comes my light-hearted giant, 'Is ut Bills ye're wanting, shure and ye shall have them with all the pleasure in the wurrld.' You couldn't be angry, and you couldn't resist him, most especially when he said he would let me pay for my own work, and would come himself and bring the 'boys' to that same bazaar. He was as good as his word, too, about coming with me; also he brought the local band - a drum, a cornet, a French horn, and a clarionet, to lend animation. The implements were all in different keys, and made a most unholy clamour; but certainly they were lively. We were all to drive over together to Barcowie in a wagonette. O'Connor would drive; four-in-hand? Yes. No, it didn't matter the horses never having been together before, or that we had no four-in-hand whip; we should manage all right. So they picked me up on the appointed day, and greatly daring, I committed my body to Mr. O'Connor's care.

Driving! You should have seen it, it was 'all aboard there behind?' 'Right ho! get along,' and the hangers round shouted a hurrah, which started the team at full gallop through the dusty streets of the little town. Presently the leaders shied and propped, and turned round to look at us. O'Connor could not reach them with his whip, but he managed to get them straight somehow, and off we went again. At the first hill we found that the brakes wouldn't act, and though your bushmen can generally mend anything in the world with a piece of fencing-wire, these brakes were quite past all repair. It wouldn't have mattered so much, only there was a steep hill a few miles ahead; and if the leaders chose to jib just then, well, the machine would be spreadeagled. The only kind of safety lay in taking the thing at a good canter, for the collars kept getting over the wheelers' ears. My man wasn't going to be bested by a little thing like the want of a long whip. Before we came to the dip he ordered us all out, and made us fill our pockets and hats with good size pebbles, and then gave us our directions. When he gave the word, or when he saw any sign of the leaders beginning to flag, we were to volley them from behind with showers of stones, and he would take care they kept straight. So said, so done. It worked like a patent medicine. The novelty of the attack astonished those leaders, and we went down *ventre a terre,* full burst.

Truly, it was a marvellous journey, and I am not ashamed to say that I was deeply thankful when we came within cooey of Barcowie. Then the band began to play in good earnest, in hideous discord, with tremendous noise, and

O'Connor pulled his horses back on their haunches at the gates of the enclosure, cool and urbane, as if nothing out of the common was doing.

And now came back my anxiety as to the preparations my good people at Barcowie might have made for a thing they had never seen in their lives - a Church Bazaar ... I had been at the first committee meeting when the rough lines were mapped out, but while I was away in other parts of my huge district how had they filled in the details?

Behold, then, the hall in which the great function was to be held. The men had specially created it themselves for the occasion. The pillars were gum posts sunk two feet into the ground: the roof was wheat sacks and gunny bags, sewn together, and supported here and there by more posts. The sides appeared to be anything that came handy, bits of wooden fencing, strips of galvanised iron, wagon tarpaulins, and rick covers. Inside, the stalls were arranged round the walls - with places partitioned off for side shows and a refreshment room. And the place was packed when we got there, cram, jam full to the brim. What the thermometer reading was I wouldn't say: outside in the shade it was a cool 105 degrees. Inside it must have been 160 in the water bag - as they say in the bush. But the heat only made business brisker. For sheer, downright enjoyment, it was a record bazaar.

I'd like you to compare this scene in your mind with an old time, well-established English fair, under the elms, in the smell of wallflowers and new mown hay. When the Squire sends down his stablemen and servants to make all the preparations, and the country gentry turn up with their ladies in summer muslins to help the old Rector ... and, if we hadn't a Member of the House of Lords, or even the Commons, to make an opening speech, we had Patriarch Fisher, who had seen the settlement from its start. I asked him to say something, and so soon as he appeared, white-haired and sunburnt, on the rough plank platform, O'Connor led a chorus of cheers from the mob...

Mr. Fisher smiled and bowed, and knew well the respect in which he was held, and the fun of the boys. He wasn't a bit disconcerted by their barracking. 'Now, my friends,' he said, 'I'm real glad to see you here, and that's all about it. Me an' my wife knows all about most of you, and leathered some on you when you was babbies. You all look to have done well on it. Ever since my young friend from England began to come here reg'lar we've wanted a place to meet in o'Sundays. And we's going to have it, and we's not going into debt (loud cheers). We done all we can, carting and hauling and digging, an' we mus' pay a man from town to do the rest. And you's got to pay. You's got to buy dollies an' lollies an' ducks an' eggs an' Sunday dinners and Monday clothes from these here stalls. An' there hasn't got to be nothing left - not a carrot. An' Mr. O'Connor, he's come special to give an instructive and entertaining lecture, an' from what I knows of him he'll be worth the sixpence you'll pay to hear him. An' I want to say that I thanks you for listening to me, and to say that after our parson done what he have for us, we can't do less than build him this church. And I want to thank the band for making such a noise, and I think that's all.'

Mrs. Fisher declared the fair opened, and the band struck up - 'For they are jolly good fellows'. Then business began with tea. I contented myself for some time with playing the mild curate, and handing round to the ladies. One owning a weak digestion asked for hot water only. The tea was being made outside in some big portable coppers, and the water had been brought in a 400-gallon tank. I dipped her cup in the hot water copper and carried it back to the lady. She looked mystified, and said: 'May I have hot water, please'. I looked into the cup and begged her pardon, went back to the copper, and then to the tank, tried them both; they were the same colour, a thick rich brown, even before any tea was put in. What was a man to do? It was too much for me, so I turned someone else on to the job and fled. I don't know how my deputy got through with it.

Escaping into the main tent I came on a great crowd overflowing from a side show. It was the famous lecturer holding forth. O'Connor had got them all breathlessly excited about an animal he was about to exhibit to them. He would permit himself to describe it first. And this he proceeded to do with wealth of eloquence and lucidity of expression such as I have rarely heard equalled. From what I could gather, it must be quite extinct. Its habits were perfectly amazing, and the audience obviously believed every word. Apparently it was a water otter of some sort that he was carefully guarding among the straw under a mat in the corner, and finding his crowd credulous, he began to let himself go. Now the otter is unknown in Australia, and I couldn't for my life make out what he was going to show. However, he kept on piling up the agony. It was a murderous enemy of mankind this animal, had tasted human blood, and would no longer be satisfied with any other food. Government ought really to legislate against the thing being allowed to breed in a new fair country where bears and lions had never roamed. But he would show them one specimen and let them judge. At this point the straw was heard to rustle, and the mat began to heave; the crowd had been caught by fear, and there would have been a stampede if the press from outside had not prevented it. O'Connor caught the psychological moment, begged them not to be afraid, but showed himself carefully anxious to provide for his own escape; with exactly calculated exaggeration of precaution, as he stood near to an opening in the sack wall, he drew off the covering of his murderous water 'otter animal' and revealed an old tin kettle reposing among the straw!

How they jeered and roared and shouted at the 'take in', and how they rushed round beseeching everyone else to interview the famous animal. In the nature of things the sell couldn't be brought off more than once; but O'Connor was the man of the moment, and therefore proceeded to appoint himself salesman of the stalls one after the other. These showed a collection of articles exposed for sale that would have almost formed an inventory of the farms from which they came. There were bags of patent chemical manure, and little sucking pigs tied to posts; there were fowls and their eggs. Buff Orpingtons and black Orpingtons, and Leghorns and Cochin Chinas, Wyandottes, and Game birds. There were woollen toilet mats enough to stock a town; ornaments, pictures, crockery, spotted dogs from the mantelpiece at home. Here in a basket were six half-Persian kittens, with blue ribands round their necks, and a legend: 'Please buy me, or I shall be drowned to-morrow', and they did a roaring trade ...

Then came the counting-up of the takings ... A lot of small sundries brought up the total to nearly three figures.

Very late and tired, we all sought our horses and traps and made for home. For reasons which I need not expound, O'Connor was not in quite the condition to be our whip, and I had to take charge ...

The 'Water Otter' Bazaar gave the finishing-touch to the preparations for the church at Barcowie, and although the money was not yet all in hand, the foundation-stone was laid and the bishop travelled up 250 miles for the ceremony.

◆ ◆ ◆ ◆ ◆

Aborigine cradle carved from a single piece of wood, used for sacred rights within the tribe and rarely shown to outsiders. The Eagle and Emu feathers were worn in battle. When these items were presented to Charlie the feathers were stained with blood.

1 - Life in the Australian Outback

After almost a year in the outback, Charlie, still single, must have thought many times of the life he had left behind in England, his family and loved ones. It seems likely that he kept in contact with Sashie, Zoe's elder sister, as it would have been improper to write directly to Zoe. Sashie probably encouraged him, knowing that Zoe was receptive to the idea of marriage; otherwise Charlie would never have been bold enough to write the following letter to Captain Poulden, R.N., at Blackheath.

Orroroo,
South Australia

May 10, 1897

Dear Captain Poulden,

I am venturing to write to you on a matter (to me at least) of very great importance. I hope you will forgive me for introducing the subject of this suddenly. I will give, before I close this letter, the reasons which caused me to approach you now instead of, as might seem natural, before my departure from England.

Firstly, I beg your and Mrs. Poulden's permission to ask your youngest daughter Joanna *(Zoe)* to be my wife.

I ask a great thing of you - how great I realise to the full. But I can't help asking because I love her.

I know this must seem to you, sir, a stranger's request, but altho' you have not seen me more than two or three times yet your daughter Mrs Bullock *(Sashie)* at least knows me well and it is to her that I must look for a recommendation.

As to Joanna herself altho' I did not propose to her (a thing impossible without your consent) yet I saw enough of her from time to time to know that is to say the least my offer will not be distasteful to her.

My position is, of course, a humble one and my prospects are not great - they are in God's hands. But still I may fairly hope to be able to keep a wife before long. At present I am receiving a little over £200 a year and I need hardly add that that is equivalent in this country, where living is extraordinarily cheap, to nearly £300 at home. However do not think that I ask her to share this or such life as I am living here in the bush. I have already been offered two more lucrative livings in 'civilised' parts. (I refused them.) A Cambridge friend of mine of my own age who had been out here a year and a half is already working a large and important parish near Adelaide with a stipend of nearly £400 a year with a house. So the pecuniary prospects of a clergymen out here, tho' not great, are I think sufficiently good to justify him in looking forward to marriage.

46

I need scarcely add that very earnest prayer has preceded the writing of this letter. I know that it is all in the hands of our common master and that He will work it all out right.

I have not said all I wished or as I wished - it is hard to write about such things. I have been perhaps far too presumptuous in asking you such a boon. What I long for is your and Mrs Poulden's permission. Hers (Joanna's), unless a year had brought great changes, I have great hopes will follow.

Although Captain Poulden's initial reply was unfavourable, it was soon to be revised in a second letter imposing certain conditions on the proposed engagement. (Unfortunately his letters are now lost.)

Written during this anxious period are the following extracts of a letter from Zoe to Frank Homfray (the husband of her sister Mary).

16 Hervey Road,
Blackheath.

Aug. 23-97

My darling Wankie *(Frank)*,

I didn't know Mother had told Mary about the wonderful event that has happened lately.

Well, of course, I did not know it - but about two months ago a letter came from S. Australia to Father asking permission - of course you know what to do! Father replied kindly but firmly that I was too young and that he thought it inadvisable (which squash my poor dear young man must have received about now). Five days after my 21st birthday while I was still at Quorn *(staying with Aunt Jane Cox Gawler, her mother's sister)* I received some letters from home, and inside one of them was another with writing on the envelope which needless to say I recognised. This arrived at breakfast and I tried almost in vain to stifle my emotion. Prayers never seemed so long as they did that morning. Aunt J. appeared to be making a special effort to be as long as possible. At last I escaped, and on opening the aforementioned envelope found a little plain gold heart and chain wrapped in cotton-wool and paper. No writing anywhere to be seen. The most astonishing thing is that it was not registered, and how it is, it reached its destination safely I don't know. (I've become mixed in that last sentence but hope you will understand it.) Well, naturally as it had arrived here first - Mother and Lydia *(sister)* had felt it and poked it, and tried in every imaginable way to guess what it was without opening it. Mother, in her letter said they were curious to know what it was - was it a bit of the geology of S. Australia. So I had to write and tell her what it was, and also confessed my feelings towards the sender. On my return two days after - I felt quite reassured by the sight of Father's face, and then later on I was told of his former letter to Father and the reply. And then I was told that I might have the pleasure of corresponding with the gentleman (whose name, by the way, I feel a little shy of mentioning). It is necessary to say that I took the opportunity of doing so at once. Father has also written in a somewhat different strain to his last letter. But Oh Wankie dear he won't get them till about Sept 25th. Doesn't it seem a long time? It takes about 31 to 42 days in transit. But still I'm quite quite willing to wait of course I shan't get his answer till the end of October.

... My darling love to Bornee Noots *(sister Mary)*, - ask her if she remembers a certain midnight talk we had last year. I little thought this would come off so soon! - Ever so much love to yourself.

Continuing in a similar vein are further extracts from letters written by an animated Zoe to her sister, Mrs. Mary Homfray.

16 Hervey Road,
Blackheath.

Aug 31st 97

... Your sweet darling letter gave me much pleasure! You ask darling whether I'm quite sure I love him and I can only say that it is quite impossible to express my feelings towards him. I am only woefully aware that I'm not fit to be loved by him - it all seems much more than I deserve. God has been so good to me - the wonderful way He has put it all straight. Yes darling we are engaged only at present he does not know it!, and will not get Father's and my letters till about Sept 25th - I shall not hear from him till Oct 25th or there abouts... Father tells me every night where he thinks 'my ship' has got to, meaning the one that is carrying our letters out. Mother and Lydie take hold of the Newspaper, and pretend to read out that Her Majestys mail ship for Australia has come to grief, and that it was particularly noticed that one letter that was swallowed by a fish, bore the handwriting of Miss Joanna Poulden of Blackheath. Father at this point comes to the rescue, and adds that a certain gentleman was fishing off Adelaide and that he caught a fish, on its being prepared for his dinner, a letter was discovered inside - it is needless to say who the gentleman is. And so they go on concocting the most harrowing stories ... and yet Father always finds a way for my letter to get safely to its destination. Mother is quite as bad as the others! Of course it is simply delicious to be teased like this ... Charlie keeps a diary, and sends it to his (friends) ... I was reading one of them yesterday, and really the amount of work he has to do is simply alarming. He has sole charge of six churches. Last Xmas day he had to ride a huge way (he started the day before) to a place called Yanyarrie to take a service, and the heat was awful - it was the hottest day they had ever known out there. After the service he went back to the house of one of the church wardens - I suppose to stay the night and the heat was so awful that the only cool place at all was the well - so apparently, after throwing buckets of water over each other they went down the well and sat there! It was too hot to dream of sleeping in the house, so they camped out..

In early October, Charlie sends his reply to Zoe's father.

Ororoo,
Oct: 2/97

My dear Captain Poulden,

I received your second letter on the 30th ult, and I hasten to express to you and Mrs Poulden my deep gratitude for the honour you have done me in allowing me to look forward to such a great happiness. I wrote to Joanna her letter arrived a week before yours - and in my reply I said that I would write every week unless I heard that my letters also were to be limited. Please tell her that having received and accepted your limitation she will not hear from me again until a month has elapsed ...

Your second letter did indeed come as a surprise and joy to me and I thank and praise God's goodness in permitting it. I presume you mean our engagement to be provisional, I mean not a proper engagement. But as far as I am concerned nothing could be more binding than the fact that your daughter loves me.

I remain,
Yours very sincerely,
Charles E. Doudney.

Zoe, whilst staying with Aunt Jane Gawler at Bishop Auckland, receives a letter from Charlie and writes excitedly to her family at Blackheath.

20 Victoria Street,
Bishop Auckland,
Nov. 1/97

Oh my darlings, You know what had come, and I can't realise it, and I've only had a second in which to read it, and my dearest ones I do thank you for all your sweet kindness and for sending it on. And please don't be surprised if another one comes rather soon, because I can't have explained it properly that we might only write once a month, so that he is going to write often till he hears. I'm so sorry, but I'll tell him in my letter which I shall be beginning to write to-day - all being well. His dear letter is not very long, because he happened to be

1 - Life in the Australian Outback

Charlie and Zoe 'with one of the oldest inhabitants' standing outside St. Augustine's Church, Port Augusta, South Australia, with the rectory on the right.

pressed for time just before the mail went, but oh! of course it is quite impossible to describe what its like. There is a message for you. He says 'Will you convey to your parents my most heartfelt thanks for the permission they have given to our engagement. Please tell them that words simply can't express how truly grateful I am'.

In 1898 Charlie becomes rector of St. Augustine's, Port Augusta, and now has a suitable living for his bride. Arrangements are made for the wedding to take place in June the following year. They are married on Friday 16th June, 1899, at the Portman Chapel, and spend their honeymoon in Cambridge before returning to Port Augusta, South Australia.

Charlie and Zoe's first daughter is born on 13th June, 1900, and is named 'Esther Eirene'.

Opposite page: Joanna Doudney and baby. Port Augusta, August 1901.

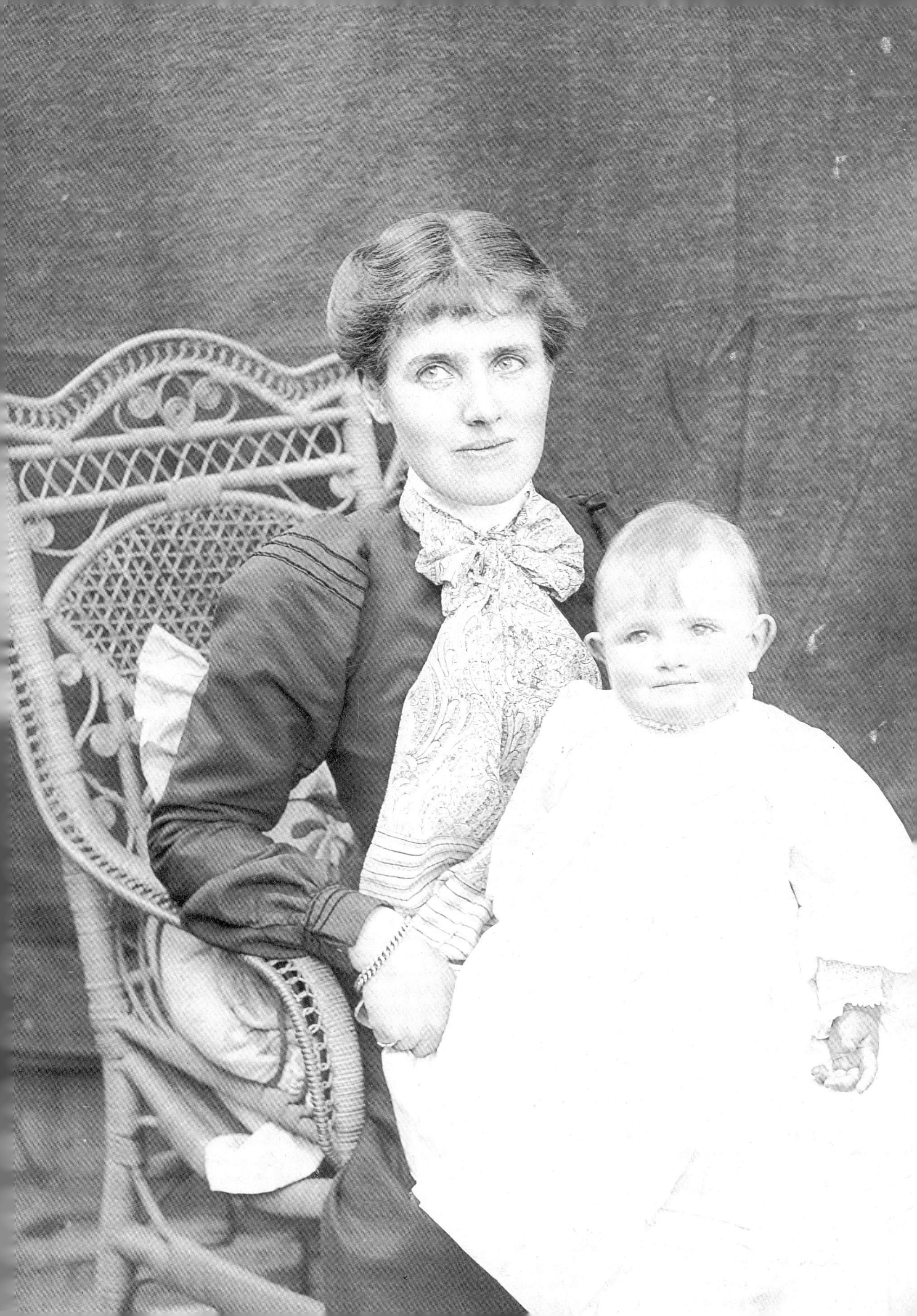

1 - Life in the Australian Outback

Early the following year in a letter to her sister Mary, Zoe writes of important guests and married life.

> The Rectory,
> Port Augusta.
>
> Jan 21 - 1901.
>
> My sweet N.B., - I wonder where you spent Christmas after all - I suppose with Aunt Jane at Brailsford. I've just opened your letter and begun to remark on the first thing that caught my eye.
>
> What fun your party must have been - I hope none of your guests had to sit on the floor - as mine did once. When the 'Royal Party' came here there were not sufficient chairs for the two little Tennyson boys to sit down so they sat on the floor - I believe Lord T. sat on the music stool which is ill suited for a man of his build - a sort of mini seat on three thin brass legs ... *(Lord Tennyson was Governor of South Australia.)*
>
> ... Our dear English friends at least some of them evidently think that one of the immediate outcomes of the Commonwealth had been the introduction of the ld stamp between England to here. They are mistaken - it has not come to pass yet. Lately we have had to pay quite a lot - though some were on account of over-weight ...
>
> We are feeling unusually drunk this afternoon Charlie and I - but have to keep up a semblance of repectability because Archdeacon French is here just for the night. The reason for our feeling this is firstly - Charlie has had one of his bad bilious attacks for the last day or two and only just managed to get through the Services yesterday - & secondly - we have had some fairly bad heat followed by a sudden cool change which always makes us feel limp ...

Extracted from The Treasury is Charlie's description of a memorable journey undertaken with Archdeacon French, who wanted to travel to Port Germein, a distance of nearly 60 miles.

> 'What facilities were there?' he wanted to know. Facilities, is it? There was the 'mail coach' - save the mark - a four wheeled spring dray fitted with two uneasy backbreaking benches, running over a sandy, bouldered, unmade road, or there was my cutter and the pathless gulf. You wouldn't have said that he had the archdiaconal manner. His overcoat was rusty and a good deal splashed with mud. His boots were very thick, and his gaiters had not been built in Bond Street. He drove a mild-mannered fat brown mare in a rattle-trap buggy, and he had a nasal twang to his voice. The clergy of all the North loved him amazingly. In his vicarage at Petersburg the spare room was always kept

ready for outlying clergy.

... They had wanted to make him Assistant-Bishop, for he had that which helps men, especially Bush clergy - strong, quiet sympathy as well as scholarship and goodness. He had left his English parish to give his life for Australia. His comfortable seaside congregation at Glenelg he had given up ...

For courage and hardness you shall not find many who surpassed him, as the following adventure shows. The choice was mail coach or cutter! He would take the cutter, please, and would be obliged if I would land him at Port Germein on Friday. Now the cutter was a badly designed, unhandy, somewhat cranky three-and-a-half tonner, in which I had taken little runs never more than ten miles out. Sleeping accommodation was so simple as to be barbarous. My passenger-to-be was a bachelor of over middle age, and I had made the offer almost as a joke, never expecting it to be accepted. He had taken me quite seriously and now it came home in bulk. Not wishing to back out, I engaged a dock larrikin to come with us, and spent a day in overhauling gear and laying in provisions.

After Evensong on the Wednesday we were to board the 'Kaloolah', the tide serving. Twelve hours' run ought to take us round if breezes were favourable, and this was allowing more than a day's margin ...

At sundown there was a blustering wind in the streets, but my sublime ignorance kept me from noticing that it was only the protection of the town itself which sheltered us from half a gale. The sky was quite black, the night overcast, as we three scrambled down the ladder and stowed our 'dunnage' by the light of a hurricane-lamp. I took a single reef in the mainsail and made all snug. Then waved goodbye, pushed off, and swung with a good tide down towards the bend. The little party standing on the half lit wharf were nearer than they thought to saying goodbye for good and all.

The gulf here is only a quarter-mile wide, and, waving like a river, broadens out as you descend, to over ten miles' width... We were in deepest darkness, and when we were once outside the break wind of the wharf down came the half-gale hurtling and shrieking. The 'Kaloolah' lay over to it as she came up into the eye of the wind, with black water foaming over her decks right up to the hatch-coamings. Smack! smack! smack! came wave after short wave, drenching us with spray as we sat in the well. Every two minutes we had to go about, which was chancy work, for you couldn't see ahead of the bowsprit and we only guessed at the channels. The waves told us a little about depth. The tide was stronger where the current was deeper, and there the beating wind raised a big-water, but the gale had now risen to more than the 'Kaloolah' could weather. In a gust she lay over, and two hatches broke adrift and went overboard. A goodish lot of water had been slopping in, and my poor Archdeacon was already as wet as his gear, and that was like paper pulp. If he wasn't dry, his comments were. He seemed to think that even an Australian coach had some advantages. As if I was responsible for the wind!

... We carried on, through it all, on the port tack till the channel, tending a shade eastwards, let us luckily anchor in shoal water behind a mangrove clump without going aground. If we had touched bottom it would have been for twelve hours, for the tide was racing out, and our food would not have lasted. But now we could take our time and close-reef the mainsail, bend on a storm-jib, and generally make all snug. Then out and into it again, thrashing gloriously down the spreading gulf, salt in our veins and nostrils, and all the nerves tingling with delight.

She carried her canvas now more easily, and our eye grew more used to the darkness. A few beacon marks we could just make out as we ploughed along but the wind came heavier and thicker every minute. As we rounded into each fresh reach it struck with the blows of a hammer, and now also there rose a cruel, angry, swelling sea. A clear gale was working up for midnight. The muddy mangrove-fringed shores of hereabouts were desolate and forbidding enough. They were less directly dangerous than the shelterless, rock-bound littoral a few miles down; so we concluded to anchor before worse befell, if anchorage there was. A little spit of island sand we found, with smooth water and good holding ground, just in time.

Thankful for small respite, we snugged her down, rigged the fire-pot in a thole socket, and brewed billy-tea to wash down 'tinned dog' and bake-meats. It was good to be there, and my Archdeacon cracked jokes on yachting sky-pilots and talked of English clergy in their comfortable vicarages... the lamp glimmered mistily on the main boom, and we hauled out long bags filled with chaff to pillow each side of the centre-board casing... We lay luxurious, smoking closely rubbed 'Victory'...

Our morning broke blue and cloudless, radiant in colour and sparkling light ...

Breakfast over, we were soon on our course with a full sail breeze for the south, working from shore to shore on lengthening boards. Towards the afternoon we raised the bare masts of the wheat ships laying in Germein, and looked to be there by nightfall. Not so ... Yesterday's weather began to come down again. Reef after reef we took in, until she was carrying her minimum. No longer river work now, but open water and a head wind up the gulf, thrashing up a sea that must be respected. The cutter was no good sea-boat, and she kept shipping in green in sloppy showers, infinitely unpleasant.

We studied our admiralty chart, and as the coastlines on both sides drew together made out Point Lowly on the west and Ward's Spit on the east. This last is a five-mile long spit of sand running out into the gulf, and awash at high tide. Over this we could see the safe shipping in the port beyond. Bleak, bare shores on either hand, inhospitable and desolate, gave no possible shelter. The chart showed no inlet or bay deep enough to run for.

But we discovered that on the east side the water shallowed to a fathom (as the tide was then); and this flat, probably dry at low water, reached two or three miles out.

Here the sea was, of course, less severe; and so we worked her up the bank, going about from the port tack when heavy seas showed we were drawing into deep water.

Thus we won towards the spit. Tantalising and clear stood out the grain ships on the further safe side, and we - we knew that we must get out into the open and round the end before getting harbourage. It is a famous place, this passage between the two points, fatally notorious for its mishaps. They called it 'The Race', and with a southerly wind blowing it could be full of danger. Slowly the day wore through as we schemed and battled. Afternoon of the second day fell darksome, and between us and the light on Point Lowly heaving black waves were white-topped in breaking spray ...

Suddenly we thrashed into a fleet of fishing-boats at anchor, and, luffing up under the stern of one of them, asked advice. It was given freely and at length, without undue modesty and with consummate choice of words. None of the fishing-boats, it seemed - and they were five times our size - dared face the passage. Nor did they think the variously designated hopper we were fooling in would get to the entrance.

We didn't argue. We anchored a cable's length from our friend and tried to imagine we were comfortable. The first business after getting her canvas off was to try and raise a fire. The fire-pot was a sort of canister with holes knocked all round the sides, and fitting on to a bent rod let into a thole socket. This, when filled with wood and coal, and once fairly lighted, burnt splendidly in the wind. But our fuel was wet with spray, and it seemed hours before we could get the fire going. Finally it cheered us by looking warm, and as it roared we fancied our clothes were drying, and we made tea. It wasn't easy to pour it or drink it in that 'heaving sway and restless roll.' But it served. The sea was short and steep. It was vexed with many cross-currents, so that the big rollers from our side were chopped into little bits ...

Somehow we managed to sup, then blocked ourselves in with wedges of sails jammed down upon each angle of our persons - and slept. At least, we pretended to, with poor success. The Archdeacon was a Mark Tapley. He never complained nor fretted, but poured out story after story, and really acted as though enjoying his 'hard lying' and wet bed.

More than once during that miserable night I scrambled on deck and crawled for'ard to try the cable. But she held well. As the second morning broke we were just where we were as regards the fishing fleet. The wind also was unchanged, and there was no rosy prospect of getting in that day. The fisherfolk would not try 'The Race,' so that was out of the question for us. But the chart gave us a single hope. We found there was a narrow winding channel, cutting right through the spit of sand, giving sufficient depth at high tide. Best of all it ran at an angle from some distance out along the point to its very root on the futher side: in fact, into the harbour of Germain. With centre board up we could have run over the spit, but we could not beat over it without its help. So we determined to try the channel. You are to remember that no land was visible as we sailed, close-hauled, out to the west along the edge of the shallow. It was only by the colour of the water that we could tell where our channel was. Suddenly we struck dark blue water, a line running into the yellowish-green of the half-fathom. Into it we shot, coming about to the starboard tack, and, as the cutting trended south-east, making a soldier's wind of it. Jumbo *(the boy)* was perched in the bows with a boat-hook, trying depths. Not that this was much good at the ten-knot speed we were making. But the colour led us right, and in a few minutes we were crunching through the little waves of the port.

The jetty is well over a mile long, to enable the big ocean-going wheat ships to come alongside. The tiny town looked hazy and unreal, mirage-magnified at the end of it, as my delightful and venerable passenger carried his bag along the endless-seeming causeway. It was as a wayfarer passing alone and unfaltering to a City of the Dawn. He never looked back. Perhaps that was what marked him off from other men. In his life he had never looked back.

Looking over events at home, a letter from Zoe to her sister Mary describes the amateur dramatics in which she and Charlie participate at Port Augusta. Amongst the small talk she mentions the Defence Rifle Club shooting competition, a sport in which Charlie excelled.

The Rectory,
Port Augusta.

Feb. 26-1901.

My darling N.B.,

I'm afraid I've been very long writing to you but got slightly mixed up as to whose turn it was and also our wonderful Concert has been taking up a lot of my time. However that is over now and I am sending you the flowery account of it written by the wonderful sub-editor of the Dispatch - the Port Augusta weekly which will save my going into it all. I haven't sent the printed account home because I thought the dear parents would be rather disturbed at Operas being mentioned etc. So I've just given them my own account about it... My gipsy costumes consisted of my dark blue linen skirt made shorter with three rows of red braid round the bottom, a white silk blouse, short sleeves and low neck, edged with gold braid, a piece of red satin ribbon round my waist, and a little square of red sateen placed on my head with gold tinsel round the edge and spangles made out of a brass trim cigarette box hung around the edge. My hair down - and awful hot it made me. I rigged Charlie up in a blue shirt, and a red sash and cap and his khaki trousers - which I turned up to make them into knicker-bockers and tied round the bottom with red ribbon and a pair of red football stockings, and black shoes ... (We) borrowed two troopers uniforms (trooper here means bobby) and one is terrifically stout. Charlie wore that one, and stuffed himself with pillows the uniform would not have stayed on other wise and between each verse they marched round one behind the other like bobbies do at home - sticking their feet out in that absurd way - and the audience shrieked ...

We have had the most appalling heat for the last fortnight it has been quite muggy and tropical but at last the rain has come. It has been threatening to ever so long but always passed off and come to nothing. Last night it rained quite half the night and we lay and listened to the joyful sound hardly daring to hope it was true. We've just been out to bask in it and revel in the damp delicious smell. Your small niece is on my lap doing her best to get hold of this letter and saying 'Oo Hoo Boo' etc., the first syllable of every word being a very high note. She is now reading Faulding's Medical Journal with interest and occasionally trying to eat portions of it.

I think I told you about the Defence Rifle Club *(Charlie)* was the means of starting. Nearly every Township or at least a good many of them have D.F.C.s and they had one here some time ago but it fell to pieces - but *(Charlie)* has revived it and there are a great many members now. Tomorrow the Wilmington D.F.C. are coming to shoot against our Club and we are going to entertain them with provisions out at the butts. It will be most exciting watching the shooting. It will be the first time ladies have been present at a match here. They've just borrowed our beloved copper to take out there for making tea etc. Mr Sykes met Charlie this morning and asked if we would mind lending it, and Charlie said without hesitation, "Oh yes, we'll lend it with pleasure", and here are Mary and I left stranded. She put off the washing from today until tomorrow on account of the rain and now they've seized and carried off our only copper and left Mary to wash the clothes as best she can!

On occasion, Charlie had to travel to 'that horrible Tarcoola', as Zoe called it, and would be away from home for some three to four weeks. The journey was arduous in the extreme, most of the way being over sand and desert. The bush tracks were scattered and uncertain, often cut away by rivers and sometimes impassable. The usual method of transport was by weekly coach, drawn by four sturdy mules which were changed at intervals along the route, 120 horses being employed for the round

1 - Life in the Australian Outback

trip. The coach set off in the early hours every Monday morning, crammed to more than its limit. Despite leaving before daybreak each day and driving until near midnight, it did not reach its destination until Saturday night, after six days' hard travelling.

One day, a Mr. Richardson, the mail contractor for the Tarcoola route, said that he was 'going for the record' and offered Charlie a lift up to the new mine. They set off early on a Tuesday morning in a light four-wheeled buggy drawn by four horses, having in the meantime collected the Adelaide Monday papers that had arrived by train the night before. Richardson had arranged for fresh horses to be staged at points along the way, and the intrepid party raced on, arriving at the camp by Thursday evening. Having had only eight hours' rest during the journey, satisfaction overcame exhaustion when the newspapers were handed out, for these gave proof that the journey time had been cut by half.

In 1901, Charlie's responsibilities were extended by his becoming chaplain to the Commonwealth troops in South Australia, and from 1902 to 1904, he was acting curate for Christchurch, North Adelaide. He continued with his shooting and, at one time, returned to England to represent Australia at Bisley, securing a good share of the prizes. He also shot in the interstate team and in 1904 was the champion of all South Australia, winning the King's Aggregate. Among his other interests were yachting and rowing and he coached the Adelaide University eight for a number of years. He became known as the most intrepid kangaroo hunter and yachtsman in South Australia.

In 1904, Charlie became rector of St. George's Church at Gawler, a small town a few miles north

¹ C.E.D. From Adelaide Rifle Club Team. Winners of Teams Match S.A.N.P.A.1902. Score 443'.

Top: 1902 Coronation Medal presented to Charlie in 1903.

Life in the Australian Outback - 1

of Adelaide. The town was named after Zoe's grandfather, Lt. Col. George Gawler, the second Governor of South Australia (from 1838 to 1841), and the church communion silver had been presented by him.

Little has been remembered of Zoe's and Charlie's everyday family life in Australia apart from the odd stories related to the children at a much later date. Joy, their third daughter, remembers being told about her 'Daddy's' motorbike and basketwork side-car, supposed to have been one of the first ever seen in South Australia. Apparently one day Charlie and Zoe went for a drive, during which the side-car unhitched itself, depositing 'Mummy' on the roadside whilst 'Daddy' went speeding on. Another memory, probably from Adelaide, is of the loan of an ex-polo pony which pulled a trap, and whenever they drove past the polo ground, the sound of the players would make the pony go quite mad.

Family tradition has it that in one of the parishes (probably Gawler), Charlie had the usual bevy of ladies amongst his parishioners who helped with church work and who, at times, were a little difficult to shake off without appearing discourteous. On one occasion, Charlie observed one of these dear ladies heave into sight down the street, and in desperation picked up his cassock and ran in at the front door, through the house and out down the garden path into the privy at the bottom of the garden, leaving Zoe, who was quite unaware of the reason for this flight, standing open-mouthed.

Zoe's few surviving letters from this time give an impression of tedium made worse by the climatic conditions. Shortly before the birth of her second child, Noelle Mary, who was born on 26th December, 1904, Zoe writes to Mary and Frank who are now living in Cheddar, and fantasises about returning to England.

> The Rectory,
> Gawler.
>
> December 12, 1904
>
> My darling N.B. It is a very hot Monday and Custo *(Charlie)* and I are feeling so slack that it is an exertion even to think.
>
> C. says that absolutely the only thing that would rouse him at this moment would be the startling announcement that someone had just given him a brand new up to date motorcar and to see it outside the gate awaiting him. Well - I don't seem to hear it coming so we must conclude that it is not going to be the method by which we are to be aroused from our apathy. My idea is that a lovely white marble spotlessly clean swimming bath arranged in one of the rooms would be the thing. Of course I mean one that is level with the floor and that you can step into or sit on the edge of and dangle your legs in the water with a glass of lemon squash by your side. Ah well - though we have a very nice cool looking blue

painted bath with a splended shower I fear it isn't quite large enough to swim in and there's nothing marble about it. There is a Methodist School just opposite and the unfortunate kids have just been singing some wearying ditty which sounds like a Cantata. Children don't feel the heat like we old folks which one can see by the way in which they tear about in the hot sun with unabated energy. Essie is always livelier on these hot days if anything - and therefore no trouble as she keeps herself amused without bothering us.

I have crowds of sewing that I ought to do but don't seem able to attack it when it is hot, and when the cool changes come I troll about and do all sorts of other things. I have to see about having the Vice Regal pram re-covered *(it had been used by the Tennyson children)*. It is terribly shabby now - its original rather bright blue cloth having faded tremendously. I am thinking of having it done in blue or green linen which will be much cooler - both to look at and touch. White is rather too glazy for this climate.

Dec 13. Your delightful letter has just come Mrs. N. B.

Whenever your letters arrive I always have a great longing to suddenly find myself transported family and all to Cheddar! I'm not in the least homesick but somehow you and Frank just exactly seem to fit us - and all your sayings and doings remind me so much of ourselves - that I long for us to be somewhere within reach of one another ... Why you can't kick your Vicar out and offer the living to us beats us altogether! Especially as he seems to be a charming man and I'm sure wouldn't object to vacating in our favour!! It only wants a strong foot and a firm hand (Frank's foot and your hand) - and the deed would be accomplished in no time. Ah well it seems that we are to stay here indefinitely and the prospect of getting home even for a visit is as remote as ever or nearly. Dear Custo has faint hopes that if he can only keep up his shooting record he might be chosen for the Team if one were sent home. His expense would then be paid - where Essie's and 'its' and mine would come from I don't quite know - the sky I expect ...

To the Padre as a token from the passengers S.S. Medic — March – April ·06

WHITE STAR LINE

COLONIAL SERVICE

PASSENGER LIST.

Wm. ANDERSON & Co.,
CAPETOWN.

DALGETY & Co. Limited.
ALBANY, ADELAIDE, MELBOURNE, SYDNEY, NEWCASTLE.

W. CROSBY & Co.,
HOBART.

ISMAY, IMRIE & Co.,
LIVERPOOL & { 17, COCKSPUR St. SW / 34 LEADENHALL St. EC } LONDON.

The Liverpool Printing & Stationery Co. Limited.

LOOKING FORWARD. DECK BILLIARDS. CRICKET.

INSPECTION. SUNDAY MORNING.

2. A Parish in Bath

Fifteen months later, Zoe succeeded in her desire to move the family home to England. They set sail on 2nd March 1906, on the steamship Medic, and the journey was accomplished in about seven weeks. Charlie took up the pastoral duties of the voyage, and as a token of gratitude was presented with a photograph of the ship signed by members of the crew.

Upon returning home, Charlie took a temporary position at West Hampstead church. But the family suffered a great loss when, in March 1907, the children Essie and Noelle came down with pneumonia. Although Essie recovered, little Noelle did not survive.

Charlie was eager to find a permanent living, and on 29th May 1907, the family moved into the large vicarage at St. Luke's, in South Lyncombe, Bath. Great happiness was brought to the family with the birth of Zoe's and Charlie's third child, Joy Poulden, on 4th July 1908.

St. Luke's Vicarage

2 - A Parish in Bath

Charlie's innovative approach to his new Parish did not go completely unopposed by the more conservative members of the congregation. Some along with certain churchwardens, strongly disapproved of Charlie's 'improvements' and alterations and held prayer meetings for his 'conversion'. However, Charlie kept one step ahead of the opposition, changing the constitution of the church council to enlarge the committee and bring in fresh blood in support of his ideas.

By Easter 1908, many changes already had taken place at the church. Among them were the installation of new choir stalls and a credence table, and the increase from one communion every month to communion every Sunday. One local paper describes the 1908 Easter vestry meeting as quite an occasion:

> 'The church room had been beautifully and tastefully laid out to represent a drawing room and there was a large attendance. Ladies were very prominent among the gathering and several musical selections were given by a string band'.

Charlie, always in support of community projects that might help the poor and needy, was to become influential in the introduction of halfpenny meals of bread and soup, to be served at the parish daughter church at nearby Odd Down. He also took part in the reorganization of the Young Men's Club, the expansion of the Gymnasium Club, the creation of a Ladies' Working Party and the reorganisation of the Men's Working Party, and helped begin publication of a free magazine. Beyond these time-consuming activities, Charlie welcomed all parishioners to the vicarage and not just the wealthy as had been in the past.

When the present church was built in 1868, it was more than

Charlie and Joy rebuilding the Church, as Zoe looks on.

*Above:
Essie, Zoe
and Mrs.
Harding.*

*Left:
Essie, Joy
and Charlie.*

*Right:
Essie
and Mrs.
Harding.*

sufficient for the needs of the scantily-inhabited district of South Lyncombe but by 1909 the local population had almost trebled and the church was always well filled. It was Charlie's intention, therefore, to enlarge the building. This project was to take up much of his time and energy over the next four years. Funds were slow in coming in and by 1911 only about one third of the money needed for the first part of the work had been found. Despite this unpromising start, the foundation stone was laid

Laying the Foundation Stone on St. Luke's Day. 18th October 1912.

on St. Luke's Day, 18th October 1912, with Charlie trusting that the remainder of the money would be found at a later date. Once work had been started, it had to go on to completion, whether the funds were available or not, and from the end of April 1913 the church was no longer useable. Services were transferred to the Parish Room or, if the weather was fine, held in the church grounds. The nave was now half built and, gratifyingly, almost every member of the congregation was taking part in the work. The Baptistry, for which the children of the parish had collected over 15,000 pennies, was consecrated on St. Luke's Day, 1913.

With only half the funds available, there was no hope of completing the full rebuilding scheme, and 1914 brought more pressing problems. Charlie had, at any rate, succeeded in enlarging the seating accommodation in the church and in providing a vestry and a school room, which were his prime objectives. In 1914 the annual number of communicants had almost doubled since 1907, to 4,300.

During this period of financial constraint, the vicar was also involved with a building project at the mission church at Odd Down. With the help of Mr. A. R. Saxty, the lay reader, a recreation room with living quarters for the parish nurse and for a caretaker was undertaken. The 'new institute was to be for the use of young people and others, to provide a means of improving their minds and brightening their lives, and by healthy recreation develop a better manhood, and so prevent the objectionable practise of standing at street corners, or frequenting the public houses or drifting in the streets of Bath - already crowded at times by undesirables.'

The last major building project that Charlie undertook was a large extension to the Rush Hill School in 1914/15. Local contributions towards the cost of the construction were raised by the Bath School Managers' Association.

In 1909 the Vicar took on a curate, the Rev. A. Chisholm ('Chizzy'). He also instigated the appointment of an overseas missionary, the Rev. Vernon Shaw, who was to be sent to India and financially supported by the parish. These increased expenses were achieved at a time when the parishioners were having to dig deeply into their pockets.

Little is written about Charlie's everyday parish work, but it included countless vestry meetings, garden fêtes and sales of work. These were usually held to raise money for some mission, with the building fund being regarded as an extra challenge. Brief notes extracted by Essie sometime in the 1950s from her mother's diaries, give only a glimpse of what life was like.

> 1909 July 8th. Cricket match, ladies v. St. Luke's men. Men played left handed. Ladies scored 49, of which 16 were wides. Zoe top score with 11 and took 4 or 5 wickets.

> 1910 Feb 16th. The vicarage dining room chimney caught fire and the bedroom above was nearly burnt out. Bath's new and first motor fire engine was used for the first time and bumped into a tram on the way up. No serious damage done.

> 1911 May. Charlie and someone called Voss widened a passage and made a sleeping porch where Charlie and Zoe slept for the rest of the time they were at the vicarage, winter and summer alike! They declared that they never caught colds from that day!

> 1911 June 14-15th. Coronation Fête, made £50. Very successful.

> 1911 Oct. 25-26th. Cinematograph on China. Zoe provided continuous accompaniment on the piano.

> 1912 April 14th. 'Titanic' disaster. Service at St.Luke's later.

> 1912 April 19th. 'Twelfth Night' at the Assembly Rooms, for the Odd Down Institute.

> 1912 July 10th. Mrs Lawson's Women's Suffrage meeting.

> 1912 Oct. 6th. Charlie preached in the Abbey for the Building Fund.

> 1912 Oct. 8th and 9th. 'Ladies of limited means' sale.

Children were not neglected in parish life. This is evidenced by the fact that, sometime in 1912, and mainly due to the persistance of Essie, Charlie persuaded Miss Connnie Chadwick to form a company of Girl Guides which was to be the first in Bath.

Although heavily involved in parish life, the vicar still found time for his own activities. He played tennis, golf, and took part in cricket matches up at Odd Down. He kept his shooting up to a high standard and it was in about 1913 that he, along with two of his brothers, Raymond and Herbert, secured between them 33 prizes at the annual shoot at Bisley.

St. Luke's Coronation Fête, June 1911.

Top: The sweet stall.

Middle: Joy, aged nearly 3.

Below: Outside the Ice Cream tree.

Opposite page:
Charles Doudney and Joy, St. Luke's Vicarage,
19th December 1913.

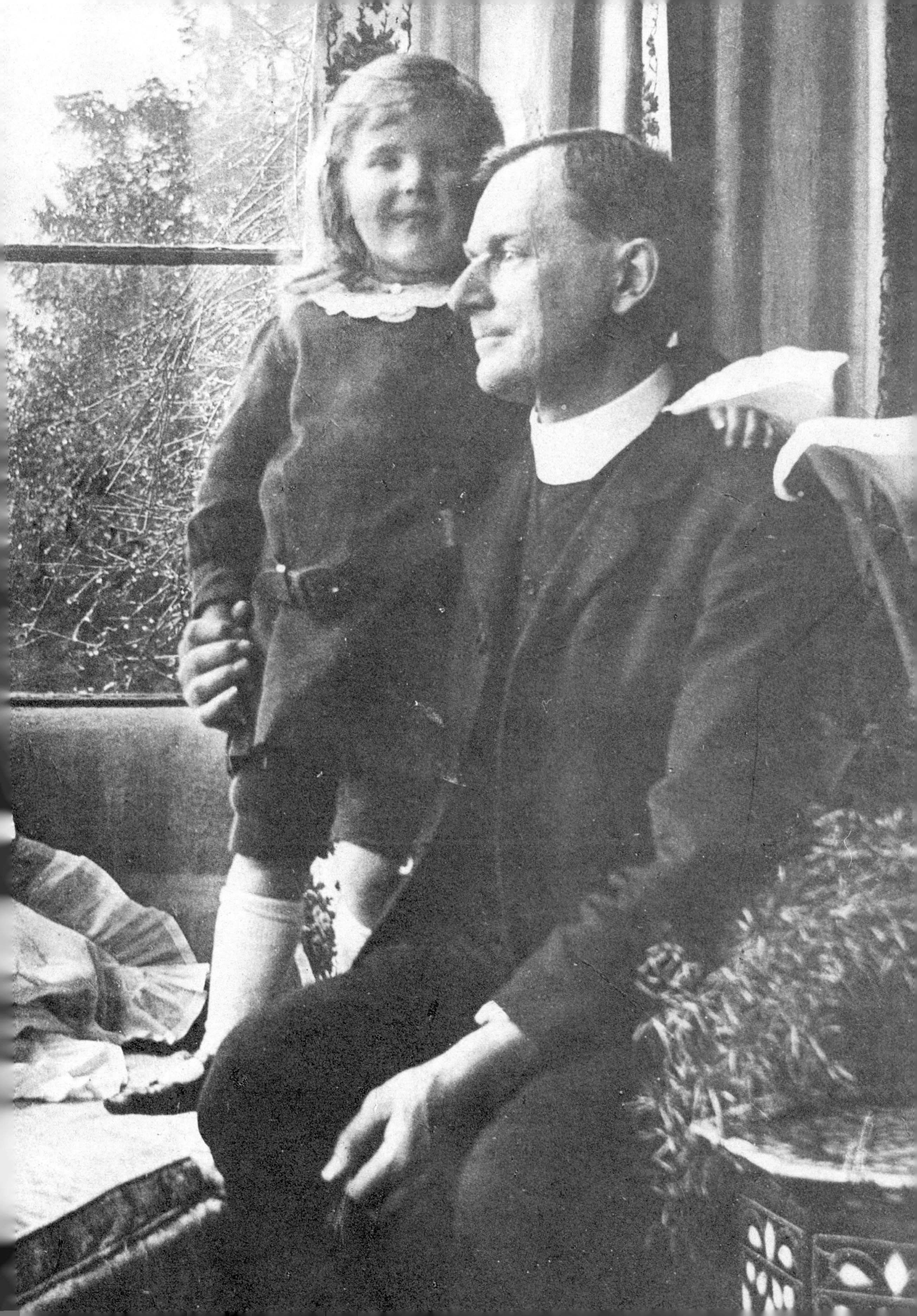

2 - A Parish in Bath

Charlie's pastimes were varied and inventive, one of his great interests being cabinet making. In about 1907, Charlie went to Castle Shipyards in London and procured some timber from his father-in-law's old ship, H.M.T.S. Formidable, which had recently been broken up. (When under the command of Captain Poulden it had been a training ship on which Zoe and the rest of her family had been brought up.) Charlie set about making furniture, which must have been difficult as the wood was so hard. The finished products included tables and chairs and a chest of drawers of his own design. The last with its hinged drawers is proof of Charlie's inventiveness *(see photograph below opposite)*. Comparative photographs show Zoe's sister, Arly unable to open a drawer of a standard chest of drawers even with the combined help of Raymond and Herbert, but Essie has no trouble with her father's new swivel drawer.

Arly, Zoe's sister, has a problem with opening a drawer which also defeats the combined efforts of Charlie's brothers, Herbert and Raymond (opposite above). Essie (opposite below) demonstrates with ease her fathers' new type of swivel drawer.

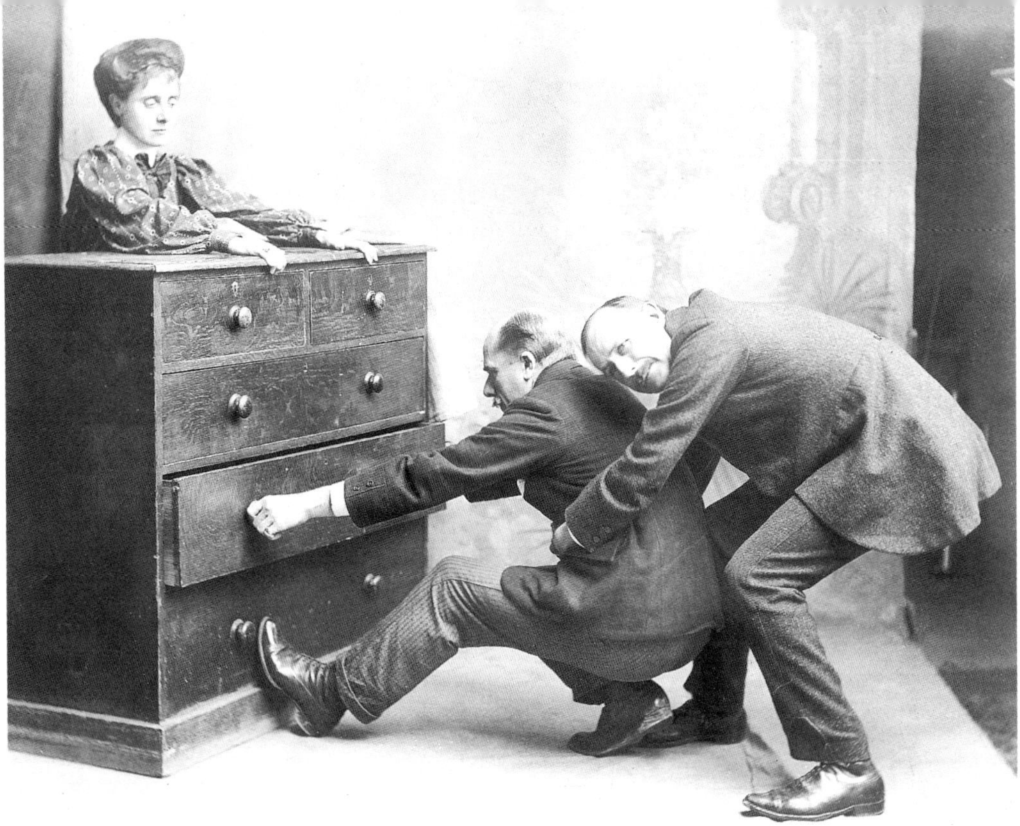

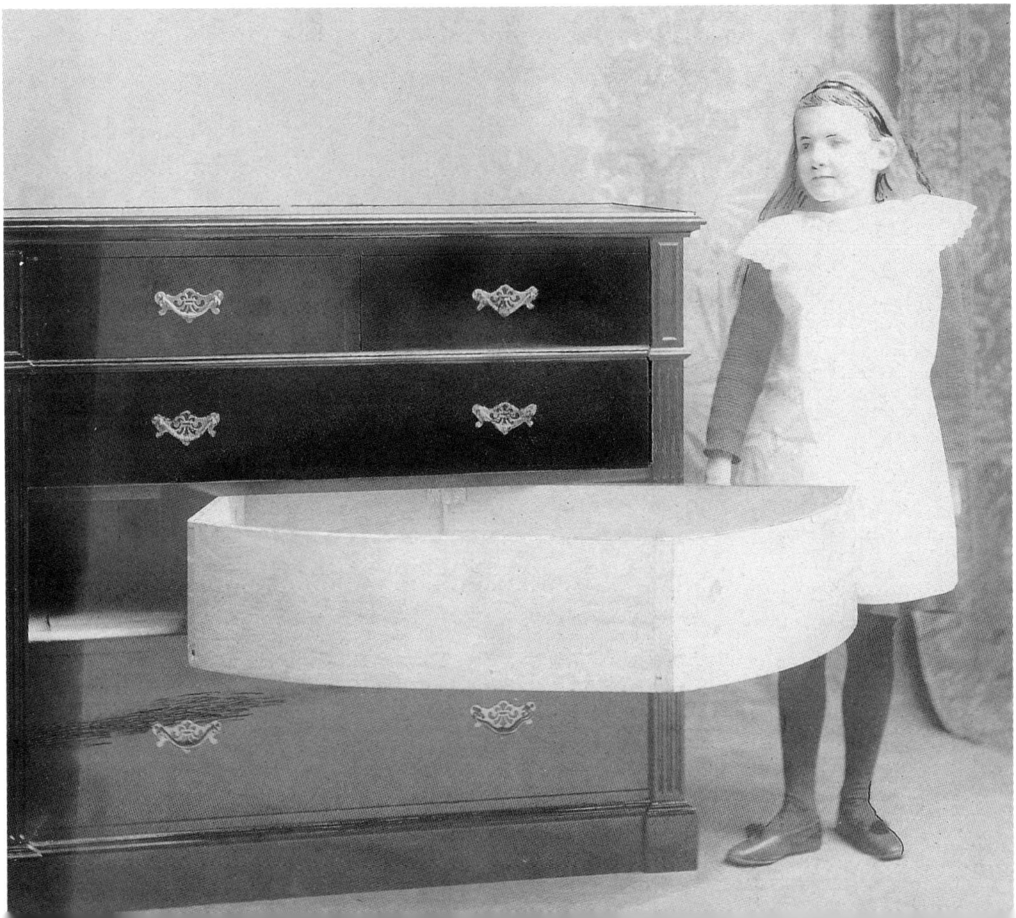

2 - A Parish in Bath

Having a creative and inventive mind, Charlie was fascinated with any new science or technology. At a garden party held in June 1912 for the Odd Down Institute, illuminations were rigged up in the gardens and were run off a homemade power supply.

With the help of his brothers Herbert and Raymond, Charlie had developed a system run on petrol gas, the volatile character of the spirit being surmounted with the use of a carburettor. The gas was generated by an hydraulic pump operated by the domestic water supply. The system was installed in the Vicarage for both lighting and cooking, and it was the first house in the area to have electricity.

Life at the Vicarage was very happy during these times, and the family was increased by the birth of another daughter, Désirée Gawler, on the 5th November 1913. Her older sister, Joy, although only five at the outbreak of the war, retains treasured memories of her father during these early days at Bath.

> The day always started with morning prayers before breakfast when we were joined by the cook and the housemaid ...
>
> On Sunday afternoons Daddy and I would go about the church scaffolding, up gigantic ladders (to me at least) and look down on Mummy. I remember Daddy taking me to the stonemason who was to carve the effigies of me and Esther on either side of the church window in the West end.
>
> After tea on Sundays I was allowed to play with Sunday games on the drawing room table. Essie and I always took part in all church social activities - e.g. fêtes, concerts etc. Mum being a brilliant pianist and Daddy having quite a good voice.
>
> Once Mummy got cross with me about some misdemeanour of mine and sent me to Daddy's study. I stood outside the door, afraid to go in, and when I did creep in, he wasn't at all cross and behaved as if he didn't know what it was all about.
>
> I remember Daddy bouncing me on his outstretched leg, and at night being tucked up in bed, rolled into a tight little bundle and saying goodnight.

Charlie's father, David, was a regular visitor to Bath, often preaching in St. Luke's, and Charlie reciprocated by visiting his father's church at Hatford in Berkshire. Christmas was usually spent at Hatford, where there would be a large gathering of the family.

◊ ◊ ◊ ◊ ◊

In 1910, Charlie spent a few weeks away from the parish as chaplain of a troop ship bound for India. The H.M.T. Plassey was to leave Southampton on or about 7th December, returning on approximately 26th January. This was to be the Vicar's first contact with troops in any number and it must have been a welcome break both for him and the Church Council. Charlie knew, however, that the trip would be no holiday as he had the spiritual interest of some 2000 men, women and children for approximately two months. He looked on it as 'a mission from St. Luke's' and felt that his experience gained while working among such a crowd could only benefit the congregation.

The following are extracts from Charlie's diary written aboard ship.

December 6 - Went aboard and signed on as 'chaplain', got a single berth on hurricane deck - no porthole, but a skylight. Bitter cold.

December 7 - Shopped, unpacked. Tommies came aboard, all carrying kit and bundles, apparently legions of them, and where they are to be stowed, 1500 in all, without crew, I cannot see. We are only 7000 tons. Drafts from all places, of all arms, artillery, infantry, cavalry, engineers, sappers, and Indian native regiment officers. Slipped down the Solent, and before dinner were clear of the Needles and had dropped our pilot. Diners left dinner one by one, casually, as if they had forgotten something, but didn't come back. Only ten of us left at the finish. Choppy.

Top: Boat drill.
Below: Deck Quoits.

2 - A Parish in Bath

December 9 - ... The ten Army nurses on board didn't rush much for their breakfast. Purser declares he's never seen the Bay worse. I haven't anyhow. You can hardly stand on deck in the teeth of the south-west gale. Pity the men and women down below, especially the children. We've no cargo, and of course are light as a cork. My! how she lifts and sends, settling with a sullen crack and crash ... But it's warmer now, and you can manage without an overcoat on deck ...

Dressing for dinner rather painful in stuffy cabin, where everything was battened down. But I enjoyed a nine-course dinner in scant company ... All night the propellers raced and shook to the noise of creaking timbers and grinding girders.

December 11 (Sunday) - ... Perfect sunshine, and enough wind to make 'white horses' and a dry ship. Everyone on deck and happy. The hundreds of new faces swarm up like rabbits from a bury. I went round the troop decks to spy out the land. But how to begin and what to do? The Tommies are thick as bees. Imagine 1235 men packed into two backyards on two decks. You can't know them all, and when you stop and chat with them they all stand to attention. I must get a choir out of them somehow by next week, and some sports going, and a Sunday-school for the children.

A boxing contest.

December 12 - Through the Straits (of Gibraltar) in the night, some of us thought we saw the Rock. Troops busy at physical drill and fire stations. This last very different from ordinary passenger drill. Has a smack of the real thing in it. Every gangway and passage and boat is guarded instantly with fixed bayonets and loaded rifles. The place where the spirits are kept is doubly guarded. In great danger there are some who will always try to rush that. The idea is to die drunk. All the unattached officers and myself had to assemble in the smoking-room.

This afternoon went down with the troop officers into the 'innards' of the ship to find a place for our Bible classes. The barrack-rooms are the ordinary 'hold' of the vessel. She carries no cargo, and right down, in tier after tier, the great yawning spaces, dimly lighted, roughly boarded, are fitted up for the men. Open hatches lead from one to another. In every part, on every deck, up and down the companion ways, lying on the rough trestle tables, lolling on blankets, singing and laughing, playing cards and concertinas, swarmed and swarmed these Tommies. In that light you could barely distinguish faces, and I only found my friends with difficulty. Then we fixed a meeting-place. There was a last hatch and a final deck, and that was her bottom, flat, of course, as in all modern steamers. There I was told I could do what I liked after 6.30 any evening. It was the storehouse for the hammocks in the daytime.

The saloon is very picturesque at mess with all the uniforms. Seeing that they are drawn from all arms, the variety is rather startling. I thought I should be out of it with such swells, and they were perhaps a shade standoffish at first. The man opposite to me at the first dinner looked like one of Ouida's heroes, the dashing superb cavalry man, exquisite in mess uniform covered with medals. He spoke perhaps four times to me. Since then we have had long walks on deck late into the night. It is great to be among men who have done things. They never brag about them, but seem to speak of them like football matches. Their faces tell the story. One had governed a province in the Sudan; another walked from India right over 'the roof of the world' through districts where no other white man ever was, through the Gobi desert and so to Siberia. Another after six years in East Africa, wandered right up the map till he came to Egypt.

December 13 - The men have physical drill every morning before breakfast, and my friend the Ouida hero asked me if I would care to join them. I was the only officer doing it, and found the work hard, as the men were advanced. It was the usual Swedish, and fortunately I had done it frequently at our gym. It was lucky I did not make a fool of myself, for the Tommies who had done their turn (they were taking it in half-hour sections crowded round to watch the pastor going through the mill. It did one no end of good.

That's Algier now, on our right, with mountains ranging back in all manner of fantastic shapes to snow-crowned peaks. I'm busy arranging to-morrow's concert. There is no band on board, worse luck! And seeing that we are gathered from many regiments, no one knows what talent there is. I got an assembly, in the second saloon, of Tommies who were put forward as 'comics'. They were, and no mistake. They stood rigidly to attention, cast their eyes to heaven, and went through their verses as if on parade, getting redder and redder in the face with each line. The bandmaster and I had to get out of sight and choke in silence. Then the Bible-class in the lower depths. A few turned up and we had a fine chat, as I encouraged them to ask questions ...

December 14 - Steaming for three hours past Malta, which looks barren enough. Had a fine view, however of St. Paul's Bay, with his statue clear against the sky-line ... Concert at 7.30. A hatch forward, rigged as a stage, with a piano and a cluster of electric lights overhead. All round on every side, standing in solid chunks, hanging on to derricks, jammed into companions, and looking down from tier to tier of upper deck and forecastle head, swarmed the troops. A seething mass of khaki and white faces. First result - four of my performers not to be found. Stage fright! and no wonder. Had it pretty badly myself when I stepped under the bright glare to control proceedings. They needed control. No officers were present until three-quarters of an hour later, when they came down with their ladies to sit in roped-off enclosure. However, the men enjoyed themselves to the full. After the slightest hint of a chorus they simply let go. Most extraordinary thing! But the average Tommy cares nothing for the average song. He cares extremes, either ultra-sentimental or ultra-comic.

December 15 - Muggy and wet for chess tournament. I beat the captain and went under to the R.C. chaplain. However, we're playing on the American method, and I may come up yet. Had the game in my hands, then made a slip, lost a castle and was done.

Another class on the keel with the men. There was only one possible chapter for these waters, Acts XXVII, and the men much interested in St. Paul's escape. They hadn't realised one little bit, of course, the history of the waters they were sailing over. These classes make me late for dinner. They only begin at 6.30. Then we get discussing things. Dinner is at 7, and I generally begin to dress at 7.30.

Outbreak of measles on board, and the case isolated in the fever hospital right astern. It makes me the more sorry, because there is a woman dying there, whom I have been visiting, and now we shall not be alone when I go.

December 16 - Officers' physical drill to-day. Far easier than with the men. We did not do nearly so much. Port Said to-morrow, and I shall be busy buying ashore for the Christmas-tree. There are seventy-five children on board, and I'm going to have a tree, even if I can only get a palm; and a present for each.

December 18 - (Sunday) Holy Communion at 7.45: rather uncomfortable. We were nearing Suez, lots of people were about and there was little quiet ... and all the ship's company far too busy to attend to anything but the work in hand. But in the afternoon we had a voluntary service, well attended, and a large number of officers present, especially the younger ones, which pleased me much.

My subject was inevitable - The Crossing and the Wanderings - for Sinai was superbly in sight, and we had that day passed the crossing-place of the Israelites.

December 20 - Organising children's sports. The officers let me have the use of the boat deck, and three of them came along to lend a hand. At first the children were too shy to come up: till I went down and persuaded a few, then soon found myself acting the Pied Piper and dragging a tail from all quarters.

December 22 - Cricket in the afternoon ... No one stayed long, and on my side four men were bowled with four consecutive balls. In the morning the officer commanding and his staff had taken me with them on inspection tour over the military part of the ship. Of course I had been many times to isolated messes and to the hospitals. It is only when you go right through the whole thing on one tour that you begin to see what it must mean to house and feed and exercise and give breathing space to 2000 people in a comparatively small ship. Each mess provides for eighteen men, and there were about six messes in each division of the decks. Collapsible tables, consisting of long boards, are fixed on stanchions, and at each end are hung the metal pans and cans required for the food. ... At night the tables are lowered, and hammocks are slung in rows. The organisation needed is a miracle. Think of the cooking alone! This is really a hospital ship, and will be so used coming home. So that there are all the necessaries for the sick besides the messes. There is one large space right in the centre of the ship, just forward of the engine room where cots will be hung. It is empty now and I have commandeered it for the Christmas parade service.

December 24 (Christmas Eve) - Curious to think of all the busy shopping that is now going on in England. Christmas Eve shopping seems as far from us as the moon. We are well in the north-east monsoon now, and it is fairly rough and cooler, though I still sleep out on deck in company with two others. The worst of it is that when no ladies are sleeping on deck they turn us off at 5 a.m. for washing decks. It's quite dark then, and breakfast isn't till nine o'clock. As it is rather early to get up, we generally go and snooze in the smoking room.

Very busy rigging the tree. The sailors put up a shelter and lined it with flags. And our tree looked all that it should do, covered with toys and bright ornaments. At three o'clock I went round the married quarters gathering the kiddies and their parents, acting the Pied Piper again. A great tea was given on deck, with a fine cake ...

December 25 - Hard to believe that it was Christmas Day when the deck swabbers turned us off at 5 o'clock. Quite dark, and rather dreary. Holy Communion at 7.15. Very pleased to see the music saloon crowded, but no men from the ranks. I think they are too shy to come up to the first class. A large number of young officers ... All the ten Army sisters were there. Some of them have seen much service, and have war ribbons. They are splendid women, always cheery and bright and ready to help. The parade service was just great. The big hospital deck was crammed, and looked an eerie picture. The serried ranks of khaki, line over line, of white faces reached far back among the posts. Impossible to estimate the numbers. There might have been 1000 men, with nearly all the officers and ladies, and many of the ship's officers.

They are keeping the day, and no mistake. Flags, holly, and mistletoe are everywhere ... The courses are lavish, not to say regal. All the Tommies and their

2 - A Parish in Bath

> wives have had a bounteous spread. At lunch in the first saloon the cook marched in great state with the boar's head round the tables, and at night the dinner would not have shamed the Hotel Cecil. Not an officer was the worse for the free champagne. Well, we get to Bombay to-morrow, and I have promised to escort four of the sisters to Agra. The amusing thing is that I know no more about India than they do.

The full voyage took seven weeks, also allowing Charlie nine days of touring whilst in India. The Vicar was particularly impressed by the temperance work going on in the army and commented that "now seventy per cent of the rank and file were teetotal, a thing that twenty years ago would have been ridiculed as being Utopian".

◊ ◊ ◊ ◊ ◊

From time to time, routine parish work would be interrupted when Charlie took time off to go down the Bristol Channel in the 'Eirene', the little mission to seamen ship, visiting lightships and Lundy Island. It was on these trips that the Vicar became interested in wireless telegraphy. He was soon experimenting at home and an account of his activities was given in the *Bath and West Chronicle* of March 1913.

> ... For some months he has studied wireless telegraphy seriously and his present installation is the result of two months application, with the exception of one part - the 'detector' - built by himself ... Mr. Doudney uses the receivers which fit to the head in the form of a cap, leaving both hands free, and such a head-gear thus becomes the winged cap of the modern Mercury.

> Mr. Doudney is in touch with most of the wireless stations in this country, and many in Europe, but with the means at his disposal - an old motor coil - he has at present only succeeded in sending messages over a comparatively restricted area. His coil, under favourable circumstances and good atmospheric conditions, will dispatch messages from his own apparatus for 20 miles ... this is possible with the aid of a home made installation, which cost Mr. Doudney £2 or so ...

> The distance over which messages may be received depends on the altitude of the 'Aerial' - the group of three wires which are, so to speak, 'hung up in the sky'. In Mr. Doudney's apparatus these wires are 60 feet high, and this gives a range of from 200 miles to 300 miles ...

Charlie himself wrote of his interest in telegraphy in the *Bath Chronicle*, 2nd January 1915:

> The stimulating cause of it all was a young nephew of mine on holidays who wanted to experiment with an old house telephone and make it respond . We made desperate attempts to make it respond to wireless signals. It worked; and

Wireless-receiving apparatus made by Charlie in one of the spare-rooms at St. Luke's Vicarage in about 1912 or 1913.

> sundry faint buzzes were communicated. This was enough to lead us on however, to greater things, and we hung a wire from some trees to the house and set to work to make some simple instruments - coils of wire called 'inductances' and 'condensers' made out of tin foil and waxed paper. All the talk was of wave lengths and 'earths' and crystals, and books were studied. But, alas the poor nephew was required to attend at Marlborough for other studies before even a wandering wave deigned to come down our aerial. But I had become much interested and set to work in earnest to tap the innumerable messages that I knew were sweeping past all day and night.

Soon, the whole household became involved in Charlie's experiments. In the 1950s, his daughter Essie wrote a few notes from memory of the disturbance that occured -

> A wide bench was rigged up in the Vicarage study, the full length of one wall, and this was soon a complete mess of wires and buzzers and coils and valves and headphones and sparks. No maid was ever allowed to touch that end of the room, but occasionally my mother, under strict supervision, was permitted to flick a duster round.

> At first it was merely a question of picking up messages and it was a great triumph to get the Eiffel Tower. (For many years as a young girl I thought that the Eiffel Tower was solely a wireless station.) The family conversation became largely interspersed with references to coils and valves and time signals, and the whole household had to learn the morse code in order to be able to stand by and help Father take down the messages, for in those days there was no actual

speech, only tapping in morse. We had small hand tappers on which to practise, and even at meal times I remember that such requests as 'Please pass the salt' were tapped out in morse.

Then as time went on morse conversations took place each night with other enthusiasts. Uncle Herbert, who was now living in Berkshire, was equally keen, and it was an immense thrill to establish contact with him. On the first occasion when the two men had arranged to try and talk to one another, Father sat twiddling knobs at the appointed time, while the rest of us sat round with pencils poised determined to take down every dot and dash that nothing might be missed on this auspicious occasion. For a long while nothing happened and the younger fry began to get a bit bored. Then suddenly Father grew tense, faint signals came through, and as we frantically wrote down the letters, we thrilled to realise that the noises we were hearing were being tapped out by Uncle Herbert sitting in his home nearly a hundred miles away. On occasions when other duties prevented Father from listening in when messages were expected, Mother and I were deputed to sit with the headphones and take down what we heard.

The time came when this early Ham was not satisfied, and bent on making contact further afield. One day he looked longingly at the tall church steeple close to the Vicarage, and thought of the wonderful results he would get if only his aerial could be fixed up there. At the next church warden's meeting he suggested it was time that a steeple jack should be engaged to see that the lightning conductor was in order. With twinkles in their eyes, the church wardens agreed that it was necessary and in due course a steeple jack arrived, and in examining the lightning conductor, happened to take up

Aerial being taken to the top of St. Luke's steeple.

with him a long length of aerial which he fixed to the very top of the spire.

After that, the reception was vastly improved, and when Father was sending messages the sparks resounded all through the house, and wherever the rest of us were, we automatically took out our pencils when we heard the thing starting, often in my case to the detriment of my school home work.

The Vicar was delighted with his new aerial and it was the envy of all amateur wireless operators in the west of England. He went on to say in the *Bath Chronicle,* 2nd January 1915:

From this aerial a wire led to the house and gradually there appeared on a long table, an imposing array of instruments until the plant was complete. And then came the supreme joy of placing the phones on your head and at once hearing the clear notes - shorts and longs, longs and shorts - of the morse code. The household was summoned to listen and switches were moved, condensers varied, inductances put in and out (all to suit the varying wave lengths of any signals that might be coming). And at almost every change a different note was heard. High notes, low notes, gutteral growls, humming of mosquitoes, sweet cello tones. Of course I knew not what they were or where they came from, but it was a joy to get them. And then one night a friendly Marconi expert happened to come in and there followed an evening of revelation. He was congratulatory but I knew that it was the high aerial that did it. But it's nice to sit and listen for the first time at your own plant and be told what all the signals are.

'That's in the Channel. He's calling the Lizard. Who's calling? Why a ship of course. Ah, there's Paris. He's sending press news to the ships. That is our Navy. All code that - secret.'

A thin clear high call sounded far above the others. 'That's Germany... Nordeich. Ugly note isn't it? Hear that? That's what we call a frog-French and croaking like one.'

It seemed too wonderful to be true, that one could sit there and be in touch with the great world. But it was true, and one soon learned to distinguish the notes and to know their wave lengths and times of transmission. Most of the big stations have fixed times, and the daily calls from several were eagerly watched for. Time signals, of course, anyone could take without any knowledge of morse, but press news, weather reports and other matters were still a foreign language. So the next step was to learn the code. It is this that stops so many amateurs. It seems so easy at first. The letters can be learned in an hour, but it takes many months of hard practise to be able to use the language. Paris is the joy of the beginner, because the weather reports are sent out twice each day with quite delightful slowness. And you feel quite a telegraphist when you can get it all down in excellent French.

I soon found that it was a good hobby for a busy town person to get hold of, because the best time for operating was late at night. And so when the long series of evening engagements are done with and the house is silent, one can listen to all sorts of interesting things.

But of course, one was not satisfied with merely listening. One wanted to join in. And so came the most difficult part. Transmitting. This requires a great deal more knowledge and skill than receiving and also some source of electric power. As to the latter, I was fortunate in being on the main lighting circuit. A licence, too, had to be obtained from the Postmaster General. Indeed, even for receiving one must have a licence, but it is readily granted whereas for transmitting all sorts of requirements have to be met.

Being inland I was allowed a considerable margin of power and was soon in touch with several other amateurs, some of whom are well known investigators. I found them all exceedingly kind and very ready to help and instruct. There is a strong Freemasonry among wireless men. Most evenings one would sit down wondering who would be 'about', and a 'general call' would be answered at once by anyone who happened to be listening and conversation or test or even a game of chess would follow.

As for actual use of the station, it must be remembered that the licence is only held on condition that the military authorities may use it at any time and it is pleasant to feel that in perfecting one's apparatus one is preparing a means of transmitting news that may some day be of use to one's country. A chain of really efficient amateur stations over the country might be of great value in times of serious national emergency or peril of actual war.

Once, some irresponsible writer stating that the Vicar was wont to hold converse with outgoing and incoming missionaries in the Bay of Biscay, nearly caused the apparatus to be commandeered.

Essie remembered the day that the Bishop of Bath and Wells came to preach in the church. It suddenly occurred to her father that His Lordship might not fully approve of the church steeple being used for such mundane purposes as a wireless aerial.

The Bishop was lunching with us that day and Father took him into the study and began to tell him about this wonderful modern achievement of wireless telegraphy. Father was always able to carry people with him and in no time the Bishop was thoroughly interested and asking all sorts of questions, and when he finally heard about the steeple aerial his only comment was 'What a splendid idea!'

Then it all came to an end when war broke out. Two members of the police arrived one day and removed the vital parts from the study bench, as of course no amateur wireless was allowed to operate, and down came the famous aerial.

Unknown to anybody in the family, Charlie had already been passing on to the military authorities foreign signals that he had picked up on his wireless receiver. The author obtained this information from the late Edward Poulden (son of Luther) who, some time ago, had reason to converse with the late Mr. Nigel De Gray, one time head of 40 O.B. De Gray stated that the Rev. C.E. Doudney had contributed useful information to the department. The government department known as 40 O.B. was part of Naval Intelligence and organised many amateur wireless operators to supply them with any foreign messages or signals received. By the time war broke out, much useful information had already been gathered.

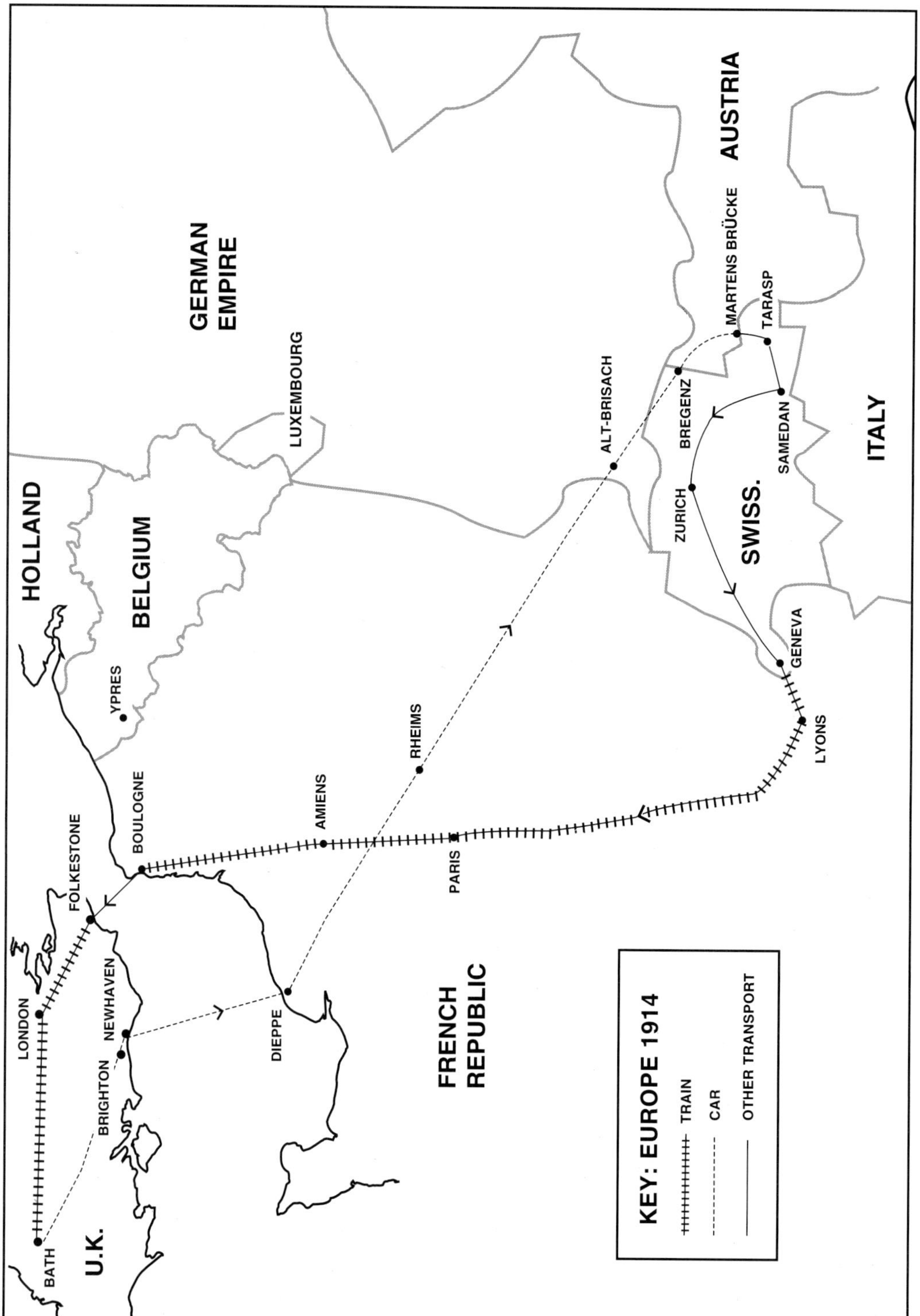
KEY: EUROPE 1914
TRAIN
CAR
OTHER TRANSPORT
GERMAN EMPIRE
AUSTRIA
HOLLAND
BELGIUM
LUXEMBOURG
SWISS.
ITALY
FRENCH REPUBLIC
U.K.
BATH
LONDON
BRIGHTON
NEWHAVEN
FOLKESTONE
BOULOGNE
DIEPPE
YPRES
AMIENS
PARIS
RHEIMS
ALT-BRISACH
BREGENZ
MARTENS BRÜCKE
TARASP
SAMEDAN
ZURICH
GENEVA
LYONS

3. Europe in Turmoil

Although war in Europe had been threatened for a number of years, nobody truly believed it would ever happen. It was therefore decided that the vicar and his wife should take a well-earned holiday through Europe, accompanied by their good friends, the Rev. A. B. West and his sister, Miss West. Arthur West had been a colleague since missionary days in Australia and arrangements were made for the two vicars to take up temporary Chaplaincies, with Charlie at the expensive Hotel Kurhaus at Terasp in Switzerland and the Rev. West not too far away in Austria.

Even without the threat of war, the envisaged journey was quite an undertaking. Many of the roads were still unmade and badly signposted, but plans were made anyway. The transport would be a hired American car called an 'Overland', and they were to meet the Wests in Dieppe.

On returning from what turned out to be an unexpectedly extended period of leave, the Vicar wrote an account of their adventures in the *Bath Chronicle*, 5th September 1914. Added to these extracts are some of Zoe's letters written to her sister, Mary.

> We started our journey on the Sunday night of July 26th at a time when matters had arrived at a crisis between Austria and Serbia, and on the Sunday afternoon a rumour was in circulation in Bath to the effect that war had been declared between these two countries. As a matter of fact there was no truth in the report. The actual position was that Austria had presented an ultimatum to Serbia and it was thought that the reply delivered by the Serbians would go far towards satisfying Austria's demands. Unhappily those expectations were not fulfilled and the declaration of war was made two days afterwards. No rupture had taken place however when we left Bath and not for an instant did we imagine that we were on the brink of the disastrous conflagration which has since broken out. I had obtained a chaplaincy at Terasp in the Engadine *(Switzerland)* and expected to be absent from England for five weeks.

Zoe's first letter to Mary gives her impressions on the start of the journey.

> Kurhaus Terasp,
> Engadine, Schweiz,
> Aug. 2. 1914
>
> Darling N.B.
>
> Just a line to tell you how we have been getting on. It was so difficult to write en route because we were too dead sleepy to do anything but go to bed the minute after Table D'Hôte.

3 - Europe in Turmoil

We left Bath on Sunday evening directly after Church - and had a send off from various parishioners. It was about 8.30 p.m. really before we finally got off as we stopped at the Dr. and Mrs. Preston King's up on Combe Down to say goodbye, and he gave me a packet of 'Mothersill'. I had another present of one of those macintosh head-coverings for motoring, from Mr. Gregory too, wasn't it kind of him. We sped on through the night, just stopping at Warminster to say *au revoir* to 'Wax' (the man from whom we hired the car, one of C's wireless friends) and by the way Raymond *(Charlie's brother)* accompanied us as far as Newhaven to relieve Charlie with the driving. Through Salisbury and Chichester, Brighton to Newhaven was our route. I slept fitfully, occasionally lying full length on the back seat and as I had one of my feather cushions it wasn't very uncomfortable. I fed the men at intervals with sandwiches and biscuits. It was very strange seeing the dawn appearing gradually. We reached Brighton about four and went along trying to find an 'open all night' garage to get a little more petrol and did so after a long hunt. Then we went to the station to try and get some tea but nothing was open so we went on to Newhaven and got there a little before five and a restaurant was open so we were able to have something and get a little washed up. Then followed a long wait but it wasn't very wearisome because there was a good deal going on and presently the A.A. men came along (Automobile Asc.) and took charge of the car for shipment and at 9.30 a.m. I took Mothersill and went and had an hour's snooze in the waiting room which was quite empty. We went on board about 11 a.m. and got seats amidship facing stern. Heaps of people came on board from the morning train and it was fairly crowded. It was quite choppy and she rolled a lot but I hadn't one uncomfortable second and ate biscuits and choc and had a cup of tea too. Heaps of people were fearfully bad so I felt deeply thankful to Mothersill. By the way it's a prevention for train sickness as well. We got to Dieppe about 2 and finding that it would be at least an hour before the car would be landed we went and found our Hotel ...

The "Overland" being hoisted aboard at Newhaven.

Europe in Turmoil - 3

Charlie's *Bath Chronicle* account continues:

On our return (from the hotel) to the harbour we found our car second in a line with three others, having passed the customs, the only remaining formality being to procure petrol at the A.A. garage, the tanks having been emptied at Newhaven for the crossing. We all started our engines and the head Customs officer magnificently waved us off. The front car swept out of the dock, but alas! our engine simmered out into silence.

I had forgotten to turn on the petrol tap. When she was going again the leading car was swallowed up in the traffic.

But nothing daunted, we shot out, desperately endeavouring to see the tracks of the guide. These of course we lost at once, but blindly guided on up and down the streets delighted to see the other cars meekly following. We all met duly at the garage and had a good laugh over the incident.

The following morning we were joined by the Rev. A.B. West *(Rector of St. Dunstan's-in-the-East, London)* and his sister Miss West, who had come over on the night boat. The crisis meantime had grown more ominous and we had a long debate as to whether we should go on or turn back. Though war rumours were becoming rife, appearances still were that no other country other than Austria and Serbia would be involved. We therefore decided to penetrate into France, agreeing that if the outlook was unsatisfactory we should turn back. So out of Dieppe, purring up a winding hill, and over an open down with the lovely views of sea and cliff. *(This description is a little misleading; according to Zoe they got lost coming out of Dieppe and did a ten-mile detour before finding the right road)* ... after five hours of steady twenty-miles-an-hour we pulled up in the big square at Beauvais, where we lunched at an hotel.

Then Compiegne, where Joan of Arc was captured by the English ... Then Soissons, and a stop for tea, and so to Rheims. It was quite dark before we got in, and the streets were crowded and badly lighted, but we soon found our hotel, housed the Overland, dined and fell into bed.

Wednesday broke gloriously and we looked out into the square and on the beautiful front of Rheims Cathedral. We had to spare half an hour to gaze at the clerestory windows - most famous of glass - and the tapestries. The glass made one understand the despair of all artists since the 15th century ...

The road given in the maps led rather too much south, through Chalons and Vitry, but a lucky mistake took us on to a much more direct one, which led straight with hardly a bend over a sort of Salisbury plain.

You would rise over a hill to see the white road ruled straight, stretching out and out until it disappeared into the hazy distance. It was very lonely, hardly a village for 60 miles, but in the middle lay the big military camps of Mourmelon, now the flying centre for the French Army. Aeroplane hangars were there in rows and rows and once a polite sentry made us leave the main road and take a detour because of the danger of flying. So the sentry said! Much more likely that they feared spying.

... we swept down to valleys at last and into the winelands, where every town and county had the name of some famous brand of wine ... and then - then a Mecca which neither my wife nor I had ever hoped to see. We have been for years admirers of the 'Maid of Orleans' ... Domremy - where she was born and lived those 16 short years of simple peasant girlhood.

It was a wrench to get away from that place but we had to set the Overland going again (two inner tubes got punctured this trip and we had to put on the stepney twice). We came through sweetly pretty country, forest-covered big hills and gleaming valleys, rich as velvet to Miracourt, where the dinner was a dream and the breakfast as fresh as air, and the coffee as only French people can make it, and the charge absurdly small.

A further extract from Zoe's 2nd August letter to Mary,

After the first day's trip when we felt extravagant and stopped for the midday lunch and afternoon tea etc., we mutually decided that we really needed neither and all we did was to eat rolls and butter (stolen from each hotel we stayed at) and cake and fruit as we went along. Occasionally stopping to make tea with our methylated apparatus. We always had a good dinner on arriving.

Charlie continues in the *Bath Chronicle*,

Thursday, July 30th, we were now to try our luck with frontiers. Of course war rumours were rife, but it was hard to get exact news in those out-of-the-way places. If we had only had a single London or Parisian paper that morning the motor's head lamps would have aimed in a diametrically opposite direction from that we did take. Who would have dreamed that all that lovely peaceful borderland with its quiet farms and still pine forest would be in a day or two seething with war.

But of course we didn't guess it and set out early for the frontier. Through busy Neufchatel-sur-Moselle, whose streets were crowded with Army Service carts and on eastward over a small pass to Epinal. Here we had to crawl along roads crowded with marching troops in full campaign kit, very hot but singing as they went. And now the mountains began ... Up and up through the pines, past delicious leaping streams, until we swept along the shores of Lake Gerardmer and confessed we didn't want to go any further. A week there would have been a joy.

And the town on its banks - Gerardmer - was most interesting.

As chauffeur I was wondering all the journey what the car would do on a real pass, and now she was to be tried. The famous Schulcht had to be tackled. It was a long pull, a steep, quite ten miles of about one in ten with bits of, say, one in five, or even steeper, but the good car never troubled the least and we throbbed up over one of the finest roads that I have ever seen, in the cool shade of great pines, winding and winding, and all the time the precipice on our right fell deeper and deeper. As for my passengers they enjoyed the scenery but I didn't see much of it. The necessity of keeping a big car from making a plunge of 3,000 feet sheer kept my eyes glued to the road. The summer changed to mid-winter and our big coats were not too much. Right at the top was a mile or so of broad safe billiard table road, and she swung into the top gear and forgot all speed limits.

Then the Douane. Now we had decided that should the frontier mean any trouble whatever, down the Schulcht, westwards again we should go. But the polite French officials bowed us out of their land and a hundred yards further on the even still more polite Germans bowed us into theirs. Of course my papers and driving licence and photo were all carefully examined and many questions asked, but no difficulty was raised. We discussed the war, but the idea of war universal was ridiculed (save the Austrian-Serbian, which of course was in progress then). We were happy then and all through the trip in having Mr. and Miss West who spoke French and German fluently.

It is almost beyond comprehension that within one short day all motor-cars were confiscated there, men were shot, bombs dropped from aeroplanes, in a few more hours tens of thousands and in a week hundreds of thousands of men fighting for life.

(On that same day, Thursday 30th July, the British Prime Minister, Mr. Asquith, made his historic speech in the House of Commons awakening the country to the gravity of the situation. He declared that the issues of peace and war were hanging in the balance.) Meanwhile, Charlie continues:

From the border down to the Rhine level was a big drop but not very interesting. We wound out of the mountains leaving them suddenly - and ran out on to the dead flat plain of the Rhine up which, at the time I am writing, the French troops are pressing and have driven the Germans back on the forts of Neu-Brisach. A big factory town lay on the flat at the foot of the mountains - Colmar - then a network of canals and small rivers and marshlands. Suddenly we came upon a menacing fort and had to go right through it, past the two moats and through tunnels, into the village in its heart, and out through a similar line of defence. Of course many sentries were passed but they waved us on gaily. War being declared between them and us within a few days!! The most serious stoppage was the Rhine. A bridge of pontoons crossed it here, dominated by the steep town of Alt-Brisach, with its fine cathedral. At the beginning of the bridge we were stopped by a strong guard whose officer came up to the car and questioned us very closely as to our intentions and destinations. Our interpreters were able to satisfy him, whereupon he directed a private to escort us over the bridge. The Rhine here is a broad river, apparently not very deep, but moving with very great speed. It was really a very impressive sight to see that great mass of water swirling past with irresistible power. The bridge was of pontoons and each pontoon, as we crossed it, gave one the impression that it was a boat moving up stream at high speed and cutting the water into two waves at its bows.

From the Rhine the road rose gradually into mountains again, which began to loom ahead ... Up and up to the cool highlands and over the watershed and down again to Neustadt, a place in the heart of the forest. Here we put up at a delightful inn, and were much amused by the merrymaking of a bridal party. At least we were until we went to bed. Then our opinion of them changed, as they kept up the shouting of their national folk songs and dancing until the small hours!

We had great debate as to whether we should pass Lake Constance to the north or south. It was a question of roads. In both cases it meant terrific hills and very roundabout ways but acting on the advice of the innkeeper, we decided on the southern route, and made for Douane Schingen, a place which has since been a centre for mobilisation of troops. It was a perfect run - mountain roads, but absolutely perfect in surface. At one place, it is true, the motor gave up through choked carburettor, which meant a couple of hours work to get at and clean it but that did not mar the best run of the tour. Down a sudden hill with a simply appalling gradient the frontier appeared and we were duly passed from Germany to Switzerland. A bang a little further on indicated a burst back tyre. The Stepney (oh precious Stepney) was put on in a few minutes and we pulled up in Schaffhausen for repairs. As these would take about two hours we went by train to the famous falls of the Rhine and saw them from all sorts of points of view, including partly underneath.

From Schaffhausen to Constance and right along the shores of the lake to the Austrian border was perhaps the worst section of the whole tour. That is from the point of view of the driver. The roads were shocking, villages with narrow winding streets occurred about every 2 miles - in some parts of the 30 miles run down the shore the 'village' seemed almost continuous. All the dogs in Switzerland except the ones on duty at St. Bernard had elected to spend the day stretched fast asleep across the road. The Pied Piper had just been along that route and left most of his train playing there in the dust, and in one place the main 'road' was up, and we had to make a decline through some back alleys and work the big car over a small wooden bridge ...

We crossed the Austrian border at a point just south of the lake near Bregenz, and the hostile attitude of the soldiers ought, perhaps to have made us turn back...

In Austria we found intense excitement. All the Landsturm were being called out and the men were assembling in all villages; 1,200 from one small town and 700 from another through which our road led that day. Every market square was filled with a gesticulating crowd and we were greeted with what sounded like hostile cries. And now, on each side and in front, loomed the Alps, snow-covered peaks gleaming in the setting sun.

We followed the course of the Upper Rhine as far as Feldkirch, where one road turned sharp to the east and led over the famous Arlberg pass. We had half a mind to try this at night, as our time was very short and only one day remained for us to get to our respective chaplaincies. It was just as well that we gave up the idea and turned in at Feldkirch for the night, - a somewhat uneasy one again, this time disturbed by the shouting marching in the streets. Parties of students went arm in arm through the town singing the 'Watch-on-the-Rhine' and other martial songs.

August 1st. We were delayed in our start because the hotel keeper would not take an English £5 note for his bill. So we had to wait until the banks opened, which they fortunately did at the early hour of 8 a.m. Even there they would not honour the £5. We did not realize why till later, i.e. that the strain was very severe in all Europe and no foreign paper money was cashed. However, they did cash a circular note. I wonder now why they did this, as I have not been able to get another honoured since.

The Arlberg was superb. One long pull up, at an easy gradient for about 20 miles, winding in a mighty precipice up the face of which the road crawled in 'hair-pin' bends. The gradient got steeper and steeper and yet the good car swept up bend by bend and the valley dropped deeper and deeper, first on our right hand and then on our left. But it was so steep that the bonnet looked as if it were cocked up in front of us.

She held on and on till suddenly the engine faltered, stopped, then rushed on again. I shouted to the passengers to jump out, which they did nobly, but it was not want of power, but want of petrol that caused the failure. A few more rushes and a final stop. I backed her very cautiously against the low wall (guarding the precipice) - it was right on a hair-pin bend that she stopped. The ladies walked on up the pass and Mr. West and I set to work to find out what was wrong. This we soon discovered to be that the gradient was so steep that the petrol would not flow to the carburettor! With this car that could not happen even on the steepest part of any hill round Bath. If the tank were full it would have been right, but it was only about one-third full. We put the contents of a spare tin in (two gallons) but even that would not raise the level sufficiently, and we were discussing the idea of cleaning small stones carefully and putting them in the tank to raise the level when, far below, we saw a tiny insect shape, like a car, coming crawling up the road. It contained two Germans, who nobly stopped on the steep hill and sold us enough petrol to bring up the required level.

The two ladies had got to the top of the pass among the snow by the time we came up. The hill on the other side was just as steep and we took it about five miles an hour, but I think the passengers were not quite happy till we were down. I went down on the second gear alternating the two brakes to prevent them from heating. The summit was just over 6,000 feet.

Landeck next, and then southward again. This time up a gorge with a river raging by our side. The scenery got more and more terrible and awesome. The road rose higher and higher above the river until it was almost hanging over it at an immense height, cut clean out of the rock.

Occasionally we dashed into a tunnel, sometimes crawling round a sharp bend hooting vigorously. Again the poor driver didn't dare to see much else than the road.

Nauders, the place where our party was to separate, was reached at three o'clock, and here we found that the West's coach would leave at 4.30 for Trafoi, and that we must go on to a place called Martens Brücke and catch another at four o'clock. So no time was available for farewell tears. The luggage was hastily divided and we two started on alone, and almost at once found ourselves descending by a new road, the face of a cliff.

Just at the bottom a soldier rushed out of a house waving a red flag, and there followed a desperate attempt on my part to explain to him that we did not wish to take the car into Switzerland, but to leave it just over the bridge at Martens Brücke. It must be understood that no cars are allowed in that part of Switzerland. How we missed our interpreters! The Wests. I don't know how we managed but at last he let us go over the bridge, where of course the Swiss Douane stopped us and tried to make us go back again. Fortunately relief came for a difficult situation, in the person of a waitress from the inn, who spoke English excellently. By her good services we pacified the soldier, hired a coach house for garage, locked the car up and caught our coach. We caught it by half an hour - the last one which would land me in my chaplaincy in time for Sunday. Not bad after a whole week's run.

But, oh, the luxury after having steered a big fast car for six successive days, from early morning till late evening, over entirely new roads, to loll back on the high back seat of a coach and really look at the glorious mountains! felt as if I wouldn't care if the driver let the whole concern over one of the precipices. It wasn't anymore my responsibility. But oh! how slowly the four good horses seemed to take us.

(Monday, 3rd August) At last the lovely valley of Terasp came in sight, and our long journey ended. But only, alas! in gloom and anxiety, for we found the great hotel, Kurhaus, which contained 350 guests the day previous, now almost empty, and people still hurrying away. War was begun with Russia, France was on the verge, and even England might come in!

(German troops moved into Luxembourg on the night on 1st-2nd August, and Belgium on 3rd August.)

I may add here that we have now been here in Eastern Switzerland for twelve days, and have had no news except through foreign sources. No English papers since the war began, and in common with many other English people, we are wondering how we shall get back to our country. Our case is complicated by the possession of the motor. It, is of course, quite impossible to drive it back during the war. Fortunately it is just out of Austrian territory, and in neutral land, so in case of war with Austria it would be safe.

Terasp is a resort after the style of Baden, with special treatments for rheumatism. A large number of very wealthy people have come from all parts of Europe for the cure, as well as for the climbing. Many of the guests were millionaires but their wealth, unless it was in hard cash, was of not the slightest use to them. Nearly all who could do so were leaving the place as fast as they could, and most of those who remained did so because they could not get away without actual cash. No cheques could be changed, and even English bank notes were no good. A large number of rich Russians were perfectly destitute. I could tell stories of millionaires who hadn't got ten francs in their pockets. I was myself speedily reduced to such a state of penury as I hope I shall never experience again. Soon I had only thirty francs left, and ten of these I lent to a very wealthy Englishman whose wife was sick, and who had no money to buy medicine for her.

Zoe continues in her letter to Mary, started on 2nd August,

We arrived here about six p.m., our trunks that we sent on from Bath haven't arrived yet and this is Monday *(3rd August)*. The key has, so we hope the trunks will follow. Meanwhile it is doubtful if this letter reaches you I suppose. The war cloud is very terrible and we hardly know what to do. Our being here as Chaplain is a farce. There are only three Americans in this hotel, all the other people are German and everyday they flee on account of the war. The manager is in despair, it is usually packed, and it means of course a dead loss to them. Charlie had walked to Schuls to see if he can get some money as we can't move anywhere without it. We have had a card from Sash at Samedan *(it so happened*

3 - Europe in Turmoil

that Zoe's sister Sashie and her husband Ashton were also on holiday in Switzerland), and if we can't take the car back thro' Austria and Germany we must leave it and get home thro' Switzerland by train - only we can't desert the Wests and I must get hold of them somehow *(the Wests being still in Austria!)*. I see by Saturday's Daily Mail that tourists to Switzerland are being turned back at Dover - so that looks as if we might have difficulty in crossing.

Here is Daddy back again - he hasn't succeeded in getting any money actually, but some delightful people we struck this morning (a German banker and his wife a native of Rugby - They keep a shop of all things) and he is going to do his best to get Charlie some cash. There has been a run on his bank and he says there's not 40 fr. in the place! So we can't move from here if we wanted to. Charlie is going over to Samedan perhaps tomorrow to see what Sashie and Ashton are going to do. He says that the news was a little better at Schuls this afternoon but it is so difficult to get at the truth.

This is perfectly gorgeous and of course the Hotel is the essence of luxury. Huge big salon - and salle a manger and a smaller room for lunch. We get up about 8 a.m., go out and have cafe au lait, honey and rolls, on a lovely gravelled terrace, with a rushing mighty torrent below us (snow water), snow mountains above us, sparkling fountains and flowers around us. We hadn't spoken to any of the other people until this afternoon when we were trying in vain to translate a German telegram pinned up on the notice board. In desperation I went to one of the American ladies and asked her if she could translate it for us.

Charlie's *Bath Chronicle* account continues,

Great Britain declared war against Germany on the night of Tuesday, August 4th, and we heard the news at the Hotel Kurhaus the following morning. I came downstairs and entered the big salon of the hotel. A number of Russians, Germans and Americans were talking together, and as soon as I came in somebody turned to me and said 'England has declared war on Germany'. The Americans made no secret of the fact that all their sympathies were with the British, but the Germans, of whom there were still a considerable number in the hotel, were furious. Life at the Hotel Kurhaus was very strange after this, and relations between the various nationalities were decidedly strained. We waited there for some days trying to get into communication with Mr. West and his sister, and at last a telegram came from them in German - no English telegrams were allowed - begging us to join them at Nauders, and return to England as quickly as possible. But by that time Britain, France and Russia were all at war with Germany, and we knew that to return by the way that we had come was absolutely impossible. Besides we had no return tickets, having motored out, and without money we could not move. With considerable difficulty we managed to get a telegram through to Mr. and Miss West begging them to join us at Terasp, and after two or three days, days you may be sure of great anxiety to us, they managed to get across the Austrian frontier and joined us. England had not, at the time, declared war against Austria, and they got through principally, I believe, because they made themselves very pleasant with the Austrian soldiers at the little customs place at the bottom of the Engadine where we ourselves had crossed. Needless to say we were very much relieved when the party met again.

Around this time, Zoe sends a second letter to her sister, Mary.

> Kur haus Tarasp,
> Engadine.
>
> Aug 6 - 1914.
>
> Darling N.B.,
>
> This is a funny birthday. I am writing because I can't do anything else. Our trunk has not turned up and we are very short of clothes - indeed Charlie has had to borrow a shirt from a nice old naturalized English-German His own being absolutely beyond the pale. People are very kind and have offered me clothes galore - but I am clinging to what I have as long as possible and this morning have managed to send one change of garments to the wash. One very nice American lady has offered me silk 'shirt-waists' - I happen to have one old one with me and two black ones and two shirts - but we only brought a suit-case each because room in the motor was limited.
>
> I mustn't write anything about events going on now because letters have to be sent open and if they have any reference to things that are seething around they are sent back. Indeed we hardly know whether you will get any news of us. Anyhow we are quite safe, in the safest place they say - but we are told that we must stay where we are for the present, - until arrangements are made for our safe transit home ...

Charlie continues in the *Bath Chronicle,*

> For three weeks after the declaration of war we were absolutely cut off from any information from England ...
>
> In the meantime the management of the Hotel Kurhaus were allowing us credit, for the very good reason that they could not get anything else, but the position was such that we decided it was no use remaining at an expensive hotel, especially as Mr. Bullock and Mrs. Bullock (my wife's sister) were staying at Samedan, in the Engadine, not a great distance away. We therefore expended almost our last pence in travelling up by the railway to join them. I left a circular note with the hotel people as security for my debt. This will be converted into cash later on when the war is over.

3 - Europe in Turmoil

Thence forward we stayed in a delightful little chalet, simple, sweet, and clean, kept by some charming Swiss people who also gave us credit. We could have spent a most happy time there had we not been so anxious. The cows used to be brought in every night and were stalled inside, on the ground floor. Insanitary? Well, from the English point of view, it may seem so, but nobody notices it there ... for a fortnight we had to remain quietly at the chalet, passing the time away by occasionally doing a little mountain climbing.

From Zoe's 6th August letter to Mary,

On Monday last (Aug. 10) we came here to be near the Bullocks ... I hated leaving the Kurhaus Tarasp altho' there was only one pure American lady there - no English and two nice families of German-Americans who spoke English and who regret Germany's folly very much and were quite friendly to us. The rest of the people were mostly Russians and a few Germans. But we have come on here because there is a British Consul at St. Moritz and he is getting passports for the English people and is supposed to tell us when arrangements are to be made for us to return home.

... why we can't stay quietly where we are and finish our holiday I can't think. Charlie thinks he ought to be at home bucking the people up in the Parish and helping to keep their spirits up etc. But I don't expect they need it a bit, if the rumours of England and French success so far is true. I believe he would sit quite still if only you people would send him an English newspaper even dated a week back. We haven't had an English newspaper for nearly a fortnight and yesterday when it was discovered that Sashie had one at Samedan in the Hotel lent her by a gentleman, Charlie and Mr. West nearly went down on their knees to her - to be just allowed to kiss the margin. It was eight days old but reverenced as no newspaper ever has been before ...

Charlie continues,

All this time the Engadine was gradually filling with soldiers. Switzerland had mobilised her entire military resources, and was pushing her troops up to the Italian border, which was within eight miles of us on the East. There was no disorder, but martial law was very strictly enforced. Soldiers with loaded rifles and fixed bayonets were everywhere ... Switzerland on the east side is naturally very pro-German. I do not mean to imply that we had any difficulty with these people, but their sympathies were obviously antagonistic towards the English.

After many days spent in anxious waiting for financial assistance, a Swiss gentleman came one day to the chalet where we were staying and inquired for me. He said the Swiss Bankverein wished to know what my address was and this gave us hopes that some day, some how, money might reach us. How the Bank found us I don't know, but I imagine that it must have been due to efforts made by Mr.

Herbert Harding, of Lloyds' Bank, Bath. The day after that I received a letter from the Swiss Bank offering every kind of help money, or any other assistance that might be required ... Thanks to our friends in Bath our money troubles were at last over.

A day or two after that the relations between the Swiss and the Italians were becoming so strained, and so many troops were being massed all round us and sent up to the Italian border that we determined we must leave. The place at which we were living had been offered for the reception of wounded and it really did seem as though, at any moment, an Italian raid might come down the very road and past the very house in which we were living. Italian feeling was most strongly pro-British, and it is perfectly certain, in spite of denials in the papers, that the Italians had mobilised, and are still mobilising, over the border some eight miles away. The Italian papers explain that it is only the summer manoeuvres, but it is very significant that they have never had summer manoeuvres there before.

As it seemed more than likely that, if we stayed where we were, we should soon be in the actual theatre of war, and having now received money to bring us back, we determined that we would make an effort to get home. Throughout these weeks of waiting we had been in constant communication with the British Consul in the Engadine, and reports which reached us as to railway facilities were so very conflicting that we hardly knew what course to take. The significant fact that no letters had come through, and that for three weeks no French or English papers had reached us, was pretty good evidence that railway communication was thoroughly disorganised. Still, we decided to make an effort to get back, and accordingly we left the Engadine on Sunday, 23rd August. We *(with the Bullocks and the Wests)* started very early in the morning, and got to Zurich that night, what is ordinarily a four-hour journey having taken us the whole day. We consulted the English Consul at Zurich as to whether it was advisable to wait for one of the special trains which were being made up for English people, or whether it would be better to proceed independently on our own account. The confusion and uncertainty were such that the Consul advised us not to wait for a special train, and we were very thankful afterwards that we took his advice, for we learned that the hardships suffered by the passengers on the special trains were very great.

From Zurich we went on to Geneva, where we arrived last Tuesday morning at one o'clock. We found the station packed with people. Masses of American and English folk were lined up in queues waiting for one of the special trains which was about to start. We heard that they had to wait most of the morning .

From Geneva to Paris it was a case of simply taking any train you could find which seemed to be going in the right direction. Nobody seemed to have any idea what trains were running or at what time they left. It was absolutely impossible to ascertain at what stations particular trains stopped, or whether one had to change. We generally had to fight our way to it, and sometimes we had to stand up in the corridors all night. As for railway tickets, nobody seemed to worry about them at all. For whole stages of our homeward journey our tickets were neither examined nor inquired for. Apparently, so long as you were English you could travel where you liked. But at almost every stage we had to show our passports, these being carefully examined and revised at every stopping place, so as to show whence we had come and where we had to go to.

On Wednesday morning at four o'clock we reached Lyons, where pitiful evidences of war were to be seen on every hand. The station was packed with soldiers, many of whom were wounded and had just been passed back from the front, while there was also a large contingent of the French Corps Alpine on their way to the fighting line. We saw a great many wounded men lying in the waiting-rooms, poor fellows and we ascertained that the four large military hospitals in the town were simply crowded with wounded.

As we had to wait the whole of that day before it was possible to get a train forward, we tried to find an hotel where we could get a few hours rest, but none of them were open, and we had to put up with what was little better than a common lodging-house, a sort of all night shelter where the ladies had to put up with a great deal of discomfort. They had never been in such a place before, I can assure you, and I hope they will never have to suffer in such a way again.

There was an air of settled depression upon Lyons. War notices were exhibited on an immense board in front of a big building in the public square, and crowds of people hung about reading them and waiting for the lists of dead and wounded. Very bad reports of the war were coming in, and it seemed that France was in great trouble. I was rather struck by the large number of young men remaining in Lyons. Elsewhere young men were conspicuous by their absence, but in this city the great majority of the crowds consisted of men, and I assume that they remained in the city for some special purpose.

While we were waiting at Lyons we saw a good deal of the famous Corps Alpine, and a cheery, high-spirited lot of fellows they were. For two hours our train waited alongside theirs, and schoolboys going home from their holidays could not have been more delightfully excited than they were at the prospect of soon being at the front. They were singing songs and dancing, and some of them gave their comrades rides on the luggage trucks, tearing up and down the platform and racing one another till one of the trucks would be overturned and the men in it pitched out. They seemed delightful fellows, and amid the general depression which prevailed it was cheering to watch them.

We left Lyons the following morning, and as our train moved out of the station in the misty dawn a small crowd of perfectly silent men stood in the station yard with bared and bowed heads, whilst a poor wounded soldier about whom they were grouped passed to his rest. The poor fellow lay on a stretcher in the open air - the hospitals were all over-crowded - and he drew his last breath as our train left.

After suffering much discomfort in the train, we arrived in Paris on Thursday morning last, about seven o'clock. We were not allowed to stay in the City, but were hurried through as fast as possible. Everybody, however, was most kind to us; it was indeed a feature of our journey all the way across France - the extraordinary kindness and marvellous help we got from everyone because we were English. Every possible courtesy was shown us and no trouble seemed too great to take to help us. A very great number of the shops seemed to be shut, but there was no excitement and the City seemed to be exceedingly quiet.

There was a marked depression but it is very different from the depression which prevailed during the Franco-German war of 1870 which resulted almost immediately in insurrection and despair. The present mood is one of grim determination rather to die than give in. It is just the attitude that Great Britain would adopt in similar circumstances of invasion, personally I do not believe that the Germans will get to Paris, but it seems very likely they will succeed in turning our left. The French soldiers were full of confidence. Whenever we encountered them they cheered us to the echo. It was 'Vive L'Angleterre' everywhere; it was very cheering and inspiriting to see them.

From Paris we were able to continue our journey on Thursday to Boulogne and now for the first time on the whole journey, we had a comparatively empty train and were exceedingly comfortable.

Our emotions were deeply stirred when we got to Amiens. For four hours our train was stopped just a few miles from the station, and it crept on slowly, stage by stage, behind one train of wounded Englishmen and two trains of Belgian refugees. And alongside our train, on a parallel line, were trains of British soldiers on their way to the front. We cheered them tremendously. There were Royal Engineers, some of the 20th Hussars, and other regiments, together with members of the Army Service Corps. There were also guns, and war impedimenta of all kinds, and train after train of cattle and sheep, evidently intended for the troops. The English soldiers looked delightfully clean, strong and splendid; the change was striking after we had lived so long among foreign soldiers.

As our train stopped frequently alongside troop trains we fraternized with our gallant fellows, and frequently the passengers in our train jumped out and chatted with the men. Every Englishman on our train emptied his pockets of tobacco, cigars and cigarettes, so that Tommy Atkins might have his supply of the 'sovran herb' increased. We also gave our lunches to them. All the British soldiers were in great heart, and they gave us a number of letters to post to their sweethearts and wives - commissions which we duly executed as soon as we got to London.

From Amiens onwards we had what I personally felt was a very anxious time, because we were now within twenty miles of the actual German front. The invading army was at that moment, we learned, endeavouring to turn our left; German cavalry reached Arras and were apparently making a dash to Abbeville, which we passed through. We even listened for the boom of the guns, when the train stopped, but could not catch any sounds of firing. The populace was in a state of very great excitement. At every station, and every railway crossing, peasants and others were assembled waiting for news; and it looked as if the whole population of the countryside were preparing for flight.

At last we got to Boulogne - six hours late - and missed the boat. We found the place in a state of tense excitement. Troops had been withdrawn, leaving it an open town, apparently quite at the mercy of any sudden descent which might be made by the German cavalry. Grave anxiety prevailed. The town was under martial law, and everyone had to be within doors by nine o'clock in the evening.

The scenes which were here to be witnessed on every hand were the most pathetic I have seen in the whole course of my life. Multitudes of Belgian refugees had just arrived, fleeing from their ruined homes, most of them possessed of nothing at all except the clothes they stood in. The women looked worn out and their eyes were red with weeping. A large proportion of them were obviously of the upper classes. There were many well-dressed ladies, in summer costumes. They looked as though they had just sprung up from the table, or from the ordinary occupation of every day life, and raced for safety. Then there were little children, the babies - it was a sight that made one's heartache. Some of the little ones carried bundles, mats and rugs tied together at the four corners, containing obviously any little valuables and necessaries they could grab at the last moment before their flight. It was simply heart breaking to reflect that these were innocent people from a neutral country; it made one feel very embittered towards the Germans. The refugees were being passed on to Paris as quickly as possible.

There was no boat for England until the following morning so we stopped at an hotel at Boulogne for the night. Early the next morning a boat left for Folkestone and we stepped on board. We came out of harbour escorted by three submarines and a French torpedo boat, which turned back after having seen us safely out of harbour. After this we did not see a sign of a battleship, or war vessel of any kind, all the way across. Having disembarked at Folkestone we came straight on to London and spent Friday night at an hotel.

We are indeed glad to be in England again. None of our luggage has yet turned up, but we know it is on the way. It was a remarkable co-incidence that on the very day we left Switzerland to come home our main luggage arrived from

England. It had taken over a month to get there, and how it managed to get through at all I don't know. During the whole of that month, the only change of clothing we had was contained in a hand-case. We registered the luggage for the return journey, but it has not yet arrived.

News of the party's safe return was welcomed with great joy amongst the parish, and many wires and letters were received from friends and relations.

It was not until 1920 that Herbert Doudney went to Switzerland and collected the car. He found it had been untouched by the war and was just as it had been left six years previously, still containing blankets, tinned milk, etc.

Life back in England had not been uneventful during the Doudneys absence. Connie Chadwick, a close friend of the family and the guardian left in charge of baby Désirée, wrote to Zoe on 30th August. She notes that since the Doudneys had been away, a new phrase had entered the vocabulary: 'Bandage Parties'.

> It must have been thrilling to see the British troops at Amiens. It made me "guiddle" all down the back to read that part.
>
> I warn you that Wednesday and Thursday there is to be a bandage party 10-1 and 5-9 and if you show your heads in the Parish Room you will be simply smothered by embraces from the whole Parish!
>
> Tell the Vicar that he must expect to be embraced by all the old ladies who have been in a continual state of tearful anxiety, notably the Misses Byfield ...
>
> We, the Guides, had a busy day yesterday. We had two decorated barrows and placards 'Gifts for Bath Territorials' and collected tobacco, pipes, cigarettes and magazines for our Territorials on Salisbury Plain.

The Germans at this time were passing through Belgium, a neutral country, and sending thousands of civilians fleeing for their lives. The sight of those refugees had left a deep impression on the Vicar, who wrote in the *Bath Chronicle*, 5th September 1914:

> We people who live in this island do not understand what war is. I wish I could make them realise what it means. If they could only see what we have seen, those Belgian refugees, the homeless women weeping, the suffering little children, and the awful destitution, there would be a great rush to join the colours. Absolutely the whole of Europe is under arms. The nations know it is absolutely war to the death ... England does not yet seem to have realised all that is at stake.
>
> In France ... All the manhood of the nation is out in the fighting line. What a

3 - Europe in Turmoil

> contrast when I get to England, to London! On the Continent theatres, cinematograph shows, exhibitions of all kinds are closed. Games and sports, and every kind of amusement are suspended. You come back here and find cricket and tennis going on as usual, the theatres all in full swing. I was amazed and disgusted. Let me put the position plainly, and I intend to speak of it at every possible opportunity. It is not for England and the British Empire alone that we are fighting and that we ought to fight to the very last ditch; it is for the liberty of Europe and for the peace of the world ... France wants all the help and encouragement she can get in this hour of her greatest trial. It is up to Englishmen to give it to her.

On returning to Bath it became Charlie's primary task to help the Belgian refugees, and accordingly he was elected secretary of a new committee, whose aims would be to find homes and jobs for as many as possible.

One of the first accounts of refugees arriving in Bath was given in the *Bath Chronicle,* 24th October 1914,

> A party of fifty wounded soldiers for whose reception Bath has been in a state of preparedness and expectancy for many days now arrived on Thursday evening. As soon as the need of accommodation of this kind was mooted, two hospitals - the Royal United Hospital and the Mineral Water Hospital cleared a number of beds.

> Really, how news travels! The time of the arrival of the Belgians was only known to an official few and yet there could hardly have been a bigger concourse of the general public about the G.W.R station entrance ...

> The time of the arrival of the train from Southampton was 4.32, and before that time came, a considerable number of private cars were waiting to convey the wounded to their respective destinations.

> ... The public in the street caught sight of the ambulance coaches as they were brought into position, and hearty cheers were raised. So little time was lost, that a few of the more active wounded were already hobbling along the platform before the coffee and biscuits provided for them had arrived ... Those who needed a helping hand were promptly assisted by ambulance men or eager city councillors.

By February 1915, through the actions of several committees and individuals, Bath had received 360 refugees, acting as a clearing house for the local districts and keeping and maintaining a large number of the displaced in the city itself. The hostel in Poultney Street which had been opened and maintained by the Catholic Woman's League, held 50 to 60 refugees and was a starting place for the work of receiving and caring for them. This was also the case with the house at 93 Sydney Place, which to the amusement of those concerned had once been the home of Queen Charlotte, a princess of German extraction! A convalescent home was set up in Marlborough Buildings to accommodate forty wounded Belgian soldiers as they were discharged from the Bath hospitals.

Between two and three tons of clothing were collected for the refugees. Bread, vegetables and other gifts were generously donated, the Gas Company provided free gas, rates were remitted, free medical care was administered and free education was given to all of the Belgian children.

As the war continued, the refugee problem steadily worsened and in February, when Charlie visited Aldwych House in London, he was distressed to see so many Belgians 'loafing about' awaiting adoption, there being some 10,000 still in the capital. It was therefore unanimously decided by the refugee committee to extend the relief work.

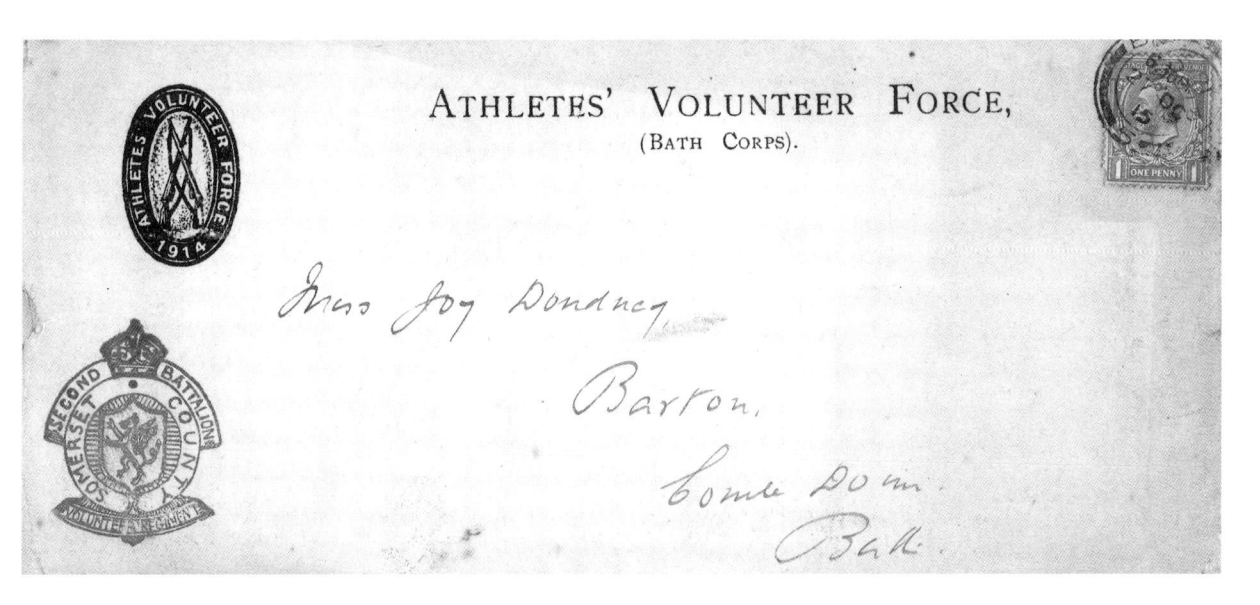

◊ ◊ ◊ ◊ ◊

Private Thomas Smith wrote a letter to Joy on 27th October, 1915, thanking her for 'the very nice scrap book you made for us poor wounded soldiers ....' and used the old A.V.F. envelope overstamped in blue, for the Second Battalion Somersetshire County Volunteer Regiment.

In preparation for the impending crisis, the Bath Volunteers was formed on 10th August 1914. Its aims were to train young lads under the age of seventeen in the rudiments of shooting, along with practising elementary drilling and route marching. Charlie's brother, Raymond, had agreed to command the unit and, naturally, on Charlie's return home from Switzerland, he became very involved with this new challenge, setting up a rifle range in the parish room.

3 - Europe in Turmoil

By November 1914, the possibility of a German invasion was a very serious consideration. Bath responded by forming a corps to be known as the Athletes Volunteer Force, which seems to have enveloped the earlier Bath Volunteers. The duties of the Force were to take over from the regular army and the police in time of need.

The Force was divided into three companies, with Raymond Doudney, now Captain, as O.C. of 'C' Company. Charlie was in command of the No. 1 Platoon of that Company. The age limit had been changed and a great number of volunteers were over 40 and 50, three being in their 60s. Those of an enlistable age had to sign an undertaking to join up if required by the Government.

The strength on the first 'route march' of the Force was 542 and the following extracts from an account written by 'one of them' was printed in the *Bath Chronicle,* 19th December 1914.

> ... How history repeats itself! The very phrase 'Saturday afternoon soldiering' conjures up visions of the old-time volunteers. After all, the new movement is only a manifestation of the same proud national spirit which says that 'Britons never shall be slaves'...
>
> As our "uniform" had not arrived, we all, for uniformity's sake wore caps. Some probably wore caps who had never done so before and otherwise there were seen many quaint and unexpected make-ups. Thus one respected citizen wore a white sweater which, together with his cap, gave him the appearance of a prize-fighter - a thing quite alien to his natural bent ...
>
> We formed up on the North Parade in the presence of a large concourse of people ...
>
> We had two bands, one composed of members seasoned to the work, the other a bugle band containing performers who were none the less ardent but certainly more exuberant. Picture us then standing at 'Shun' in our respective squads on the parade ground. Then came the order, 'Fours, right, left wheel', and hey presto! we were marching in column ... The assembled crowd was too awestruck to cheer, but many admiring youngsters were held up by their proud mammas to shout at Dad, now turned soldier ...

By January 1915, Charlie had been promoted to Captain, and under his command, he had trained and drilled a squad of some 50 Belgian refugees who for the first time paraded with the Athletes Volunteer Force. Three months later, on the afternoon of Sunday, 20th March 1915, the A.V.F. held its first church parade at St. Luke's. Over 500 men, including the band, were present and they marched from Queen's Square via Union Street to the church. Once there, Charlie gave a forceful sermon to the assembled volunteers. Within four months, the A.V.F. had become the Bath Battalion of the recently formed Somersetshire Regiment.

Virtually all Charlie's energies were now turned to the war effort. At the Harvest Festival of 1914, floral decorations were dispensed with, and the congregation was asked to provide fruit and vegetables and other food for the 4th Somersetshire Regiment. Some 5,000 bandages made by church workers were sent to the Front. At Christmas, decorations were curtailed and the money saved was spent on gifts for parishioners in the fighting forces.

In January 1915, the Vicar published his regular New Year's Letter.

> 'As 1915 opens we see uncertainty, insecurity, sorrow, poverty and perhaps death in its days, for many people and for ourselves, but it is quite wrong ... to lose that optimism which is our Christian heritage ... Though 1915 may see a world in distress and us with it, it will see Heaven nearer - perhaps with us'.

Before the year was out these words proved to be only too true. By now there was hardly a young man left in the parish. Then, what Charles Doudney's friends had expected and feared came to pass. At the request of Bishop Taylor-Smith (Chaplain - General), the Vicar was asked to join the ranks as a temporary Army Chaplain.

On Monday, 12th April 1915, the Belgian Refugee Committee held a special meeting in the Mayor's parlour in order to wish their secretary farewell and God speed, refusing to accept his resignation and hoping he would be back within six months.

Charlie describes his speedy departure in the *Bath Chronicle* of Saturday, 3rd April 1915.

> I was very suprised to get a telegram on Sunday (yesterday) asking me the earliest date I could go to the front. Since then I have felt very humble. I hardly expected having to go to the front at once and thought I would be put to work for some months at home before being drafted. This afternoon I received another telegram saying that I must sail on Wednesday and must report to the War Office on Wednesday morning. That means leaving Bath tomorrow. I feel I am the proudest yet humblest man in Bath and I never felt more elated than by this honour placed upon me and yet I feel very humble realising what little I can do.

Although at very short notice, the parish made a collection amounting to 20 guineas in order to provide their vicar with a number of comforts and necessities for use at the front. He was now equipped with valise, sleeping sac, canteen, lantern and case, knife, fork and spoon, mirror, air pillow and case, chair, stove and fittings, bath, basin frame, table, bucket, ground sheet, rug, trench belt, wristlet watch, uniform case and gloves, all of which were kindly supplied by Messrs. Lords at nett cost.

> The Rev. C.E. Doudney left Bath on Tuesday evening on the 6.10 train to London. Many of the parishioners of St. Luke's saw him off and the Bishop of Bath and Wells was also present to bid the Vicar farewell. The cheering for Mr. Doudney was hearty as the train pulled out of the station.

Charlie.

4. Base Hospital ~ Rouen

Charlie was now on his way to London to sign up and was about to enter a different world. In order to keep the parish informed of his activities, he sent back vivid accounts of his adventures, written in diary form. Luckily, these texts have survived, as they were regularly published in the *Bath and Wilts. Chronicle*. Although all correspondence was censored and names and places were not allowed to be included, it has been possible to fill in some of these omissions by studying the appropriate 'War Diaries' at the Public Record Office, Kew, Surrey. Charlie's first account in the newspaper appears on 1st May 1915. It may be seen that sending the new chaplain to the Base Hospital at Rouen was a means of preparing him for the horrors that lay ahead.

> The main impression left on one's mind on joining the Expeditionary Force in France is one of admiration for the organising genius of the War Office. Red tape we are fond of talking about and complaining of, but it may be that very asset that is the ultimate cause of the smooth working of the great war machine. My reception at the Chaplain-General's Department at the War Office was kindly and cordial, and I was passed like a parcel from hand to hand and office to office, with which an American would call 'some' slickness. Indeed after three days' travelling under the iron hand of military rule one felt like a parcel. My valuable signature was required on an endless succession of documents, and it grew less and less legible as the day waned, until on visiting the august room of the Chaplain General finally, I overheard the clerk at the phone say 'it is spelt D-o-u-d-n-e-y'. I laughed and he politely explained that another office I had just visited had been at pains to read the marks I had set down there.
>
> And so to the station, where two other chaplains joined me, and we journeyed luxuriously seawards. At the port it was a case of passes at every turn. Passes to go into the hotels (the latter reserved for officers), and most stringent ones for the boat. No one seemed to know when the latter went, and as it was pretty late I turned into a delightful cabin - provided by the fatherly Government for me! - and went to sleep. Woke up to find she was at sea, and not relishing being torpedoed in my bunk, I dressed and went on deck. It was broad daylight and a sparkling flashing sea, smooth as oil. I was greeted by an officer and at once allotted a boat, with instructions to help get into it certain Belgians in the event of a wily submarine appearing. After breakfast, of course, I sought the skipper and got leave to visit the wireless man, in whose room I spent the rest of the crossing. I mustn't tell anything of the way we crossed or our escort or other details, though they are interesting, especially as I am now the censor (or one of them) and strike out with a big blue pencil similar information that I find in other people's letters!

4 - Base Hospital, Rouen

Passed the poor X *(censored)*, submarined the other day and only her upper works showing. Landed and was politely showed into a bus and told not to think of one's baggage. A Tommy added carefully labels to any thing not so marked. I reported to the Base Commandant, and was told to go on by a certain train that night, but the senior local chaplain said no and got us off. He was going on himself next day and knowing the ropes said we should get on better with him. A charming man and a warrior to look at. He had been right through the retreat from Mons, the Marne, etc., and had been under fire continually. He regaled us with yarns which are fascinating.

Next morning, on in the usual luxury - no trouble at the stations and first-class in the trains. As officers we can go anywhere in the stations. The French never say a word. No tickets; only the order from the proper person saying where you are going. And so to Rouen, the city of a thousand charms. But I'm not going to make this a guide book so will take all the interest and beauty for granted.

We went straight to the head and fount of authority for us chaplains and, of course, were on tenter hooks till we knew where we were to be sent. One was to go straight to the front. But as he is a first-class chaplain and a great man of 28 years' service it was not to be wondered at. We other two, being only fourth class, were to be kept at the base for a season. I was told to report at No. 8 Base Hospital and the Padre there (who was to go to the real front) would tell me my duties. So I took a tram and went up a long hill to the village of Boisguillaume, where I found a great collection of huts in the ground of a big institution. The latter had been turned into an ordinary hospital and the huts (15 in number) had been added later. Six hundred and fifty beds, clean, fresh, and dainty, awaited day and night the ghastly convoys that continually roll in.

I entered the premises and the very first person I met was one of the nurses I had voyaged to India with on the 'Plassey'. She, I found, was matron of the big hospital. She remembered me instantly. Then I sought the officers' mess and found a dozen or so lounging in a bare stone floored place furnished with one long table, some ordinary chairs and a piano, the men all rose and greeted me very cordially. They were of course all doctors. After tea one of them escorted me over the premises in the hunt for the other Padre. He was soon found and I began my initiation into the work of a chaplain of a military hospital. He however did not leave until the following Monday - it was now Friday - so we had plenty of opportunity of discussing things.

I stayed at the hospital until he left, being accommodated with a nice bright room in the institutional part and on Monday took over his billet which consisted of an office in the local village Mairie. There I dwell in an airy room lined with cupboards and stone-floored. A bed and washing stand, a table and chairs furnish it and the wife of the caretaker makes my bed and does my laundry.

When I first arrived the hospital was very empty and there was not much for me to do. No bad cases, and I could see all the men in a couple of afternoons. There are 23 wards altogether and in several there were but two or three patients. But, later, we have become crowded out. In one day and night there arrived no fewer than 458 wounded and all the staff have been pressed to desperation. But the organisation is so perfect that there was no hitch, no disorder and just steady, quiet work. All day motor ambulances rolled in and deposited rows of stretchers in the yard - in the shade - the poor torn fellows lay silent and patient till their turn came for the clean cool bed and the fresh dressing. And oh how they joyed in it! I stroll through the wards seeking the worst cases and trying to say some heartening word. All around are busy nurses and orderlies and white-robed doctors. And the sights! I am so thankful that my nerves are all right! One poor Canadian for instance with all one side of his face including the eye gone! I don't think he can live but he's so bright and patient. Indeed it all makes one ashamed of oneself and any grumbling one had ever done. I have spoken to many hundreds here, but have not heard, as yet, one single word of complaint, seldom a groan. This last rush is the result of the last battle and most of these men suffered from the German gases.

22nd April 1915. I have had a somewhat strenuous and exciting day. There is a most complete X-ray plant here, with a specialist doctor in charge. At breakfast he announced that the assistant was ill, and as I had been through the apparatus with him before he roped me in to help. Well we worked at it all morning, and did about 12 men just in from the last battle. Then after lunch, he had to go away, and there were six more to do. So he collared another doctor and left us there to do the work. The other man, a most decent chap had helped an X-ray man about 10 years ago for a season and had forgotten all he ever knew and said so. As to the electrical part he knew nothing. So there was I in a maze of dynamos and coils and switches and terrific high tension current. The doctor fixed the patients up and I worked the thing. We didn't kill anybody and succeeded all right. Very few had bullets or splinters in them, but they X-ray them on the chance of there being something.

I had a long talk with the matron after tea. She says the scenes here early in the war were awful. Men brought in who had not been off their stretchers for nine days. The screams and groans were heartrending as they cut their clothes and bandages off them. Now it is very different, though rather ghastly. The men today had been wounded only a day and a half and were pretty bloody sometimes. They were just as they were bandaged in action, and were X-rayed straight off so as not to disturb them again. I think 12 heads were wounded, one a bullet in the eyes and one in the jaw. They were most extraordinarily cheerful, though of course, we ratted them about having their photos taken for their sweethearts.

May 14th 1915. Perhaps I had better give a typical day's work, which may make clear what I have to do. 6.30 - called by my servant, who brings my charger round at 7 o'clock. Then a glorious ride in the great forest, whose edge is reached in five minutes. 8.30 - back and am met at the hospital by the man who takes the horse to his stable. Then comes letter-censoring for say one to two hours until (nearly every day) an orderly appears with 'Please sir would you kindly go to the X-ray room'. And there I work for the rest of the morning. We have photographed well over 100 cases in the past few days.

After lunch comes the visiting. The wards are straight by that time and I am not in the way of doctors and nurses. And so I go from ward to ward until about 6 o'clock. Then a game of rounders - officers v. men or officers v. N.C.O.s or sometimes a service in the recreation-room. Mess at 7.30. After mess there's nothing that can be done - unless someone is dying and needs a visit - and we sing and play but all go to bed early.

Sundays, of course, are pretty hard as there are services to be taken at other places. Last Sunday there was celebration here at 6.40, another at 8 two miles away, parade service at 11 and two evening services, one in Rouen and one here.

It must not be thought that this is 'at the front', but it seems that we are sent there in turn and we chaplains stay at these base hospitals until our call comes and then, one by one, disappear in that mysterious region where life must be much more strenuous. Meanwhile I am trying to learn all I can of the work, getting inured to horrors and getting fit for big exertions by my early morning rides, and so trying to train for the time when I shall join the troops in real action.

The Bath and Wilts. Chronicle, 22nd May 1915, published Charlie's second report:

Just got a wire saying, 'Prepare to fill every bed in the hospital tomorrow morning', so I am afraid there has been more slaughter. What we shall do I hardly know. The full staff of doctors is 21. This has lately been reduced to nine, owing to pressure of work. The telegram means probably over 800 wounded. The senior surgeon told me tonight that he would probably ask me to anaesthetise for him in the theatre. I don't know, of course, if he meant it, but they will want all the help they can get. Operations are going on all day - sometimes half the night - and to take another doctor for that in these times of stress is rather a waste. I am getting simply saturated with stories of battle. Endless accounts are given by the men who are straight off the field. There seems no question that the Germans drive our men (prisoners) before them. The evidence of many who have seen them close is too strong. Also that German officers with swords simply stab the wounded as they go along, killing them. It's too ghastly for words.

Scene, the Orderly Room. Three sergeant clerks at tables and the Registrar and Censor, the two latter doctors. I, by the side of the Censor *(Lt. Macnaughton*

R.A.M.C.), helping him to reduce the big pile of Tommy's correspondence. This is always a long job, but when the hospital is crowded as it is now, it is one that carries the poor Censor through the whole morning and well on into the afternoon. So, I'm a very popular person with him, and I can steal his tobacco, or take any other liberty with him that I may choose. A threat to resign my post of Assistant Censor will bring him rapidly to a state of abject servitude.

To the student of human nature the Censor's work would be a study of some value. Of course the great majority of the letters are commonplace and consist of plain statements of fact. But no morning passes without some revelation of a deeper mind. Some are very pathetic, some sad. But a few are hopeless; most, far the most, cheery and optimistic. Monday usually means a few references to the Padre's sermon the day before, and not seldom an excellent resume of it.

An orderly enters with a telegram form, 'Receive 140 cases at 10.30', we will say. That's not an unusual number; 458 arrived in 26 hours last week. We've had over 1,000 in the past week. Presently a bugle sounds, and quickly with no sign of bustle and excitement, the big yard fills with men, officers and orderlies and a long line of ambulance cars buzzing in through the gate.

From each, gently and quickly are lowered two or four stretchers, with broken men on them. I am sitting with the doors wide open, right opposite me is a

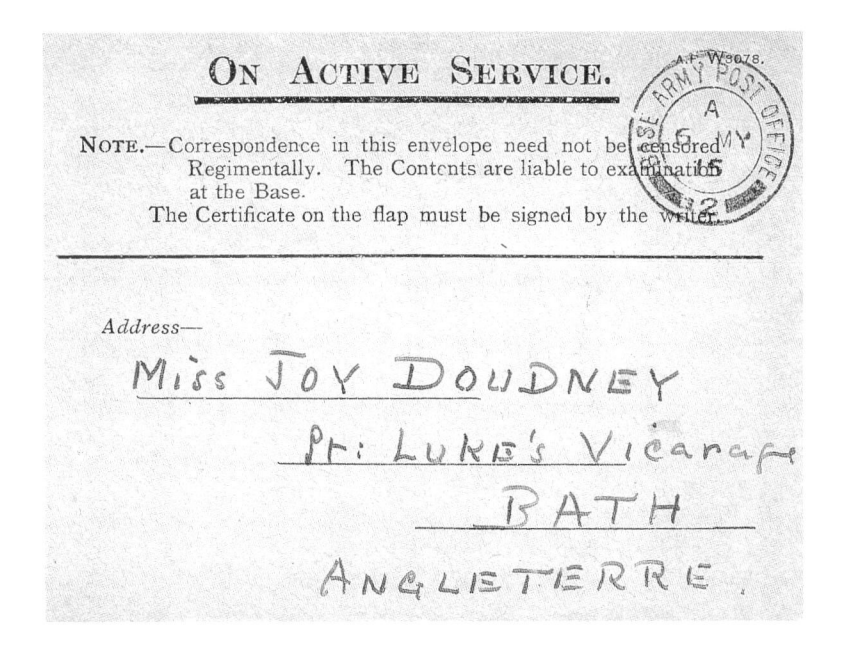

Posted 6th May 1915.
"My Dearest Joy How are you? Here's a green envelope for you. They are very scarce. Much love from Dads".

4 - *Base Hospital, Rouen*

A.-L. — BOISGUILLAUME (Seine-Inf.) — Le Mont Fortin.

Posted 11th May addressed to Joy:
"This is a view close by here. I sometimes ride along the top of the hill in the photo".

wide table. In the centre sits the registrar; other doctors stand by. Two stretchers are lifted on to the table, so that two white faces lie on either side of the Registrar as he sits. He bends to each and gently asks his name, regiment and nature of wound. A moment later a terse command 'Surgical' or 'Hut B2' as the case may be and the stretcher moves on to the ward in question, and possibly for the first time for months the tired warrior is laid in a clean, cool, fresh bed. It's certainly 30 hours and perhaps three days since he was wounded, and oh the relief to have the trench-soiled and blood stained and torn khaki ripped off, and the wounds re-dressed, and the body washed, and a clean, sweet nightgown put on, and just to sink back and not to be moved and lifted and carried and jerked anymore.

These periods of frantic activity are interspersed with quiet spells which gave Charlie time to write home. His third report appeared in the *Bath and Wilts. Chronicle* on 31st May 1915.

And so 70 pass on, and there follow the 'Walking Cases', a motley crew hobbling and hopping and leaning on each other. In one case a lame man leaning on and

112

steering a blinded man! These all go to the huts, and will soon pass out to convalescent camps.

And it's all so still! It's a breathless day, the masses of livid green chestnuts there behind the offices are just murmuring, and two blackbirds are making liquid music, and a cuckoo is calling in the distance. And into this peace every two minutes comes the tramp of bearers and the silent heroes file past. You never hear a cry. Weary beyond words, aching and throbbing these lads never murmur. Truly we don't know what they are. No words can describe their heroic patience. But in saying this I do not mean to limit the credit to the patients. Nurses and staff are alike splendid. A hospital in war should be a certain cure for 'the grumbles'. They would be driven out for very shame!

And now comes my work. In some trepidation I open the door of a long ward, well knowing that in that one ward alone (and there are 23 of them) is at least one hour's work, work that demands one's very best, all one's manhood, tact, skill, knowledge of men - not to add nerves to see, without flinching, sights that are simply ghastly. Need I say that I personally cannot tackle the job without the prayer outside the door that calls down the strength.

There's the long ward. Four orderlies are working like Trojans. Two sisters, in spotless white aprons and red Army capes and graceful head arrangements (don't know what you call them), looking the very essence of efficiency and cleanliness are there, one sterilising instruments at a table and one assisting two doctors - the latter with white overalls over their uniforms - in something they are doing to a patient. And so one begins and works slowly up all one side and down the other and woe betide you if you miss any. You'll catch it from the sisters afterwards! But you couldn't (unless pressed for time), for you've only got to look across the ward as you go up and you see eyes fixed on you. They know the Padre's uniform, and though they've never seen you before they're waiting for you with a grin as you come round. And of course the ones you know - they're all too few for they go out, to England or convalescent camp, at the rate of about 100 a day - are well on the look out, and its 'coming to you laddie, in a minute'. 'All right, sir, no hurry'.

And so one drifts up the wards. Ah! here's that poor Canadian lad - 22 years old - and half his face is gone. I saw it once when the surgeon was dressing it. And they've made a hole in the bandages over the remaining eye which twinkles through and with his poor torn mouth he makes weird American jokes about the nurses. Pluck, sheer stark pluck, is what that boy is made of. His nose, one eye, all one cheek, upper jaw on one side gone, clean gone.

Then there's a Jew, highly educated and intelligent, and full of faith in his own religion, but awfully mangled. So grateful to me, though I'm a Christian! Over there there's an old friend of nearly a fortnight's standing. Here's a little foxy man, with comic face, and he's sitting up in bed, admiring his two legs which are fixed in a cage. The dressings are off, and he's positively proud of a hole in one thigh eight inches long and four broad, and a most complex smashing of tibia and fibula of the other. He calls your attention to the healthy look of the flesh, but as it looks like ordinary raw meat one is not quite so appreciative as one ought to be.

In such a war as this it must, of course, happen that deeds are done meriting the glory of the V.C., but which are recorded in other than earthly books - splendid self sacrifice, with no 'gallery' or danger deliberately faced for wounded mates who died before they could tell of it. And instances innumerable where the chances taken were too great and death was the only reward.

Even here, in the quiet peace of a base hospital, one glimpses now and then the flash of true heroism and daily one sees the inspiring example of true grit bearing pain with no grumble - you learn to read pain in their eyes - the strong faith in looking forward to the life of a cripple, and unflinching facing of the slow approach of death after the hope of recovery.

A young volunteer of the London Rifle Brigade, a Kitchener draft, and a man of good education, is in with a wound that could not be treated properly for days, and gangrene has resulted. He is told his only chance is to lose the leg. His reply is 'I'd rather go'. He had to be convinced that they would rather have him crippled than dead.

I was talking to a Sister at the bedside of a man just back from the theatre, discussing with her his chances, when a feeble voice from across the ward attracted her. She moved over. 'Is that the chaplain? Please ask him to come here'. A Corporal of Horse of the 1st Life Guards, one arm torn off and a bullet right through his brain from side to side of his forehead. 'Please pray that I may recover. My mother depends on me'. Not a word about his own future. There is such a simplicity about them. They don't reason or argue or philosophise. They take it - the bitter cup of pain and the more bitter cup of a fine young life ruined, and they lie there so quiet. I think that is the impression that grows on one most. They're so quiet. Surely down at the bottom of it all, under the rough surface and the ignorance, there must be the sense of that same sacrifice that in the same manner was borne on the cross.

Perhaps some who read a former article that I wrote may care to hear the story of the Canadian boy I mentioned then. He is doing well, and has just been sent to an English hospital. I had to drag this account out of him at different times. It was only by dint of persevering questions that I got at it at all. He didn't want to tell it and sees nothing in it. I cannot reproduce his quaint Canadian talk but the facts are these:

It seems he had the duty of carrying dispatches from the battery he was with, and one day started from some place east of Ypres with an urgent message to the ammunition column for more ammunition. As he galloped in, a shell brought his horse down headlong.

'His fore leg was smashed, so I could not leave him. Had him all the time since we left Canada. I was fond of him, so I waited to shoot him with my revolver.'

'You had not got your wound then?' 'Yes sir, it was the same shell that got us ... Yes, we got mixed up in it all right.' (You may remember that half the boy's face was blown away, including one eye.) 'But weren't you drenched in blood?' 'Oh yes' (quite casually).

Well, it appears he wanted to get that dispatch in, and found a loose horse saddled and bridled ready - some other poor fellow gone - mounted and rode through Ypres. What a sight he must have been!

Not the least interesting (and inspiring) part of the work here is the surgery. There are men whose skill could only be commanded by the wealthy, slaving here with a lieutenant's rank and pay, and doing those wonders that only modern skill can attain.

A man came in this week, the whole of whose forehead had been torn off, or rather a wide strip of bone right across from temple to temple, and even the brain damaged. He was operated on yesterday, and today said he felt a slight headache! One, of course, inquired of the surgeons as to his future. They are quite hopeful, and speak of an artificial frontal!

But perhaps, the heart of the war here, I mean the war with disease and death, is centred in the big room where a gentle kindly young man - with a big degree *(Lieut. John L. Annan R.A.M.C.)* - patiently pursues his daily hunt for the deathly microbe. Armed with high pressure steam and bottles and tubes and stains and sugars and a microscope, he tests and isolates and identifies the virulent scourge that would slay even more surely than bullet or shell. And typhoid and tetanus, cerebral meningitis are found and cornered and slain. Trenches and parapets and cover may save their hundreds but this quiet doctor has saved his thousands.

And so the wonderful life goes on. There's nothing else here but just the two classes, the two bands. The sufferers, fighting their splendid fight of silent bearing night and day, and long night again, and the healers bringing to bear their patient skill. And I, whose office is to try to teach the inner meaning of it all, am beginning to read deeper and to find traces and more than traces of God Himself, the Sufferer and the Healer, in rough soldier and cultured doctor, in sister and orderly, in quarter masters' staff, and the cook's mates, from colonel to bugler boy, and it's good to find it there.

Dear Joy,
  It was very kind of you to send me the nice toffee. I keep it locked up so Daddy can not get it, except when I give him a bit.
I had a nice label ready to tie on him but he has run away from me, & I cant catch him, so I cant send him home.
I have to write in red pencil because the blue one is lost today. I hope to find it

again tomorrow

I hope you are better

This is another picture of me

with lots of love from

The Censor

8 General
Hospital.
19th May
1915

Dear Joy,

Your Daddy is behaving most disgracefully, this morning he ate all my breakfast. He has stolen all my toffee, & I think he means to eat my dinner too.

Will I put a label on him & send him home?

With much love
The Censor

4 - Base Hospital, Rouen

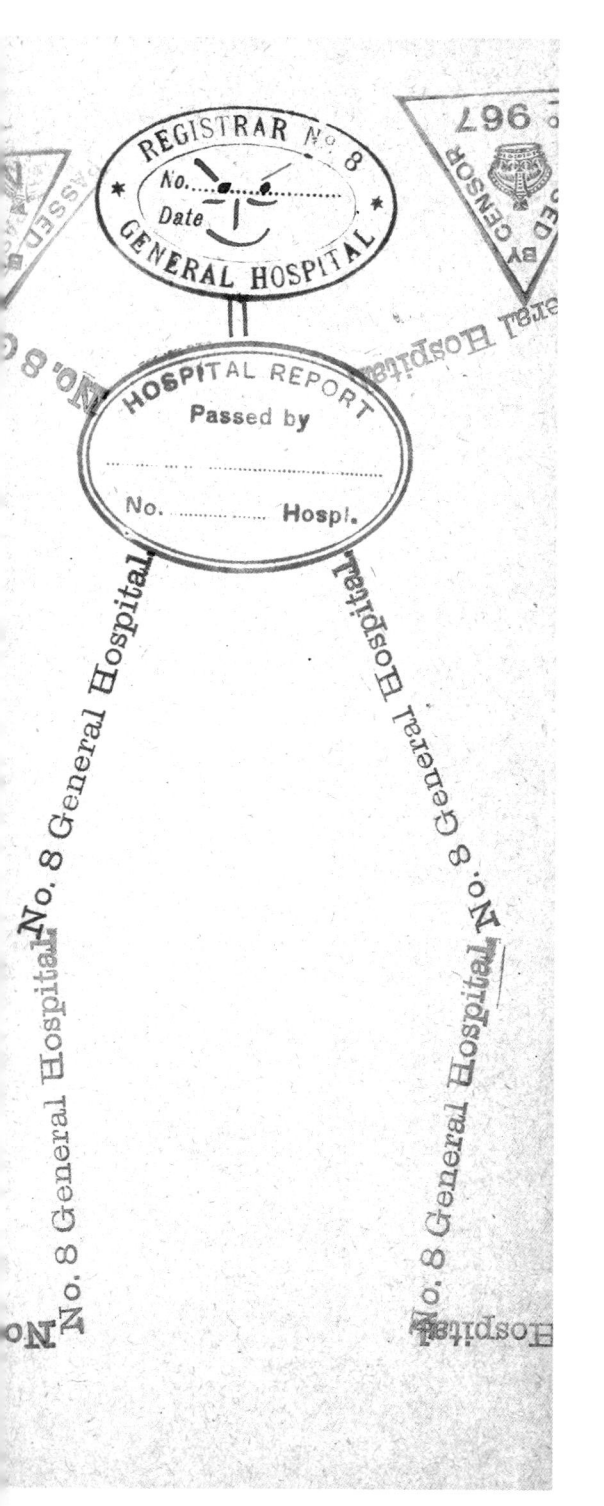

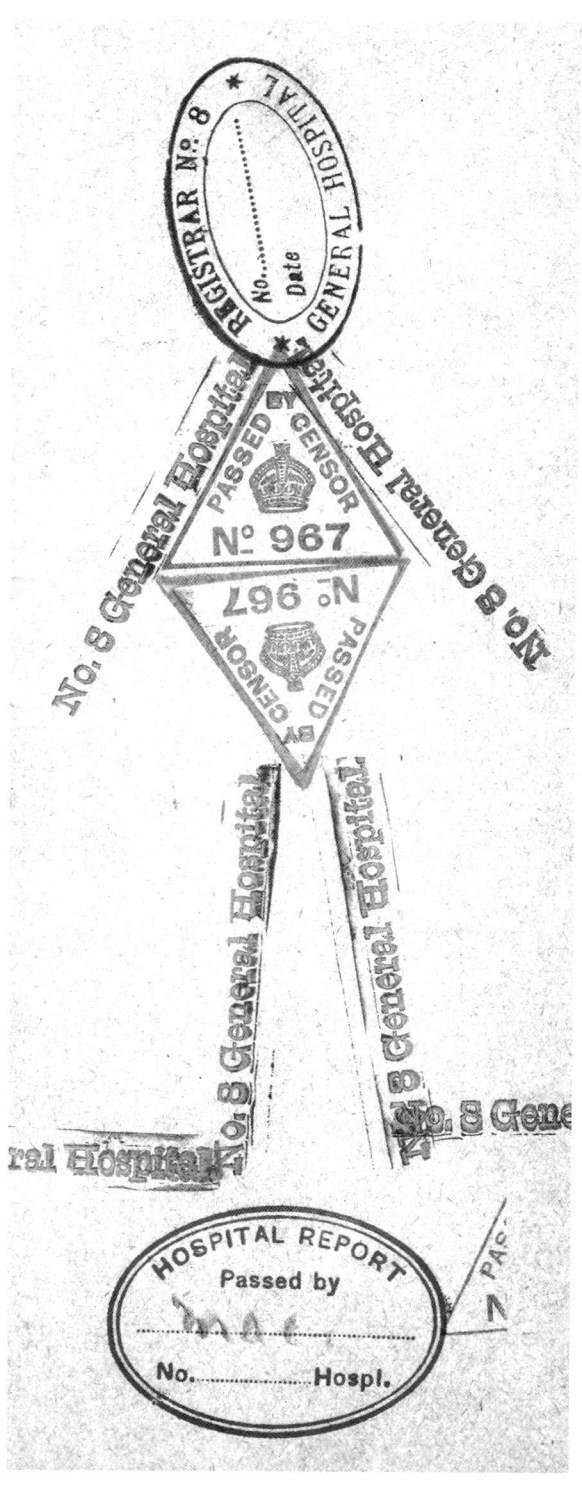

The padre   Lt. Macnaughton

Base Hospital, Rouen - 4

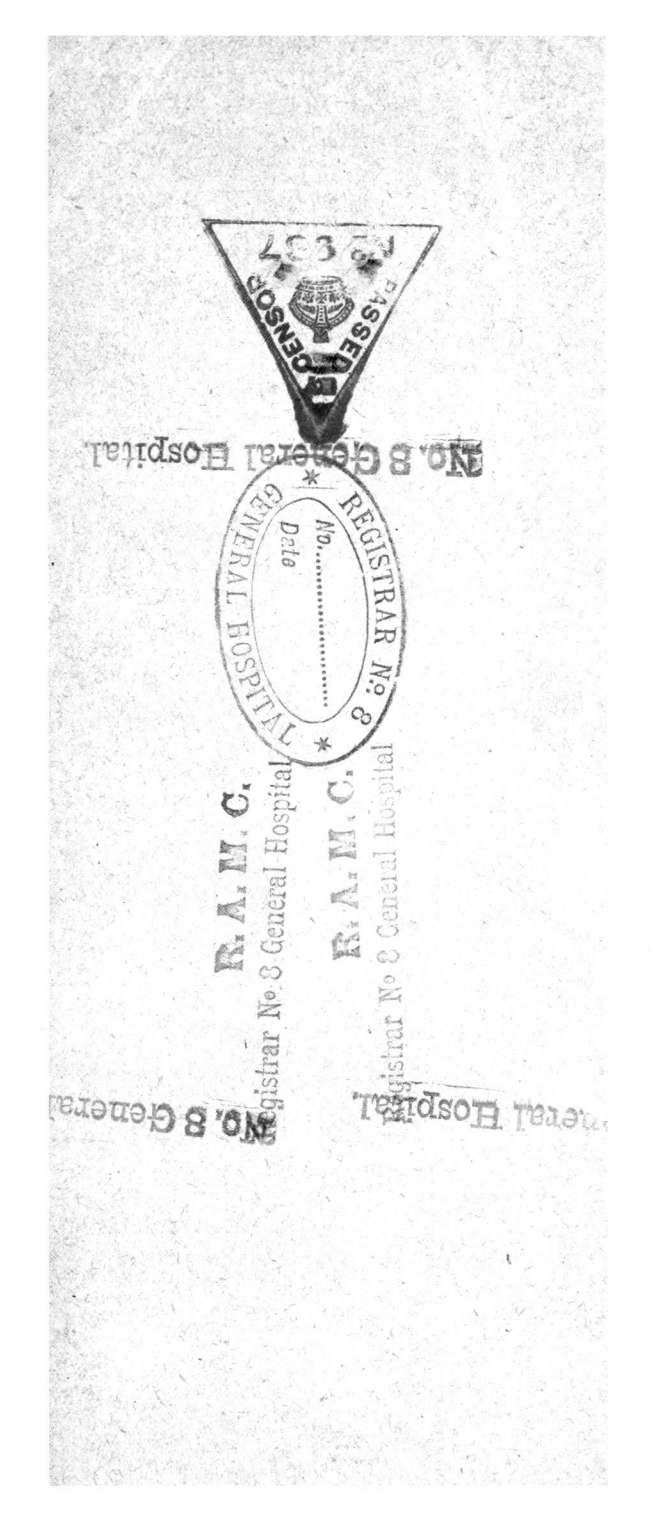

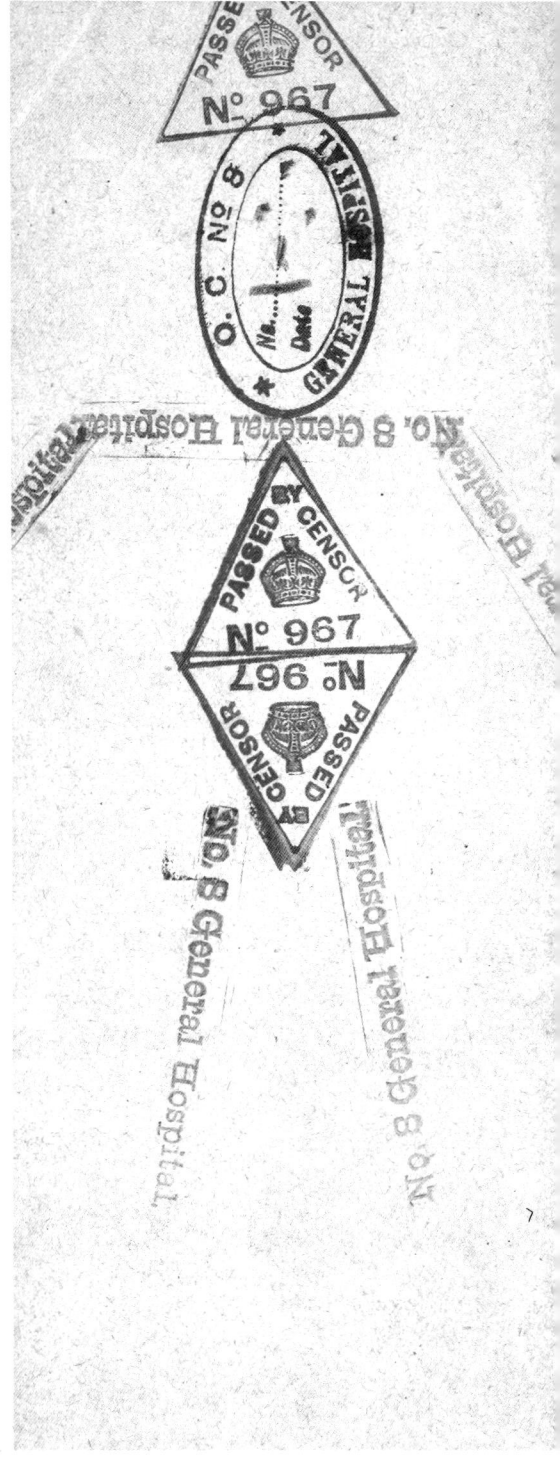

'The Censor'   The Registrar

4 - Base Hospital, Rouen

At about this time the Censor at No.8 General Hospital, Lt. Macnaughton, entered into correspondence with Joy Doudney who was not quite seven years old. Unfortunately only Macnaughton's letters have survived, having been treasured by a little girl. His misuse of the hospital stamps must have given great pleasure (see illustrations) and his comments reflect the light-hearted banter that must have prevailed between himself and Charlie. Although Charlie was sent up to the Front at the end of May, Macnaughton's correspondence with Joy continued until the end of July, at which time he became ill, was operated on and then was sent home to his mother at Airdrie in Scotland.

Meanwhile Charlie was mustering support from the people of Bath. A particular request was for any old gramophones as at present they only had 2 for 23 wards. He also requested cheap writing material and handkerchiefs. His letter to the parish was printed in the parish magazine of June 1915.

> ... the impression gaining ground steadily here is that the war will not be of long duration - it is far too severe to last - and I may possibly be soon among you again.

As to my work, you will have already heard its nature. It is at present confined entirely to the wounded. Most of the other Base Chaplains are at hospitals near the camps, and they live in the thick of the military stir, but I am quite isolated. We deal solely with crowds of broken men; and here I am quite alone. There is no Y.M.C.A. (who are doing a great job elsewhere), or any other organization whatever ... There is no other Chaplain save an R.C., who calls when needed. So I think I may fairly say that in letting me go so willingly, you have not done so in vain.

As to my prospects. As far as one can see, I shall be called to go to the fighting zone in due course. It seems they keep the Chaplains at the Base for a varying period, and send them more or less in order to the front. It has been hinted that my turn will come soon ...

Field Service postcard sent to Joy, dated 11th June 1915.

5. Called to the Front

In 1914 the Germans intended to capture Paris by a quick penetration into France. Having been halted by the allies, each opposing army then tried to outflank the other; eventually they were racing to the sea in an attempt to secure the Channel ports. The resulting front line formed as a bulge, some three to five miles around the eastern side of the ancient city of Ypres. Further north, the line was secured mainly by Belgian troops who flooded the lowlands, making penetration by the enemy very difficult. Ypres was now the northern-most bastion of the Western Front and a vital position to be held. If the Channel ports were captured, Britain would lose its main supply route.

At the end of May 1915, the 6th Division was brought up in London buses from Armentieres and redeployed within the 'Ypres Salient', replacing those troops who had been fighting the second battle of Ypres (which officially closed on 20th May). Both sides were totally exhausted.

The Germans used poison gas for the first time at Ypres. This had proved very effective and at one time they appeared to be close to victory, succeeding in making a considerable dent in the north east sector. The allies were forced to withdraw to a more defensible position, effectively losing two-thirds of the Salient.

Charlie received his orders to join the 18th Infantry Brigade (6th Division). The Brigade consisted of the Second Battalion Sherwood Foresters (Notts./Derby Regiment), Second Battalion Durham Light Infantry, First Battalion East Yorkshire Regiment, First Battalion West Yorkshire Regiment and Queen's Westminster Rifles T.A. Although he was attached to the Durham Light Infantry, his duties encompassed all these regiments, including the gunners and ancillary units attached to the Brigade.

Charlie reported in the *Bath and Wilts. Chronicle,* 10th June 1915, that as he neared the Front he found everything in chaos due to the recent troop movements.

> The nearer I get to the Front the harder it is to realise that war is on, though now it is all round me. I'm sitting in the corner of a field behind a farm - just behind me are the horse lines, and just behind them two lines of motor ambulances.
>
> My valise bed lies in the line of others and officer doctors are scattered about in all stages of dressing. One is bathing from a canvas bucket, others around the field kitchen are eating bacon and eggs. The latter are late up because they were out for the wounded and back at three. I saw them making coffee just before dawn. It is a perfect summer day and the whole surroundings are redolent of sleep and peace, except that overhead is the constant burr of war planes, and the

5 - Called to the Front

intermittent thunder of guns. Yesterday afternoon the latter was incessant and was exactly like a thunder storm on a summer night. I am really not on duty here but having spent two days in trying to find the headquarters of my brigade *(18th Infantry)* I happened upon this unit which is another brigade's own particular field ambulance. My brigade has just been moved and hasn't settled yet, which accounts for the difficulty in finding it. Meanwhile I'm stopping with this ambulance for the day as its trekking this afternoon to a place near the people I was seeking. I don't know that an account of my travels would interest anyone, but in case it should I shall try to give one.

My quiet life at No.8 General Hospital was rudely disturbed by a telegram reading simply 'Chaplain Doudney is appointed to *(18th)* Infantry Brigade'. Where that particular Force was no one that I met had the slightest conception, but I received from the Base Commandant a paper covered with perfectly incomprehensible statements, but which seemed to please every official I met for the next two days. I shall not dwell on the farewells at No.8 but for a 6 week stay they were much more sad than one would expect. And so off again to another new life of quite unknown possibilities.

At 8 p.m. I was installed in a coupe with some very young officers. The carriage was half full of kit and we had good fun settling down for the night among it. We all had rations for two days consisting of enough dog biscuits to last (me at least) for weeks. Two tins of bully, one of jam, cheese, tea and sugar and we invited each other to meals on our own particular rations. (As a matter of fact we fed for that night on ham sandwiches supplied by the kind ladies at the station coffee store.)

At 4 a.m. I left the train and was taken prisoner by the railway transport officer of the station I had reached, who insisted that I finished the night at his palace which consisted of a railway carriage. He had no idea of my destination but decided to send me on east-ward by goods train that evening. So having a day to spend I hunted out my brother-in-law *(Capt. G.E.L. Poulden)*, a Royal Engineer working on the lines of communication and spent a delightful day with him. The goods train had a second class carriage in its middle in which lived, I use the term in its full sense for he has no other quarters, the Army Services Corps Officer who commands it. There, acting practically as a guard, works the head of a very technical department of the British Museum, the winner of high classical honours at Cambridge. Such is war!! He made a perfect host and fed me and blanketed me and turned me out at my station at 3 a.m., handing me like a parcel to the Railway Transport Officer there. The latter packed me into a guards van of another train in which I bumped and rattled to yet another place which was the railhead for the particular division to which my brigade belonged.

So I found myself in a silent station at 4 a.m., listening with deep interest to the distant thud of guns. At about six a friendly officer who is in charge of the railhead took pity on me and breakfasted me in the railway truck in which he lived. You will notice that life was growing more primitive as we got nearer the line. It was not long before I found that I was no longer a parcel, indeed my paper covered with signatures and marks was taken from me by the last R.T.O. So not being a parcel it was necessary to be a person again. Not a soul would send me on anywhere, nor had I any transport but my legs to get anywhere.

So I made friends with a Tommy driving a motor van with mail who (to my joy) said he was going to my brigade. And so east again through delicious country over a pave road (stone setts) shaking till all one's internal machinery was mixed up into a kind of porridge, and the noise tried to stir it up. At one we pulled up at a field post office and I was directed to the headquarters. So leaving my kit there I started to tramp along a very dusty road, raising steadily a thirst of noble dimensions. I tramped and tramped, but no headquarters. This was but natural as I found, later in the day, that they had trekked off, bag and baggage, to a dug out some miles off. But that road was far from dull. Infantry and cavalry and engineers, motors and bicycles and ambulances, staff officers and dispatch-riders in endless streams and incessant dust, all looking as different from a military tournament as you would wish.

Well, no headquarters but news, from a sentry, of this Field Ambulance, and he pointed to a farm across country with the information that I couldn't reach it without going a long way round by road. I'd had enough of dust so I differed from the sentry and made a bee line through hop gardens and wheat fields and over hedges and ditches till I found the *(18th)* ambulance and, in a corner, a group of officers sitting on the grass having just finished lunch. The first to welcome me was an old friend of mine who is also a chaplain with this Brigade and it seems that I am additional to him. As there are five regiments plus a whole brigade of gunners, two chaplains are none too many. After lunch, the other Padre and I rode out to find the (Brigade) Headquarters and failed. We are going to try again this afternoon, and failing this to go to Divisional Headquarters for orders for me. I hope we shall be able to live together and order our daily work between us. As the Front occupied by our brigade is very limited it would be better, I imagine, than being separated. Certainly this ambulance is not the best place as it is not in touch with the troops and really only works at night. However, one will learn as the days go on what is the best thing to do. *(The 18th Ambulance were at Wippehoek on 1st and 2nd June 1915.)*

Just a word of one's feelings. I have never felt it so hard to realise the big war as now that one is in it, and strangely enough, I have far less interest in reading the news than I had at home. The really interesting things are the aeroplanes and captive balloons, and the variety of guns that are going off all the time.

Charlie's next newspaper report comes from somewhere in Flanders.

5 - Called to the Front

The orchard at La Louie Convent photographed in 1992. It was here that Charlie spent a lazy morning writing, 3rd June 1915.

June 3rd 1915.

After a lazy morning, spent mostly in writing, I trekked with the ambulance from one peaceful farm to another peaceful spot, where I am now sitting in an orchard behind a convent *(La Louie, north west of Poperinghe - temporary Headquarters of the 18th Ambulance)*. The move was most interesting. In wonderfully quick time the whole ambulance packed up and moved off, a long column, three sections (about 150) marching, then a lot of horse wagons, then the saddle horses. The motor ambulances went separately. I borrowed the Major's horse and rode with the column. He was rather a brute, and would not trot when required and pulled a bit. Considering that the road for the most of the way was like the Strand for traffic, it was rather exciting. Troops and transport swarmed everywhere and at most corners, even in country lanes, military police directed the traffic. Another Padre, V-, and myself soon got tired of restraining our horses with the column, and as I had to go on to Divisional Headquarters and had not much time, we rode on to this convent which lies close by a beautiful château with most glorious gardens *(La Louie Château)*. V- and I then rode on to the D.H.Q. *(Château de Couthoue, Poperinghe Proven Road)*, but found no one there but one officer, who gave us careful instruction as to how to find the Brigade Headquarters. The latter, it seemed, were in a dug-out right up at the trenches east of *(Ypres)*. There was nothing for it but to get there, as the General *(Major General W.H. Congreve V.C.)* was the only man who could tell me what my work would be and with what unit to live.

After tea some ambulances were going up to the advanced station so we went in one of them. Along roads inches deep in fine dust we went, drawing nearer to the famous town *(Ypres)*, the signs of war becoming more and more prevalent. No house with whole windows, and very many showing signs of shell-fire. The ambulances stopped at the advanced station and we walked on to the camp of the ? regiment *(either Sherwood Foresters or West Yorks.)*, which was one of my Brigade. This regiment was taking its turn of rest out of the trenches. Most of the officers were out, but a captain provided us with two guides, and we set out for what was by far the weirdest walk I ever took in my life. We had barely started when a bang loud enough to blow your hair off came from just behind. This was the signal for the usual little good-night to be called from our lines, and a terrific banging then set up. It was from our guns, which were at one side of us and behind. The men said that it was an unusually big shelling, so we expected things. We were soon in the town and the sight is one I shall never forget. As far as one could see not a house was intact. We went down a broad street with what were once fine buildings on either side, but now simply shattered, some gone completely and enormous holes left as if men were excavating for building. Some leaned out in a drunken manner, and some had huge holes in them. All were deserted, and it was literally a city of the dead. The sun had set and there was a weird twilight in which things looked ghostly and unreal.

Overhead screamed and whimpered and quivered and sizzled the shells, now joined by the Germans, while the shock of the appalling bangs of our big guns behind echoed and re-echoed in the silent streets. Parts of the town were burning but we did not go near them, and after a bit the enemy began dropping shells into the town, though none fell near us. What were my feelings? Well, I hardly know. It was certainly very exciting and very interesting, but it was so unreal that one hardly knew that one's own personality was moving though it.

After the town was passed we stumbled along ... Suddenly a challenge, and we were led by devious paths to a door, at which another sentry stood. In a moment we were in a very primitive sort of place, where sat General *(Congreve)* and his Chief of Staff eating a frugal supper. They greeted us cordially and we discussed our work. The General was very sympathetic and told us he would arrange for us both to be quartered where we would be most use. A telephone message had just come asking whether a chaplain could come out to the advance trenches for certain funerals. V- decided to do this, as it was his lot. So we parted, he going out to more adventures and I to return.

On my way back we had quite a firework display. Star shells were bursting all down the trenches, and on the left, heavy rifle and machine gun fire told of some attack. It was quite dark by this time, but the star shells made enough light to see where to walk. One shivering sizzle came near and a small shell burst just across the canal, but nothing came near us from it. And so back to the ambulance where I waited for the motors to return, and though the time was long, it was not dull, as wounded were coming in and had to be seen to. V- turned up at about 12 o'clock, and shortly after the motors. In one of these we returned to camp covered and choked with dust and ready for bed. But no beds were ready for us. We had to hunt for our kit in the dark, and found it had been moved in our absence. Finally, we lay down in the strange old vehicle that carries our luggage, a cross between a baker's cart and an old cab. Here, in spite of excitements and a wooden bed we slept peacefully, though the dawn was breaking before we lay down. I am still waiting, without any work, for word from the General, which he had promised today. I shall certainly be placed with the gunners and shall live with the ammunition column. The latter, I need hardly say, are in a very safe place indeed, and they all say that the gunners have lost hardly any men. Of course I shall not be with the guns, but with the reserve men, and I shall have to take services with the infantry which are in reserve.

5 - Called to the Front

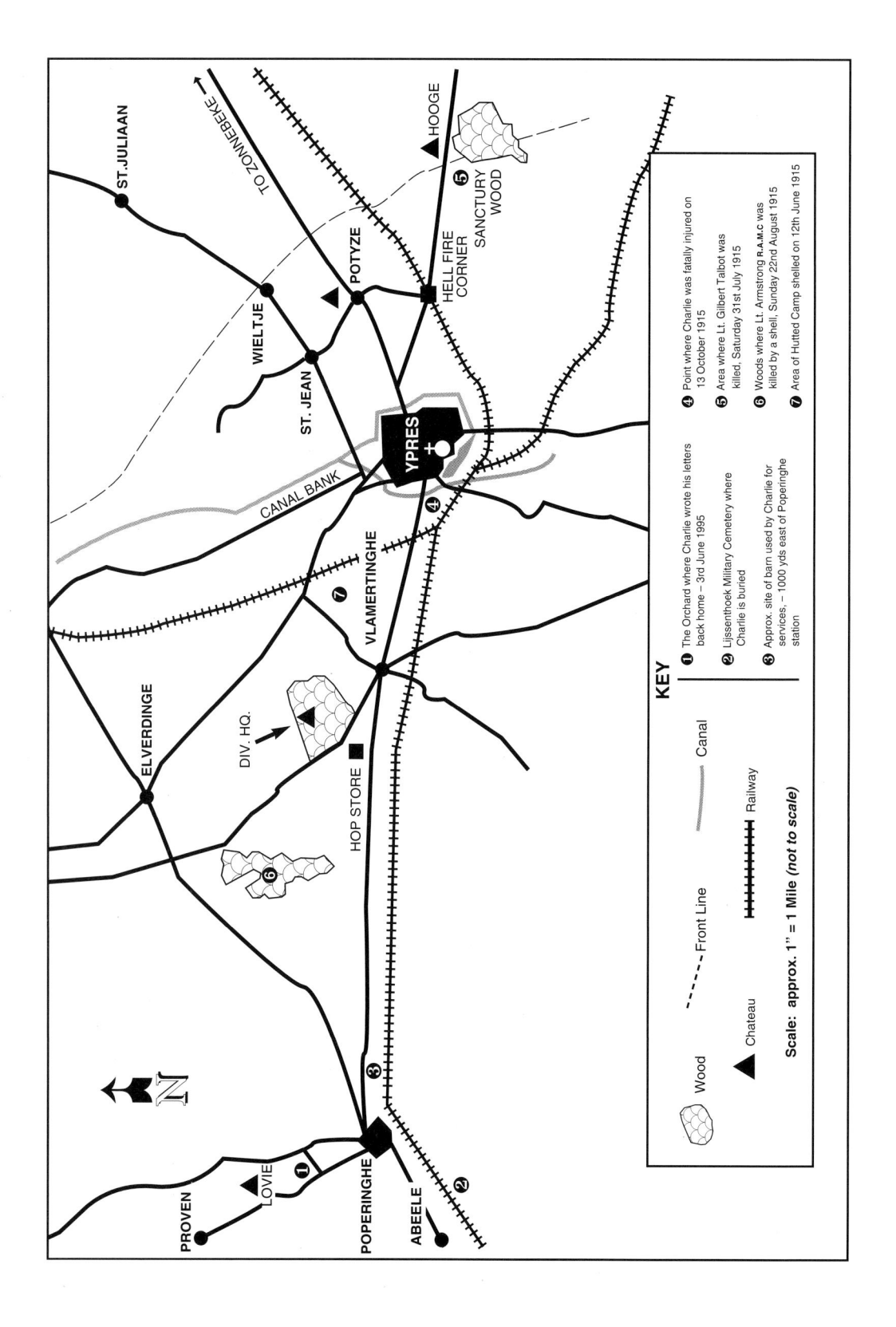

On 5th June the 18th Ambulance, to which Charlie was attached, opened an advanced dressing station at the 'Hop Store' in Vlamertinghe. As he reports in the *Bath and Wilts. Chronicle*, 19th June 1915, this arrangement suited Charlie as he could get a lift in the motors which went up to the front line every evening.

> June 6th 1915. Yesterday we trekked to a place near our lines - a village of dust, very like Australian conditions. In the evening I walked in to see the Brigadier *(Brigadier General H.S. Ainslie)* through *(Ypres)* again, and found him alone. He was very sympathetic, and at once urged me to come and live with the troops, either with his staff or with the reserve. He promised to dig us a dug-out (V- and another Padre and myself). The other Padre is in charge of the division. I arranged with him for services today. The latter will be easy, only two, as I have not got in touch with the other battalions. So this morning I walked three miles *(to a hutted camp 2 miles west of Ypres)*, and had a most wonderful service with the *(East Yorks.)* regiment. The Colonel *(Lt. Col. J.L.J. Clarke)* was very nice and keen, and men as attentive as you could imagine. Afterwards we had Holy Communion in a hut, with about a dozen men, mostly officers. After that a number of young officers gathered round me in the shade and insisted on my messing with them. I had to beg off from the Colonel, who had also kindly asked me. During the service a battery on each side and one behind started up with shattering bangs, which added to the unreality of the service, but, in a sense, also to its reality.

This morning at dawn - such a summer dawn - a terrific artillery duel set up. It was hard to think it Sunday and my thoughts went back to peaceful St. Luke's. The evening service was very nice. We united two regiments *(East Yorks. and Durham Light Infantry)*, and V- took the service and I preached. I went round and saw a good many men, and then walked over to the guns that have been disturbing us so much. Found a charming officer in charge, who explained everything. They were in action, and the bangs nearly blew my head off. All through the service shells were screaming overhead.

June 8th 1915. We are getting the most terrific heat here now. Today is just like Australia, only more sultry ...

After lunch I rode out to find another chaplain whom our senior had asked me to fetch. After riding two or three miles I was directed back to the next field to this and found him there. A fine chap, 6 feet 5 inches high! *(Rev. Neville Talbot)* had tea at his mess with some gunners, and then we returned here *(Hop Store)* for a chaplains' meeting at six - five of us altogether. We discussed and arranged the work, and then went to mess.

After or rather in the middle of that, things became rather confused, as the Germans started to shell this district. We had no wounded in to look after, so all the ambulance scattered away from the building, which is a brewery, into the fields where it is much safer. Only one man was hit and he not severely. When they had finished I went over to the gunners camp with V-'s and my letters for post, as theirs went earlier.

Whilst I was there another dose came from three directions. I candidly confess that I was in a blue funk all the time, but trust I did not show it! But it proved one thing to me and that is the extraordinary little damage these big shells cause. We had about 20 to 30 in our area, and beyond the huge holes in the ground nothing happened. They bury themselves so deep before bursting that all the charge goes upwards. On my return I found a lot of wounded just in, and went and sat with them for a couple of hours until they were all seen to. Three died in the night. They were all from the trenches.

After that we took our valises into a cornfield near by and slept there. It was all lumps, but I slept all right.

I could sleep anywhere now, I'm getting so hard! Was awakened very early by the scorching sun. It was so strange to find the tall stalks of the corn around one. We went there because we thought it healthier - not so near this building, which, by the way, was not hit after all.

(Probably June 10th 1915.) I never longed so much for the pen of a ready writer as I do now, to be able to describe the scenes I have been through, though words could never convey one fraction of the impression. One who has not been through it could never hope to understand what this war is. It is just simply hell on earth, but a hell through which moves a race of heroes, whose bravery and self-sacrifice make one ashamed. But with my feeble words I will try to tell of one little corner of the great line along which the deadly struggle wages.

Yesterday I received a telegram reading 'Can you come up to *(Potyze)* Château tonight for a burial service?' It was from the Colonel of one of my regiments *(Probably East Yorks.)*. V- and I had just moved into a camp close to the advance dressing station *(Hop Store)* of our ambulances so that by walking over to it I was able to drive up to the trenches in one of the ambulances. It was just getting dark and we moved slowly through the ruined city, picking our way past shell holes, past the shattered cathedral and going through long streets where no single house stood intact. The effluvium of putrifaction was appalling in places and all through it reeked like a charnel house.

On to the first line of trenches, with the star shells beginning to flame in front and to the right and left. We drove through the gates of some country house *(Potyze Château)* and pulled up in a curving drive among the trees. It was now very dark and raining and one had some difficulty in getting about. A good many soldiers were moving near. Various handcarts were being dragged up containing all manner of stores, food, water, sandbags, etc.

No one seemed to know where my regiment was but the general opinion was that it was on the flank of another whose trenches began close by. So I entered the latter and commenced a wearisome tramp through them. Tramp is not the right word: scramble is better. Splashing through water, slipping and sliding in creamlike mud, wandering up blind alleys. Losing direction and being redirected, pushing past men standing in rows in narrow passages, past patient sentries watching the front. On all hands was a perfect rabbit burrow of dug-outs, full of men, and occasionally a more elaborate one in which were officers. All the time a lively rattle of rifle fire was going on, which reminded me of the Century Butts at Bisley. A good many bullets whanged overhead, but fortunately there was no shell fire going on, so one had not to dodge into dug-outs. I was of course challenged by sentries and once examined by a sergeant, whom I easily satisfied. One moved as in a dream, among phantom men who talked low and were busied about their strange life. Almost everything meant discomfort and one could only try to imagine the scene when intense cold was added, when men craved for bacon fat to eat raw as they do in the Arctic. I was only a couple of hours there, but came out plastered in mud and wet to the knees.

At last I reached my line and was taken to the captain of the first company, who welcomed me to his dug-out and we sat in the low roofed mud hole and yarned. He telephoned to headquarters and I found that I had to go back to the Château. He kindly sent a guide with me and this time we did not go via the trenches but along a road to the rear. The risk was small, as it was so dark and only isolated sniping bullets whizzed by, aimed, I suppose at random. I found a burying party ready, and the body sewn up in a blanket and we started through what seemed to be a wood, along devious paths, jumping ditches, sliding down and scrambling up banks. I found it hard enough to move myself and kept wondering how the stretcher-bearers kept their feet. The sergeant in command had a torch, but he only flashed it with the utmost care once or twice to see the way.

Soon we were standing by an open grave and I began the wonderful words "I am the resurrection and the life", I have said them in strange places many times before but never had their ring come home so true. To die in decent surroundings and from a life full of comfort and loving care somehow cannot ever seem to need the comfort of this promise in the same degree as to go from this charnel-house of horror. What a contrast! The poor body in its blood-stained clothes stealthily buried at dead of night and the reclothed soul the real man - in the greater life where no death can come! I had, of course, no light - that would have meant machine guns on us in a few seconds, so said by memory the essential parts of the service. I was struck by the responses of the men every word said of each, not merely the one reply as is usual.

It was now well after midnight and no more ambulances would be returning till 2.30 a.m. so I made up my mind to walk. I say "made up my mind" because I knew it would be anything but a holiday stroll. But I am glad I did, for it left an

Aerial view of the Cloth Hall and Cathedral, Ypres, 1915. Courtesy of the Imperial War Museum "Through the great square with its skeleton building, once the pride of Flanders, one's heavy boots ringing on stone setts, and on past the great Cathedral, roofless and ruined and around it the torn-up vaults of men who lived half a millenium ago!".

indelible impression. Into the town and past the cemetery, shelled recently by the enemy till the graves had been upheaved and the poor bodies scattered. The stench was of course quite beyond description. The town I had been through before, but only in company with others. But now it was silent and deserted and the roofless houses stood gaunt and ghastly. Flickering light from the star shell shone through gaps and revealed all the debris of civilization in chaos. Everywhere, now and then a stench coming from some cellar or ruin told of dead people yet unburied.

Through the great square with its skeleton building, once the pride of Flanders, one's heavy boots ringing on the stone setts, and on past the great Cathedral, roofless and ruined, and around it the torn-up vaults of men who lived half a millenium ago! Suddenly came the startling 'Halt! Who-goes-there? Advance one pace and be recognized!' I took good care to be recognized! And a friendly chat with the sentry was no small relief to one's mind. And so back to camp and strangely enough I only remember undressing. I was asleep, I think, before my head got down on to the lumpy pillow of my valise.

Charlie's next report appeared in the *Bath and Wilts. Chronicle* on June 26th 1915.

June 12th 1915. Yesterday I walked into various units to arrange for Sunday services, and among others visited a famous London territorial regiment *(Queen's Westminster Rifles)* in a most primitive rabbit burrow on the canal. The Colonel was most sympathetic, and, though he dare not give me a full service as they were so frequently shelled, suggested Holy Communion in groups of 20 or 30. So this I have arranged to do. Also some gunners nearby want to come. When I got back I found that both V- and I had to go up to the trenches for funerals, so we carried out the usual programme, going up through the town in an ambulance, taking the funerals and walking back through the silence and the smells. The latter were not so bad last night since the rain. Got in about 12.30 and to bed at one. At three some shells came over and banged just beyond the camp. So we got up and went out, being joined by the gunner officer, whose change of horses for the field guns is just in front of us. We inspected the holes made by the shells and then turned in again.

For two more hours shells flew over us and burst some distance away, but we were too sleepy to worry so snoozed through it. Then came a terrible BANG close on our right which shook our hut and rattled it with debris. So we got up and put on boots and overcoats and went out. We then saw that the gunners with perfectly splendid discipline were getting their horses away. We and our two servants did the same with ours, and went off down the road to the south. We were not clear of the camp when shell after shell ripped into it. We nipped behind some trees and watched with interest our cookhouse, next to our hut go up in a column of red dust! It was an old brick building. The steel splinters were coming over our way a bit (you can't pick them up as they are red hot or nearly), so we went on to an estaminet (tavern) about a quarter of a mile off, and waited there whilst the enemy proceeded to plaster the camp with shrapnel ... all the troops had cleared the day previous, as it was evident that the Germans had ranged that camp.

There are some very funny things even in war, and we began to realize that our costume was not quite according to daylight etiquette, when an orderly appeared before us with Lieut.'s compliments and two pairs of trousers!! These we donned, and went back after two or three hours, as it seemed that the enemy had got tired. We found that a shell had gone clean through the next-hut-but-one to ours and burst underneath it. Another on our cookhouse, another in front, but our hut had not been touched beyond shaking everything down off the shelves and putting a piece of metal into the toe of one of my boots. We gathered a few clothes and dressed at the gunner's billet, and, after some breakfast, packed our things hastily into our 'Noah's Ark', the windows of which had been shattered, and trekked off.

We were in any case going to leave the camp in a few days, as our regiments are going right back out of shell fire for the period of their rest. So we made for the neighbourhood of their new quarters *(east of Poperinghe)*. Stopped at the ambulance to learn that they, too, had been shelled again, and there I got an urgent request to conduct a funeral in another brigade whose padre was away. So I stopped and took that - it was close by - and followed the ark on horseback, to find that V- had seen the quartermaster, and had been billeted in a farm. So here we are in a large, clean, old fashioned room, and well outside range, and listening with what, I must confess, is relief to the storm which cannot reach us.

Sunday, 13th June 1915. We had a glorious night last night, safe and peaceful. Our two servants are splendid, such simple fellows, who revel in looting things for us and have simply taken possession of the kitchen here, and do our cooking as experts.

After an excellent breakfast I rode into the old hut camp and left my horse (or rather V-'s) with the neighbouring gunners. Yesterday we had nearly taken a billet half-way in the village *(Vlamertinghe)* where the ambulance is. It was in a house right opposite a very fine old church, and an hour after we left to come here they shelled the church and completely demolished it. I passed the poor wreck today. So we should not have had a peaceful night at all had we stayed.

Walked on to the canal, where I could not well take my horse, to the rabbit burrow of the London Regiment (Queen's Westminster). They were having a Sunday clean-up outside their holes in the sun and some were even bathing. Four had got hold of an old tub of a punt and had rigged up a sail of ground sheets and were sailing up and down, with two of them dressed up as ladies with pink sunshades - the clothes looted from the ruined houses there. They were pretending it was Maidenhead! This,

The ruins of Vlamertinghe Church, Oct. 1915. Courtesy of the Imperial War Museum.

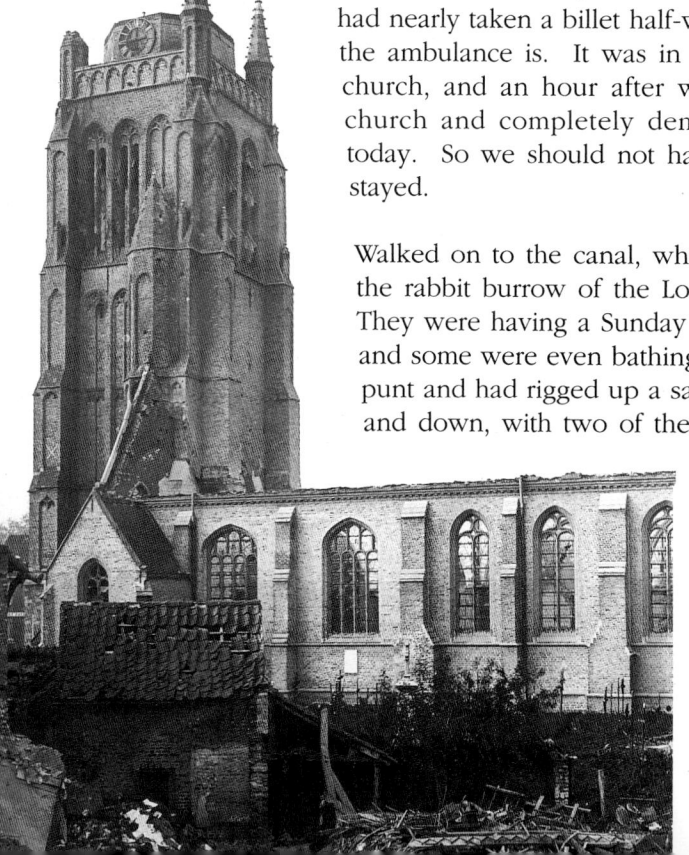

mind you, with the chance of shrapnel over them at any moment.

The Colonel was against a parade service, as the only place where we could have it was small and would be very crowded and he dare not risk a shell, so he asked me simply to conduct a Celebration. It was one of the most wonderful sights I ever saw - a small level space crammed with kneeling men ... The General came over. Lunched with them and then walked back to the gunners. I went over fields literally honey-combed with shell craters and past a number of well-hidden guns, which startled one every now and then with a terrific bang.

Held service with the gunners in a lovely garden. Two shells screamed down during the prayers and exploded a field or two away, but nothing came near, and then I came home. A very easy Sunday, but all our regiments are in the trenches and one can't get up by day there. Next Sunday they will all be out and we shall have a proper parade service. Coming through near the wrecked church *(at Vlamertinghe)* my horse shied and slipped down on the pave (setts). He came right down on his side. Fortunately I was shot clear of him and got off with a slightly sprained arm and wrist.

I was stopped a few yards farther on by a polite corporal who asked me very deferentially if I would take a funeral for his unit near there. I did so of course- and returned to our peaceful home to find that one of us had to go to the trenches for four funerals. They were all V-'s regiments, so the poor chap, after a hard day, had to be out there all night. We are putting up a Wesleyan parson for the night. Also a major of a crack regiment (with an eyeglass) came into supper. I fancy the Padres' mess will be a sort of Hotel! I'm very well, I am thankful to say, and seem to be able to do more every day without fatigue.

We are really in clover, feeding like fighting cocks. The past fortnight has, of course, been a trifle rough. But now we are billeted close to the transports and the quartermasters are most kind. We have tea, and sugar, bread and Army biscuit (very nice), bacon (the best I have ever tasted), ham, meat, tinned butter, jam, marmalade, dates, cheese, bully beef, etc., all good and in absolute profusion. We buy eggs and milk at the farm here. So want for nothing. V- is a first rate linguist and speaks French and Flemish and German perfectly, so we get all we want. One of our servants was taken ill last night, so the other drove him into the hospital. I went too, to see what was wrong with him. It does not seem to be much. While there they examined my arm which had bothered me during the night. Nothing is broken or sprained - but the ends of the bones at the elbow and wrist are jarred. I have been ordered to keep it in a sling for some days. So I shall be compelled to take a rest, which is not unwelcome, though I am so fit that I feel able to go all day and all night. I shall be able to walk about and go to the trenches, to take funerals, in the ambulance, but cannot ride or drive. We are enjoying our life here immensely. It is such a relief to get beyond shell-fire and we don't mind a bit going in on duty. It is quite different to living in continual daily danger of shells.

5 - Called to the Front

Charlie kept in touch with the parishioners of St. Luke's via letters in the Parish Magazine, such as this one in the July 1915 issue:

> Last month I wrote you giving certain opinions as to the duration of the war which were being expressed by people at the base. Now I fear I can give none. The nearer one gets to the line of battle the less one knows. You know far more than we do. We understand, of course, the work of our sector, but it's such a small one and has such a limited effect on the great front.
>
> Well, here I am rushed up from the most distant part of the peaceful base to the most advanced portion of the fighting line, and am working among the men who are struggling and suffering in deadly earnest for the great cause ... I'm picking up the threads and trying to get used to the new conditions. I doubt (at present) if I shall ever get used to the shells. Their scream is so vicious, and their coming so unexpected and the crash so appalling, that one's heart gets down into one's boots.

6. The War Continues

Potyze Château was the front line aid post administrated by the 18th Ambulance, and this is where the motors drove every evening to pick up the wounded. Charlie, taking advantage of the free lift, came to know this strange place all too well. His vivid and horrific description was printed in the *Bath and Wilts. Chronicle,* 3rd July 1915.

> A year ago it was a charming villa set just back from the main road leading from *(Zonnebeke)* and two miles east of *(Ypres),* a famous old world city. Flanked by a small wood, a serpentine lake in the rear, and grounds laid out in the French style, in which every point of view gives a finished picture. Inside everything showed the sign of culture, rare furniture, paintings and sculpture. Last June it must have been perfumed with flowers. I never saw it by day, but a somewhat chequered series of scrambles on several nights about the place gave one a fair impression of the kind of residence it was. And now! The flowers are gone, and their perfume is replaced by the all-pervading stench that one is even beginning to be accustomed to - of putrefaction fraught with chloride of lime; in some parts of the ground one has the predominance, in some the other. But it's the smell of a charnel house, and in places is added the strange effluvium, indescribable, of new-shed blood. The garden is an area of mud or dust, according to the weather. The shapely gate posts are rent and the iron gates gone. The kitchen garden at the back is lined with little mounds, marked with wooden crosses. And all over the premises, under the bushes, in the wood behind the stables, everywhere, are the larger mounds which tell of an under-earth village where dwell varied units connected with the war.
>
> But come inside the house. It's just as well, for a shrapnel has burst just over the gateway, with a scream and a deadly bang, and its contents have swirled and clanged into the drive. A number of slightly wounded men standing there drop flat as one man. 'Anyone Hurt?' calls a voice, 'no?' 'Right'. And the men begin quietly climbing into a line of ambulance cars. Through a small porch and into a good sized salon, dimly lighted with candles. The door is slammed quickly lest even a gleam should reach through the bushes to the enemy, whose trenches are not 800 yards away. Indeed, all the time, all through the night, bullets are coming past, hitting the trees, richochetting away with a bi-r-r, and reminding one most exactly of the Century Butts at Bisley. Indeed, the impression is just that of being behind the targets at a big rifle range with the protection mounds cleared away.

Left: Ruins of Potyze Château, June 1915. Courtesy of the Imperial War Museum.
"A year ago it was a charming villa - perfumed with flowers - and now replaced by the all-pervading stench that one is even beginning to be accustomed to".

All the windows of the salon are boarded and blanketed to exclude every gleam of light. The rich curtains are torn down. The painted ceiling has fallen in (the upper stories being ruined). The mirrors are smashed. All round the walls are tables, carved dressing tables and washstands, oaken bureaux, and on them glisten the bright horrors of the surgeon. Bandages and dressings, splints of all sorts, blood stained stretchers litter the place. Sitting and lying about are a dozen R.A.M.C. orderlies in their shirt-sleeves, resting till another stretcher party come in. Bravo, oh! brave beyond words, these lads who slave there night by night in that deadly atmosphere, week in, week out, month by month.

Another big room leading out of this is quite dark but as one stands in the entrance one catches the sound of confused breathing. There are 50 men there, sitting and lying on the floor. Their wounds are dressed and they are awaiting the next convoy of ambulances. All slight, reports the sergeant. There's no talking. They are silently, patiently waiting.

An arched opening, covered with a rich curtain. A little room with crowded easy chairs and five doctors in easy deshabille. Candles in a shattered chandelier. Round tables with tea things and English biscuits and Fullers sweets and smokes. 'Hullo, Padre, come in and have some tea'. And we settle down and yarn of old days of peace, and rake up mutual acquaintances, and they describe yesterday's awful battle on the right which they watched. And every now and then the house shakes with the shock of 'Crumps' falling about the cross-roads hard by ('Crump' is the name given to a high explosive big shell bursting in the ground).

'Yes, we'll have one in here some day'. 'But don't you live in a dugout when you're not working?' 'No, we sleep here during the day. You see, they don't shell us much in daylight, as there are no men moving about'.

These are the regimental doctors, whose regiments are all in the trenches, and here they stay for all the time they are 'in', in close reach, and ready at any hour to tend the stricken. Young, all five, but only showing by their faces to those who watch them - never by word or action - the strain their life must be.

Two o'clock comes, and one, whose head has been nodding for some minutes, wraps himself in a priceless piece of embroidered curtain and lies down to sleep, asking them to wake him if wounded come in. Soon after, a whirr in the drive tells of ambulances. The 50 men in the dark room are passed out by 7s or 8s according the space of each car. I strode past the convoy. If there's no room for me it will mean a long walk - eight miles - to where my billet is now. So I confess to some anxiety, especially as the road is now being shelled again, and one can hear the shrapnel going over it. The cars will take another way in consequence, and will go four times as fast as I can walk past the danger zone. So it's with relief to me that the driver of one beckons me up. His mate (there are always two drivers) will sit on the step. The big Wolseley - built for such different work - slides out of the gates and is cleverly and tenderly guided, lightless of course, over a road shattered by shell. Past blazing houses, dead horses, through deadly smells, we swing silently till I am dropped off the ambulances and trudge a dusty road in the fair dawn for three miles to my peaceful but not soft bed - a blanket on the stone floor of a kitchen.

Saturday 19th June, 1915. Have had a quiet day. Rode into the Hop Store to the field ambulance before breakfast to see what patients were in. There were some very bad cases. The ambulance is in a brewery among bales of ancient hops, rather sour, and the smell will, to my dying day, remind me of these scenes of blood. Spent the rest of the day in arranging services for tomorrow ... I have borrowed a horse from a friendly gunner for the day. I have indented for a horse for myself, but expect it will be a week before it comes.

The Hop Store at Vlamertinghe, June 1915, being used as a 'dressing station' by 18th Field Ambulance. Courtesy of The Imperial War Museum.
"The ambulance is in a brewery among bales of ancient hops, rather sour and the smell will, to my dying day, remind me of these scenes of blood".

20th June, 1915. *(On this Sunday the whole of the 18th Brigade was out of the trenches, giving extra work for the padre.)* Have had a wonderful day, full of excitement. Parade service at 10 with *(Sherwood Foresters)* regiment, followed by Holy Communion in the open in a wood *(east of Poperinghe)*. I rode over on an immense black gunnery horse. He had never been ridden separately and caused me considerable trouble later. Then on to another wood, *(1½ miles north west of Vlamertinghe)* where a large congregation was awaiting me / drawn up among the trees in a great square. Two whole regiments of begrimed warriors straight from the trenches *(East Yorks. and West Yorks.)*, the General and his staff and practically all the officers were present. It was perfectly wonderful. And the singing ... !

Back for lunch and out again at 1.30 on the big horse. We had to pass his 'lines' and he said 'no'. So for over half an hour I fought him with spur and whip. I tried everything, kindness included. I led him a mile and got other men to also, but when I mounted he simply reared and turned round. At last another officer came along with a groom, and sent the latter back with the black and gave me the groom's. With this I went on - he shying at everything he saw. When I arrived at the batteries (five altogether) three-quarters of an hour late the men had dispersed. You can imagine how wild I was. However, they want a midweek service instead. Then to the ambulance Hop Store, where I had a nice service, including Holy Communion with them. About 20 stayed to the latter. Then on to the huts (our famous huts, where our slumbers were so rudely disturbed by shells), and had tea with the officer who lent us the trousers. Had a fine service with two companies and left here, getting in at 8 p.m. The services here are certainly most inspiring. V- in addition to his services had a voluntary one here in a big barn with a scratch band, and the place was crammed.

Monday 21st June, 1915. I have got leave to loot a piano out of *(Ypres)* and am going to try to get a wagon and some men for the purpose. 'Leave' consists of telling the Provost Marshal that you're going to commit the crime! He says you mustn't be caught doing it and at the same time tells you where the best piano is to be found. My servant went in on Saturday, and came back pleased as Punch with a load of crockery and cooking pots. Our billet is proving more and more of a centre. The young officers constantly drop in. We are going to have a midweek Holy Communion early here, which several of them are keen to come to. In the evening I went to my regiments for a concert in the woods. It was perfect. We sat in a big circle in the moonlight in a clearing and the singing was excellent, to the accompaniment of the looted piano.

Tuesday 22nd June, 1915. Another appeal! We want a car badly and can't get it from the authorities here. It would render our work safer, besides saving much time. However quiet a horse (and they are seldom that) when a shell bursts near them, they simply swing round and go anywhere! And there is barbed wire everywhere and ditches and holes galore. A car does not shy and would carry one past dangerous corners so much quicker. A small second-hand one would do admirably, say a Ford costing about £80 ...

Charlie was also writing to friends back home to try to get support for the motor car project, and Zoe solicited the parishoners to help their vicar and his fellow chaplains.

In a letter written about this time to his sister Edith, Charlie refers to the summer holiday that the family had just had, 'So glad to hear that you have had a good time at old Bexhill. What memories that brings back. But it seems like another existence'. He was remembering happier times of his boyhood when the family had lived at Ore, near Hastings. What a contrast to Charlie's next report in the *Bath and Wilts. Chronicle* of 6th July 1915 which begins by describing a torn and shattered town.

Ypres Cathedral and part of the Cloth Hall, 1915.
Courtesy of the Imperial War Museum.

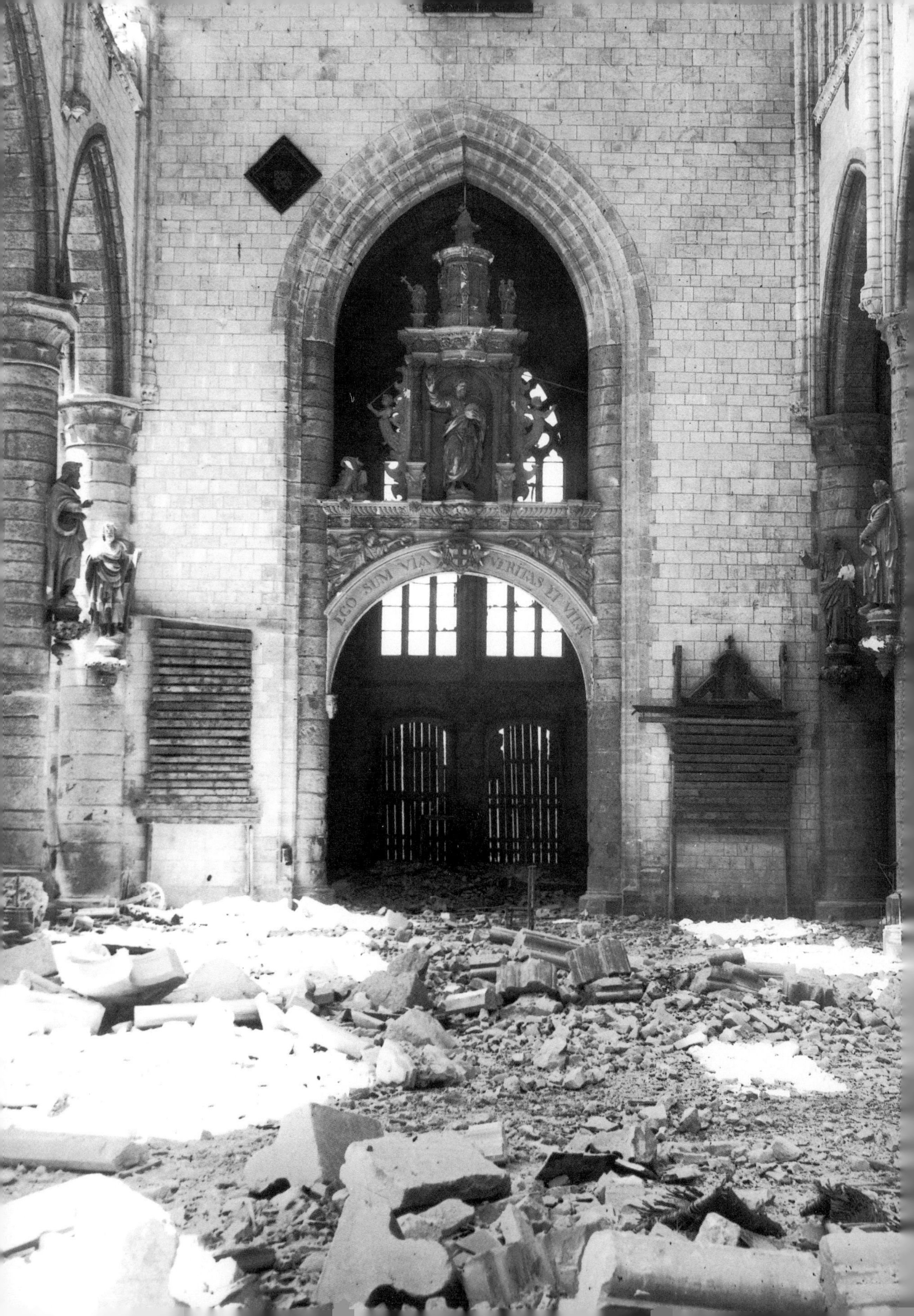
EGO SUM VIA
VERITAS ET VITA

Thursday 24th June, 1915. V- and I went into *(Ypres)* to try and loot another piano. It was the first time we had been in the daylight and, though the impression was not so awesome, yet it was interesting to see clearer details. We went down street after street and into the Cathedral, which is, of course absolutely wrecked. The walls are standing, though sadly torn. Huge stones are heaved about in all directions, pillars broken, and the big organ smashed. The beautiful Cloth Hall next door is still more done for. How I should like to loot some carvings for St. Luke's! One church had been occupied by French soldiers, and when the shelling began they had evidently gone out at once, for everything they possessed was littered over the floor. You never saw such a mess. We just picked our way through, and did not stay as the smell was not good. We found some pianos and chose one, which the transports are sending for.

It was pathetic to see decent houses, some quite splendid, torn to pieces, whole fronts gone, exposing the rooms on each floor like dolls' houses, with all the details of civilized life open to the air. Inside, everything was in utter and absolute confusion, and we went from room to room, furniture all over the place, and sometimes the staircase gone, or ceiling down, or roofless. But by far the greater number of houses are gone altogether, and nothing left but a heap of bricks and stones. For a wonder the afternoon was quite quiet, not a shell fell into the town or near the road.

Friday 25th June, 1915. To-day I have been preparing for Sunday. I generally try to do this on Friday in case of accidents on Saturday. I visited six units, which meant a good tramp over fields in pouring rain. Got a drive back in a very swagger car ... Any ordinary vehicle I stop as a matter of course, from a coal cart (in one of which I rode three miles today) to a bumpy ammunition wagon, you know the kind, a box on two wheels, no springs ... All my regiments go into the trenches again to-night, and they (the trenches) will be full of water again as the rain has been very heavy to-day.

Sunday 27th June, 1915. Have been busy today. Borrowed a great big fat chestnut and rode in near to and had a ripping service with the men of the wagon teams of the field guns, i.e., those who wait near the front to take the guns in and out of action. About 150 came to a big hut. Holy Communion afterwards, with about a dozen present. There were no officers, as none stay with these horse lines. They were a rough lot, but real good stuff and very attentive. Then off to the big guns. Again about 150 men and all the officers of the battery in the open beside one of the monsters ... During this some big shells came screaming over and burst in a field behind us. Just as I was consecrating came the first

Left: West door, Ypres Cathedral - 1915.
Courtesy of the Imperial War Museum.
"We went into the Cathedral, which of course is absolutely wrecked. The walls are standing but sadly torn. Huge stones are heaved about in all directions".

6 - The War Continues

vicious rending, biting scream. No one stirred! Had lunch with the officers, to the accompaniment of more shells. They burst about as far away as the Bear from St. Luke's, throwing up great clouds of mud.

Off again at once to some more wagon lines. I had to go past the place they were shelling, so made a detour through some fields. I don't take more risks than I can help. Another service with about 100 howitzer men. These small voluntary services I make very informal. All sit down and sing some hymns - a few prayers, and then a very straight talk, the chaps' eyes rivetted on one, and every now and then a broad smile and even a word from them as something goes home. These are the services I like best. Sometimes they provide a table which I generally sit on when preaching. I am supposed to give them about six minutes' discourse, but these informal affairs get much longer. I usually stop at about ten minutes, and say 'Time's up' or something of that kind, and they always say 'Go on sir', in a chorus, so I do for a bit, but not too long as I want them to come next time.

Then back to our transport lines. Here they were busy starting to move camp to another field close by, and not many could be spared. About 11 came, however, and they had a piano. I asked for someone to play, and a man volunteered.

As we had to wait a few minutes for a section I asked him to play a voluntary. He at once broke into Rachmaninov's 'Prelude', and played it superbly! Then home for tea and now I'm waiting for our special evening barn service, for which I have borrowed a piano, and also the Rachmaninov pianist. So already I have talked to 55 men to-day, although this is an off Sunday, and the brigade is all in the trenches.

Monday 28th June, 1915. Ten shells just gone over. We went out to watch where they landed. Only four burst and did no harm. They never come near us, but go on to a railway station about 1,000 yards further.* Last night very few turned up to our barn service, but we had a lot of hymns and the men enjoyed it immensely.

An officer came and asked for a service today and said he would bring his men over, so I fixed it up for this evening. At first no one came so I went out onto the railway line to look for them and saw a small column bearing down on me. There were about 30 and we had a short service and address and then sang songs for an hour, and the piano man played a lot. Our men seem to be having an easy time in the trenches, as there have been no funerals there. They have been up four days now and I have not been called up once. I fancy this whole

The Germans were probably shelling Poperinghe Station and therefore the barn stood 1,000 yards to the east of this, near the railway line. This area is now covered by the Poperinghe ring road.

week will be easy, a thing I don't like. Plenty of work makes one forget time and it goes much quicker.

Tuesday 29th June, 1915. In the afternoon I had to go to the trenches again. *(Kinnear)* was also wanted, so we went in together. Got in close to - on a motor wagon and walked the rest. It was early, about 6.30 p.m., and for a change I took two funerals by daylight, both behind the canal banks and so safe from rifle fire. The poor chaps *(probably Durham Light Infantry)* had been blown to pieces at mid-day by a shell, and we buried them close to where they died. Two pathetic bundles in sacks - the poor limbs gathered up and put together as best they could! The German shells were coming over in a stream all the time, but falling well beyond us. Afterwards I walked along the dug-outs and talked to the men. Suddenly a line of four big shrapnels burst together over a road, near where we were with a very fierce flash and bang, but no one was touched. Then *(Kinnear)* joined me and we walked back past where the shells had been pitching.

At length we were caught up by an empty ammunition limber wagon, which we 'took'.

Talk about seeing stars! I've been shaken up 'some' since coming here, but that beat all. It was of course a bit unhealthy (as they say here) and the Tommies put the horses to a gallop for some miles. It was simply a case of grip with all your legs and arms, the empty limber leaping like a bucking horse.

Wednesday 30th June, 1915. Today *(Kinnear)* and I went to see some motor machine gun people. I casually asked the O.C. if they had a chaplain. He said no, and that they had been four months there and had never had a service. His earnest reply, when I offered one, was the kind of reward one gets here. There were sixty of them when they came out and there are only 15 of the original ones left *(see page 156)*. We are picking up a good many odd lots of people who are in nobody's "parish" and they are all so grateful for our help.

Thursday 1st July, 1915. Rode in before breakfast to the ambulance Hop Store to see the new patients in. Then Holy Communion with five chaplains (all our division men), breakfast and a talk over our work... *

---

* *The five divisional chaplains frequently had policy meetings. Amongst the items discussed were the formation of a church club, a place where soldiers of any rank could relax when away from the battle lines. Charlie also discussed these intentions with Zoe but unfortunately never saw his plans fulfilled. A few weeks after Charlie's death a house was acquired in Poperinghe for the purposes of the club and it was left to his replacement, the Rev. Tubby Clayton, to fulfil this mission. The house was named after the Rev. Neville Talbot's brother, Lt. Gilbert Talbot, who was killed on 30th July 1915 (see pages 159-160). The British soldier came to know the club as Toc H, this being the radio call sign for Talbot House. The organisation of Toc H still thrives today as a Christian charity.*

6 - The War Continues

Then on to *(the hutted camp)* for a funeral, the place where we were first shelled and which they continue to pepper every day. On to *(Ypres),* the City of Ruins to see the Provost Marshal about the piano which he had not succeeded in getting. He sent me on to another officer, who told me that no one could give leave except the Belgian authorities, and as the town is now policed with Belgian gendarmes it is impossible to get anything out now. So I came back forlorn.

However V- went, after lunch, to see the head boss of the Belgian troops in these parts and got a paper authorizing me to take that particular piano. So I went over to some gunner pals and got a service wagon with four horses and two postillions and off we went, a charming corporal on the box with me, his trade at home that of a 'bobby', and four men sitting inside. It was a case of walk all the way in, except a few short trots and walks, as they were heavy horses and the road was bad. In *(Ypres)* we were stopped several times by town guards, both English and Belgian, but my paper was an open sesame. They were shelling the place pretty heavily but nothing came down our street. After we entered the house we soon whipped out the piano and drove off in triumph. The way home was quite a triumphal march, as everybody ragged us for looting. I met various men I knew and crowed over them. As they had prophesied failure it was a score. I felt happier when we began to draw out of range. We got in at about 10 p.m. and put the piano in the barn. A lot of good music was on it which we took. So now we have our own instrument for services and concerts and the units round are very keen on it.

In the *Bath and Wilts. Chronicle* of 12th July 1915, Charlie describes going up to the front line in daylight for the first time:

Sunday 4th July, 1915. I actually took all my services without hearing a German shell screaming. First I went to the wagon lines, where the gunners came in such numbers that we couldn't get into the big hut we were in last Sunday. So had a ripping service in the open ... Lunch and off again on the horse to the ambulance *(at Vlamertinghe).* Had the service in the great hop store of a brewery. There were no wounded men in for a wonder. I shall ever connect the smell of hops (rather sour) with that of blood. Last year's hops have a very nasty sour smell. We used a piano with a shell splinter right through it, which had smashed the middle notes, but some genius had taken the bass notes and put them in the centre.

Back to our barn *(near Poperinghe)* and found waiting a crowd of transport men, who overflowed, and spread out from the big doors in a wide circle. Among them 20 of the ? Regiment, who had just come out *(from England).* These lads were just going into the trenches, and looked rather dazed. I had a little chat with them. Tea, and a fine Daimler car waiting to drive me to the Motor Machine Gun Corps. Here even the sentry was withdrawn to attend service, quite voluntary mind you, and every single man and officer came, and we sat in some new mown hay and sang hymns, and I talked to them sitting amongst them (my services are getting more and more informal!). Back in the car, the gunners who helped me loot the piano came over and we had an A1 service. The officer (there is only one with them) told me that the men were so keen to come that the Roman Catholics had to be put on duty to take ammunition up. One or two were left in their camp. The rest all came, even the French interpreter ... I was dead beat, but quite healthily; indeed, I am marvellously fit.

Tuesday 6th July, 1915. Just had a wire from the trenches for a funeral tonight. My brigade is in another part, about a mile to the left of where they were. I shall have to find my way over unknown ground, but I hear that it is safer than that rotten old château *(Potyze)*. I saw some photos of the latter taken before the war. It must have been a lovely place. I hear rumours that we have smashed the German naval gun that shells these villages. Anyway none have come since Saturday morning.

The Brigade took up new positions on 26th June. The line included Wieltje and extended north west for 2550 yards, with a second line south of Potyze having the reserves and headquarters in the canal bank.

V- insisted on coming with me to the trenches, where I had to take the funeral. I think he likes being under fire! We caught a motor lorry as far as Z - , and after walking on for half a mile and watching some big German shells bursting under our airmen (not the usual small air-craft guns), one of our own ambulances picked us up, and we went with them to the canal bank. Here we visited our brigade headquarters to find out where the regiment was to which I was bound *(probably the Sherwood Foresters)*. The General *(Congreve)* was in, and we chatted for quite a long time, whilst an orderly phoned up to the trenches to find out where and when I had to go. The answer was 'Any time I liked', so off we went with a friendly warning, called by the General from his dugout, for us to be sure and get under cover if they fired at us. And now for the first time in daylight (for me), we walked over the fields immediately behind our trenches, and, of course, kept behind rises of ground and hedges.

A fairly heavy shelling was going on on our left, about a mile away, where our troops had attacked that morning. We could see the 'Jack Johnsons' bursting in the big fountains of earth. On our right they were plastering the roads with shrapnel, so we kept to the fields. And every few minutes a big shell fell in the city to our right rear. Arrived at the little village we were making for *(St. Jean)*. It was nothing but utter ruins. Debris of every kind littered the streets. A fine motor car destroyed, bits of bicycles mixed up with pictures and smashed furniture and clothes. The fine church was a shell and the graveyard torn up. The cross roads in the village were visible from the German lines, so we didn't exactly dawdle across them! At the headquarters of the regiment we found that the pioneers were not quite ready, and they insisted on us staying for tea. Whilst

The Village and Church tower of St. Jean, August 1915.
Courtesy of the Imperial War Museum.
Tuesday July 6th, 1915 -
"For the first time in daylight (for me), we walked over the fields immediately behind our trenches, and of course kept behind rises of ground and hedges - the little village we were making for (St. Jean) - was nothing but utter ruins - the fine church was a shell and the graveyard torn up. The cross-roads in the village were visible from the German lines, so we didn't exactly dawdle across them!

there we were much interested in examining the country and the lie of the German lines, and what interested me much was the beautiful grounds of the château, the back of which we now looked on. The Germans very seldom fire in the afternoon, but yesterday they must have been angry at their defeat, for they pumped in the shells like anything over the château and beyond. I found that the internment was to be made in the old ground behind the château. Thither we walked, the corporal cheering us on the way by saying that the road we were on was in full view of the enemy, and that they were very fond of putting in a small very high velocity shell, termed a 'Whizzy Bang', or 'Little Willie', when they see any party on it. A single man they don't worry about. Personally, I rather wished I were alone!

However, they let us pass and we arrived safely at the field. To my great surprise and pleasure I found the lines of graves tended with loving care. You will remember that I had always been there by night. Crosses marked each grave and the latter were planted with flowers and neatly finished off. Isn't it nice of these chaps? And when you think that it's a mighty dangerous place. After the funeral we discussed going back through the city, or over the fields around it. Chose the latter, and luckily too, as a few minutes later they sent a perfect shower of shrapnel over the road we should have been on. The walk over the fields was interesting if effluvious! War signs everywhere, blown up wagons, one ammunition wagon burnt and lots of cartridges not gone off, bits of soldiers' clothing, burst shells, empty English shell-cases - it was quite an interesting ramble.

Presently we came on a crater no less than 50ft. in diameter (150 feet round) and at least 20ft. deep, torn in heavy clay, great masses of which were lying all around. On the edge we sat and marvelled - caused by a 42 centimetre gun, of course. Then watched an exciting air battle, and came to the conclusion that the planes, of which there were flocks, were safer than we were. West of the city we were picked up by an officer in a car and taken halfway home and the rest in a springless transport wagon. The trenches are being made so much better that the losses are much less now than when we first came here. This is only the second call I have had from my Brigade to bury up there and they have been in 11 days. A few have died of wounds and I have buried them at the hospitals out here.

Thursday 8th July, 1915. *(Kinnear)* brought out a small 28 bore gun with him and the other day he shot five pigeons with it. D- (my servant) cooked 'em and burnt three to ashes, and as we sat down to eat the other two, two officers came in, and we had to ask them to stay, so we each had one bite and a half! This morning we had Holy Communion and two other chaplains came, including the new Senior of the Division. After breakfast, *(Kinnear)* and I went into *(Ypres)* as I had to take two funerals. I went on to the same village that I was at two days ago *(St. Jean)* and found they were not quite ready. Whilst waiting I had the strange experience of watching a battle. The colonel of the regiment took me up to the upper storey of a house, not quite ruined. I moved to the window - no glass of course, every pane in the area is smashed - but the colonel pulled me back, quietly remarking that the window was in full view of the German trenches!

So standing well back we watched with glasses a real big gun duel. We had taken some trenches a mile away to the left, and the Germans were trying to regain them. Both sides were bombarding the opposite trenches, and as they were apparently quite close to each other it was easy to see which were which. All over the area huge black and yellow fountains of earth and dust and smoke sprang up and drifted quickly off in the strong wind that was blowing, whilst the pure white balls of shrapnel broke out again and again over the lines of trenches.

But it was hard to realise that it was a battle going on. Not a soul could be seen and yet, in that ground over which we gazed, lived and breathed tens of thousands of men.

I could not stay to watch a possible attack of infantry as my funeral was ready. So I walked over to the same ground as the other day and found the grave ready - only a small one, for there was just a sack to be put in. 'That's all we could find of him Sir' said the corporal. Then I had to walk over the fields behind the trenches to another hamlet to bury an officer who had been killed last night ...

Picked up *(Kinnear)* on the way home; he had been wandering about visiting people, and we came home through *(Ypres)* none the worse. *(Ypres)* was looking none too safe as there is a big wind for the first time since it was destroyed and tottering walls have been falling about the last day or so. Walking about beyond *(Ypres)* I had another good look at war's destruction. The trees are almost all damaged, some torn up, some snapped in half, the roads littered with branches and leaves. Every single house and barn and cottage torn or blown up; crops coming up but untended. Gardens trampled, but still showing lovely flowers. The land literally scored with trenches and dug-outs everywhere. Discarded ammunition, odd cartridges and clips, mess tins, broken motor-bikes, and ordinary bikes, shell-cases numberless, big chunks of crosses, ill buried horses. It's certainly interesting as a promenade. You never know what you are going to come on next, or for that matter what is going to come on you!

7. Home on Sick Leave

In the afternoon of Monday, 12th July, Charlie departed the front to begin a two week medical leave for the treatment of eczema, probably brought on by the traumas of the previous three months. He was on his way to Bath, having received permission to take the soothing mineral waters there, rather than rest and treatment at the base hospital recommended by the military medical staff.

In the early hours of Tuesday, 13th July, Sashie answered her door at No.10, Albion Street in London, and was overjoyed to find Charlie standing there. After spending a short time in town, he went on to Bath, arriving at home on the following evening. Early next morning, he began his 'water cure', under the supervision of his old friend, Dr. Preston King.

Besides the great pleasure that Charlie must have felt at being home once again, imagine his joy when he discovered that his prayers for transport had been answered by his parishioners. He was presented with a brand new Triumph motor bicycle with all the extra equipment: leggings, luggage case, plugs, etc. (all bought at the cost of £50 18s. 9d.).

Medical treatments could not keep the Vicar away from his ministerial duties and he took the morning service at St. Luke's on his first Sunday back. The church was filled to capacity and Charlie took as his text John XIX: 17, 'And bearing his cross went forth into a place called the place of a skull'. His sermon was published in the *Bath Journal,* 24th July 1915.

> ... I hardly know what to say this morning. Perhaps ... I will deal only with generalities - just a sort of bird's eye view of what it is ... Anyone who has spent a number of years in perfecting a machine, naturally wants to see how it works ... Thus some of us have given our very lives to the service of religion, and some of us have made it our profession and work away in times of peace, when there was no strain upon it, and have often wondered what would be the result when that machine was put to work in the realities of life. And now we have seen the religion put to the severest test which any system could possibly be put to; and we have seen it come out absolutely triumphant ...
>
> It is perfectly possible, of course - indeed it is a thing which I expect to find among such large numbers, when men find themselves in the middle of horrors

Left: Charlie home on sick leave.
From left to right: Zoe, Charlie, Raymond (in car), Herbert, Chizzy, Olive (wife of Herbert), Connie Chadwick.

so awful that words can never possibly describe saying - 'Where is God? Can there be a God? We hear all through the piping times of peace about the mercy of God, and about His loving kindness; is it possible there can be a God who can allow these things to happen?' But, instead of the faith of men being shaken, we have seen it getting stronger and stronger ... the important part which really matters is not the body, but the soul. So it is still true that a thousand might fall on the right hand, and ten thousand on the left, but it cannot touch thee.

What is the message that the chaplains take, that gives us such a welcome ...

... We believe and teach that God will not stop these things unless men come and rank themselves with Him to do the work. It is the idea of co-operation in the work of God that the men reach for, and hold on to, and drink in so thirstily. And this idea gives a meaning to my work ... They are not fighting alone for men, but it is a spiritual war they are fighting, side by side with God to get rid of sin in the world.

One hears a great many tales about what is called 'The White Comrade', again and again He has appeared in the battlefield. There is a very short distance between the opposing trenches - three or four hundred yards, and sometimes considerably less than that. In the day time it is impossible to get into that piece of No Man's Land, and after dark there is the constant light of starshells so no man can even crawl across. Often and often it occurs that men have been left wounded in the area - left to die. Attacks are nearly always made early in the morning, generally, recently, between three and four o'clock in the morning, right through the terrible heat we have been having lately, with no shelter from the burning sun, and with that awful thirst which must of course follow almost immediately on a bad wound. Men lie, not one or two here and there, but often, in my own brief experience, in hundreds throughout the day. It is impossible to imagine anything worse, or more awful to bear. There are their comrades within a few yards, longing to help them, but dare not and can not, and there the men die. Well might it be said by them 'God has forgotten us' as they rave in their sufferings. But it has been said, again and again, that through that horror walks a man in white - the men call him the White Comrade, but they know who He is - tending the wounded. The story has been doubted of course; and men cynically say it is the heated imagination of the wounded in the agony of their fever. Possibly it might be so ... but they see with spiritual eyes far more clearly than this congregation, that God is with them and that the White Comrade moves with them. Men whose lives have not been known to be religious in the least, upon whose lips perhaps blasphemy has been more frequent than any decent words, men who have been known perchance to their comrades as 'a bad lot' have, in their agony on the battlefield, known the presence of the White Comrade.

It is possible that other miracles have occurred, such as the one so often told of the angels who appeared and shielded a battery from a German charge; but I know that a greater miracle even than any physical miracle is going on, day after day. Tens of thousands of men, hard, rough working men, who perhaps never attended church at home, and never thought of it are finding definitely that God is their close Friend ... Oh, if you the congregation could only see, only get a vision of one of those companies going into the trenches at night just in the fading light; or stand at the side of the road and watch them swinging past, and see the faces of those lads who know thay are going to death! For the word has been passed 'Put in more ammunition', and the load of the ammunition cart is doubled. I have seen it happen twice, - the lads going up when they know there is to be an attack, and that half of them would not come back. And the officers, mere boys many of them, know that nearly all of them will be killed that night. We watched those faces, white, drawn, and anxious as they are, but filled with a determination that could not possibly be misread by those who know how to read it. I am talking absolute bedrock truth when I say that a miracle has happened in the hearts of these lads, who have never made any profession of religion and have told me so as I have gone among them chatting about these things; but, as they go by with their drawn faces they know they are walking along that road bearing their cross to the place of a skull, and that their companion by their side is He who was crucified more than eighteen hundred years ago, and is with them in the trenches as they wait and as they go out perhaps to die ...

That same Sunday evening, Charlie preached at St. Phillip's, Odd Down. His sermon was very much in the same vein as the morning but he did interject that after this conflict, life would never be the same again. Continuing in the *Bath Journal*:

... This war has shown that our much vaunted civilisation is only a veneer; and that this world is very far from being the comfortable place which we have hitherto imagined it to be. This conflict means the end of the old world; and this fact has been realised by many of the thinking young men in our Army.

During operations on a 20 mile front in May, 120,000 fine young soldiers have been seriously injured, and 30,000 have been killed. I believe most sincerely that those who have thus sacrificed their lives at once became the inheritors of the glories of a new world ... and when we think of those who are the bravest of all, those heroines who sit quietly at home, and who receive unflinchingly the news of the death of their dear one, I feel that in those who are spared to return will be found the inheritors of the new world which will soon be.

On the following Thursday 22nd July, 1915, the Vicar held an informal meeting in the vestry. The room was packed with parishioners eager to hear Charlie's first hand account of his war experiences (these are condensed from the *Bath Journal*). He started with some observations on the pronunciation of that much abused word, 'Ypres' ... The correct Flemish pronunciation, he said, might be represented by the form 'Y-per', but 'Tommy' had soon devised his own pronunciation, and the form

7 - Home on Sick Leave

'Wipers' had found its way even into despatches. The size of Ypres might be estimated by forming a mental picture of Bath minus its suburbs. Without a solitary exception every single building in this town had been wrecked and about 75 per cent of the place had been demolished. Though the cathedral was battered by bombardment, sufficient remained standing to constitute an exceedingly picturesque spectacle. In the remains of the priests' vestries, torn and tattered vestments were still to be seen. These now bore yellow stains, and this, along with the smell that clung to them, suggested that lyddite had been employed in the German shells. As far as could be ascertained, however, no military object had been attained by this destruction. The bombardment of buildings which might possibly be used for billeting troops was a recognized military expedient: but there was only too good a reason to believe that Ypres was destroyed by the Germans through pique, because it was the only town in the occupied area of Belgium that the Germans did not occupy.

On 25th July 1915, the second Sunday of Charlie's convalescence, he put in a full day's work in the parish, taking morning, afternoon and evening services with full congregations every time. His morning sermon was written up in *Keenes Bath Journal* (31st July 1915) and describes the work of an army chaplain.

> Sunday 25th July, 1915. Rather than preach you a sermon, I want to give a business description of the way in which we spend our time and how we are doing the work ... I want to tell you what we are doing, in order that your prayers and interest in the work might not only be continued, but increased. There was an article in a daily paper, two or three months ago, describing the work of chaplains at the Front, and dividing chaplains into three kinds. First (it said) there are those chaplains who endeavour to carry out the Church's order in all its details at the Front, and who lay more stress upon the exact nature of the service and what robes they wear than upon the men they are ministering to. Secondly, there are the amanuenses, who spend their time helping the troops, looking after their material comforts, writing their letters and procuring cigarettes for them. Lastly, there are those whom the writer called the missionaries - filled with the highest possible ideal, which at all times they hold before the men who are fighting. I must say that I have come across some chaplains of the first two types; but nearly all I have met belong, most decidedly and definitely, to the class of missionaries who do not rest until they have brought the highest possible ideal into the hearts of the brave men who are fighting. Certainly we do try to help in the writing of letters and in the concerts and the games, but this is apart from our real work, which is to deliver the message of the other world.

> There are two distinct divisions regarding the religious organisation for the Army, work at the base - principally hospital work, of which I have not time to speak, and the work at the front. The chaplains are the only people connected with religion allowed there. Whilst the Y.M.C.A. and other organisations are doing noble and splendid work at the base, they are not allowed within 30 or 40 miles of the firing line.

In each army division there are now seven Church of England, two Roman Catholic and two Nonconformist chaplains, for a total of, say, 20,000 men. Until quite recently there was only three chaplains to a division. The great majority of troops put themselves down as Churchmen, and at the Church services 80% or in many cases 90% of the troops attend. Seven might seem a large number of chaplains but a division is very scattered, and each chaplain has something like 3,000 men under his charge. The area on which we work is, roughly speaking, about two miles by ten miles in depth. In this area some 20,000 or 25,000 troops are camped and they are scattered as widely as possible on account of shell fire, little groups here and there. In order to get over our work we have to travel a very great deal; and, in this connection, the motor bicycle which you have so kindly given me will be an invaluable time saver. My particular unit consists of one brigade, and my colleague and I divide the work as carefully as we can. The brigade is composed of five battalions of five different regiments, four regulars and one Territorial; the transport of each regiment, about 50 men in each; three batteries of field guns, each with its supporting units, wagon lines, men looking after the horses as near as possible to the guns, but hidden among trees or behind any cover etc. There are also three other batteries in the neighbourhood, which don't properly belong to our brigade, and then there is the ammunition column, companies of engineers, and a whole host of other details I have not time to enumerate. To all these we try to minister, and have very little spare time after visits and holding services on the Sunday. Last but not least is the work among the wounded. Each brigade has attached to it a special ambulance consisting of nearly 200 men of the R.A.M.C. - about 12 doctors and the rest stretcher-bearers and drivers of cars. This is generally three miles behind the lines, and the patients are taken there in the motors in order to have their wounds properly dressed but not for operation. Further back and out of shell range, is the convalescent part of the ambulance, where men with slight injuries rest a few days, where regular services are held for the wounded and the workers. Roughly speaking such is our parish.

The most important work of all is the glorious Sunday when we go out with a sense of being armed for victory, not against physical things, but against spiritual powers. Services are very seldom on the week day, but I have had a long conversation with my Brigadier, *(Brigadier-General Ainslie)* in which he suggests that there should be an official Sunday, because at present it often happens that the regiments are not out of the trenches on a Sunday and the Brigadier quite agrees that one of the days when the men are out of the trenches should be regarded as a Sunday, and if put into practice, would greatly increase the number of services. The Sunday services start with Holy Communion near our billet. Little services are often held for scattered groups of men - sitting along a ditch, behind a hedge, hiding among the trees, or assembled close round the guns. That is the most nervy part of the Sunday; very seldom a service goes through even 20 minutes without some excitement, or without having to make a very quick change from the open-air to the dug-out.

Motor Machine Gun Unit photographed in 1915.
Courtesy of the Imperial War Museum.
" - the famous and devoted little unit which earned for itself the soubriquet of 'sui-sidecar corps'. They came out 60 strong, only 15 remain, for, more than any others, they live absolutely in the presence of death - every week I miss some of their faces."

At 6 p.m. a service is held for the famous and devoted little unit which has earned for itself the soubriquet of 'sui-sidecar corps' *(Motor Machine Gun Corps)*. They came out 60 strong, only 15 remain; for, more than any others, they live absolutely in the presence of death - never out of action one single day. They are all volunteers, men of education mostly engaged with the motor trade. Every week I miss some of their faces; they have gone. The half past six p.m. general service is for all who have not been visited during the day, and is held in a barn capable of holding about 200 men, but I have seen them outside in a large circle on the grass. It is a hymn service, perhaps 12 or 20 hymns, and then a little straight talk. Nothing reminds them, say the men, so much of their homes as singing the hymns, and to illustrate the devoutness of these men who attend this service, a battle between two airplanes does not draw their attention away from their hymns and prayers. And so closes the great Sunday.

That same Sunday evening, another large congregation gathered to hear the Vicar give an address to the younger members of the parish. The service was attended by the Boy Scouts and the parochial company of the Church Lads Brigade, the latter in their khaki uniforms, under the command of the curate, the Rev. A. Chisholm. The St. Luke's company of the Baden-Powell Girl Guides commanded by Connie Chadwick were also on parade.

This was the last time Charlie preached at St. Luke's.

The following Friday at six o'clock in the morning he set off on his motorcycle, en route to Folkestone, once more to take up his military duties.

The Church Lads' Brigade with wooden rifles under the command of Rev. Chisholm (seated third from the left). Photographed at the church parade held on Sunday 25th July 1915.

7 - *Home on Sick Leave*

'Near Poperinghe' - a watercolour by Charlie's close friend Lt. Col. Buchanen-Dunlop, Leicestershire Regiment.

8. Return to the Front

Much refreshed from his convalescence Charlie returned to the Front, only to find that his old billet had been occupied by an ammunition column. He was directed carefully to his new lodgings, as he describes in the *Bath and Wilts. Chronicle* of 18th August, 1915.

Monday 2nd August, 1915 ... another farm, really better than the old one, although to reach our bedroom we have to pass through another which is apparently occupied by the farmer's family. For a living room we have an outhouse with no door (just a space) and no windows, another for a kitchen for the men, and a tiny room in the house, which we use for our daily prayers and as an office.

We are short-handed again. Unfortunately one of the other chaplains has been sent home on sick leave, and another was thrown from his horse and got a broken collar bone. But they have sent us another one to help meanwhile.

This morning I had occasion to test my new method of travel as services had been fixed in two places beyond *(Ypres)*. Instead of relying on passing vehicles or slowly working in on a horse, I swung down the road at about 15 miles an hour, and was in the city in about twenty minutes. At that pace one is not bumped too much, appalling as the road is. Then came the advantage. Instead of the slow weary tramp, I went right up to Z-, round Suicide Corner like a streak *(this is probably a pseudonym for 'Hell Fire Corner', a well known location, the name of which would have been censored)* and was at the dug-out in no time. Here I held a celebration for a regiment that had not had one since I took one of them six weeks back. Very few present as they were preparing to move and it was Monday. The Colonel was present, and gave me such a hearty welcome. It was worth coming back for that. Then I rode into J- and took a service for advanced gunners of my batteries, whose wagon lines I have taken so often before. Only one battery turned up. I think, judging from the noise close by, that the others were in action. We held it in a brokendown warehouse. Very hearty service, though so few were there. Then I came back *ventre-a-terre*, and so had accomplished in far less time and under safer and easier conditions what used to be such a long and dangerous business.

After tea a message came for one of us to go to the trenches for a funeral. We were just debating who should go when *(Neville Talbot)* rode up and offered to take it as he is at present living there. Poor chap, his brother was killed on Saturday leading a charge. None of his party came back, so *(Neville)* went out last night and crawled out of the front trench through the wire and actually found his brother and others all dead. Incidentally he found six wounded men and got some volunteers and brought them away.* My regiments come out tonight to rest *(the whole of the 18th Brigade were being withdrawn to a rest area near Poperinghe)* but I hear that they have to go and relieve the troops at another place so perhaps they may go in again next day. Hard luck on them isn't it?

Charlie only had been back a few days when, on 5th August, the Brigade was repositioned south of Hooge in preparation for a big offensive. The Durham Light Infantry were deployed at Sanctuary Wood with the Sherwood Foresters in support. The East Yorks. were at Zouave Wood, the Queen's Westminster Rifles at Maple Copse and the West Yorks., with the Brigade H.Q., were within the Ypres ramparts. On 9th August, spearheaded by the Durham Light Infantry, the British launched an attack to regain Hooge village and crater. This commanding position had been lost some ten days before when the Germans had attacked using liquid fire for the first time.

Charlie's involvement in the campaign was reported by him in the *Bath and Wilts Chronicle* of 18th August, 1915, and continued on the 21st.

> Sunday 8th August, 1915 ... Then came Sunday night, with the awful bombardment. You will have read all about it in the papers. The attack ... came off splendidly and we are all hoping that it may be the beginning of a real advance.
>
> Monday 9th August, 1915. In the morning I rode into the Hop Store quite early after breakfast and from then till 1 o'clock, and 3 till 6, and 8 till 11 o'clock, I worked with the wounded ... We had only three surgeons and about half a dozen orderlies for them. The other doctors were right up at the Front.
>
> There was nothing for me to do but to remove my coat and set to. Very diffidently at first for I hate to push in where expert knowledge is needed. But I soon found that there were many plain wounds that anybody could do, so took those. The stream slackened off later in the night (about 11 p.m.), so I rode back and had a good sleep.
>
> Tuesday 10th August, 1915. Was up at 6 this morning and in again before 7 and have been at it again all the morning. The others had been up all night, so there was only one doctor most of to-day. But there were not many cases.
>
> They were very bad ones and I mostly had just to assist the surgeon. All yesterday shells were coming over and bursting in the village, but when one is hard at work one does not notice them. Indeed the noise of wagons passing on the

---

* *Lt. Gilbert Talbot was killed whilst leading a counter-attack at Hooge after the first enemy liquid fire attack and is buried in Sanctuary Wood cemetery. Talbot House was later named after him.*

18th Field Ambulance carrying wounded down from Maple Copse near Hooge. August 1915. Courtesy of the Imperial War Museum.

9/10 August 1915. Between 800 and 900 casualties were brought into the advance dressing station at Vlamertinghe during the first two days of the battle of Hooge.

"We had only three surgeons and about half a dozen orderlies - The other doctors were right up at the Front. There was nothing for me to do but to remove my coat and set to ... I soon found that there were many plain wounds that anyone could do so I took those".

cobble stones and the bustle inside, made the row of the guns a sort of background. One thing bucked me up a lot. I was attending to a man rather badly wounded, to whose regiment I had preached once two months ago. Although I was bereft of any chaplain's marks (being in my shirt sleeves) he recognised me and said that the message I had given then had helped him through this awful time and last night's battle and his long wait when wounded. And he said he had handed it on to many others. I thought he might be wandering and questioned him, but he had made no mistake for he described the place and time and even quoted the words (or their sense). And that's the kind of thing that makes one so thankful to have come out. In the afternoon the stream ceased (between 800 to 900 casualties had been brought into the advanced dressing station), so I went for a joyride to a jolly hill near to get some of the smells out of my nose. Then on again with the night cases. These were very bad. They were the worst stretcher cases which could not be brought down the first day, so had lain in the trenches for two whole days. The wounds were in a terrible state, in some cases one or two limbs blown off and so on. Poor chaps, they were, as usual, marvellously brave.

> Flanders.
> Aug 11, 1915
>
> My darling Joy
> I have received two nice letters from you since I left home & I am very grateful. Old Dad likes getting letters from his children.
> I hope you are enjoying the seaside.
> I am sending you a button from a German's coat. He was caught by my soldiers & wounded.
> Much love from
> DADDY

Above: During the initial stages of the Battle of Hooge, Charlie was fully employed tending the wounded at the advanced dressing station at Vlamertinghe. As if to take his mind off these scenes of horror, he found time to write to his little daughter Joy.

Opposite page: The Hop Store viewed from both sides, photographed in 1992. The building has changed little since 1915 (see page 139). To the rear is the little cemetery where those who died at the dressing station were laid to rest.

Wednesday 11th August, 1915. About 1 a.m. the last lot came in and with them a doctor who had been working the advanced post with two others and 60 men. From Sunday night till then - i.e., two whole days and two and a half nights - they had worked away under fire in the appalling noise and confusion. He was dazed and dropping and had no kit and there was no bed there so I brought him here for the night, or rather the rest of it. He came in an ambulance and I rode behind on the motorbike, not easy in the dark with no lights. We fed him up and put him to bed in a farm bed and he slept like a log well on into the morning. After breakfast he rode in on my bike-carriage.

This afternoon I buried one of the stretcher bearers. There were three killed, but only this one was brought out; he died in the ambulance-car. The whole ambulance turned out with all the officers and we had a very impressive service ...

8 - Return to the Front

Afterwards I visited the *(East Yorks.)* regiment, which had just come out after the fight. They were engaged in re-forming and estimating wounded. There was some difficulty in getting returns from the ambulances engaged so the motorbike came in again and I rode round to certain of them and made the necessary enquiries. I made a proposal to the Colonel about holding a memorial service for the dead and that will be held tomorrow. The motor-bike has been simply invaluable these last few days!

Thursday 12th August, 1915. At night I held the memorial service. The whole *(East Yorks.)* regiment paraded in the dark and formed in a hollow square. Then, standing on a box, I read out the names of the fallen and those of the missing - a long list. I gave a short address and portions of the Burial Service. I had an electric torch for the names, but managed to remember the service more or less accurately without a light. It was certainly most impressive, and the stillness of the massed men profound. Afterwards had supper with the staff, and the poor Colonel, dead tired, slept in his chair almost before we had finished.

Friday 13th August, 1915 ... In again to the ambulance this afternoon for a funeral, and found there some poor wounded chaps who had lain out in the front of our trench since Monday morning. Today is Friday. They were found by a hero this morning, who thought he heard a cry, and got out over the parapet to see what it was. He himself was shot in the leg just as he and others had got them in. There were three, and one was not so badly wounded but that he could have got back, but he would not leave the others. They had had no food or water for four days and nights ... Pouring rain this afternoon, but in my leggings and mac I went ploughing through it on the bike in great form.

Saturday 14th August, 1915. Today I had lunch with the staff of one of my regiments, and afterwards the Colonel, Adjutant, Sergeant-Major, and four guides and I marched out to view a place I had found for tomorrow's service. It was the same that I had used last Sunday for another regiment *(near Poperinghe)* - a ripping little sheltered field.

Two stray mules came in here this morning and some of the men tried to catch them. Failing, they sent for some more helpers. Meanwhile, after a glorious hunt, we cornered them in a stable. At lunch today the General of the 2nd Army *(Sir H. Plumer)* called to congratulate the staff on our victory. He shook hands with us all and spoke so highly of the work done.

Two funerals (of Gunners) this afternoon at *(St. Jean)* up the trenches. The motor was again splendid and pipped me in through *(Ypres)* at a terrific pace. They have been putting in some 17-inch shells, and simply demolished a part of the town, but the Engineers have cleared a path along the road. I was not allowed to go through Z- as there also the shelling was pretty bad, so skirted the town and rode right up to the trenches, near to the old burial ground. Here I left my bike in a ruined house, and went along some trenches to the field. Nobody there. So I sat on the edge of an old trench, ready to drop if anything came along, and waited.

A good deal of frightfulness was going on, but mostly passed overhead. One battery just behind me seemed to be playing tennis with a German gun. The shells came screeching over, backwards and forwards, quite evenly as if they were chucking them to each other in turns. I seemed to be the net, and was very glad they didn't serve any faults!

Presently who should walk up but my friend the gunner who had lent me the trousers on a certain famous occasion. It was some of his men that I was to bury. Soon after came the bearers carrying two bodies, and to my joy, Major -, the most famous gunner here, the keenest of the keen. I had heard so much of him that I was glad to meet him. The men lined up, and the Major ordered the sergeant to go apart and keep a very bright look-out in case of a German aeroplane, for if one came over and saw the group the German guns would very soon disperse the funeral! However, none appeared, and we most reverently carried out the short service. This was in daylight, which I still think the most safe. And so back, the little motor dodging in and out among the shell holes and barricades and barbed wire and fallen trees and timber and broken wheels.

Vlamertinghe Château - photographed in 1992. In August 1915 it served as the headquarters of the 6th Division. On occasion Charlie held Holy Communion services in the Chapel.

8 - Return to the Front

> Sunday 15th August, 1915. I rode in to Divisional Headquarters *(Vlamertinghe Château, which has its own chapel)* for Holy Communion at 7.30, then back for breakfast. Off again for two regimental services *(East Yorks. and Sherwood Foresters)*, each held in my field, which again proved most convenient. In each case the big parade was followed by Holy Communion - a table in a corner of the field - and a good number stayed ... One of the regiments *(East Yorks.)* was one that had led in the recent attack and that had suffered so much, so of course, they were feeling it. Just off again to the advanced ambulance for service. The great day has closed with a splendid service with terrific hymn singing in our hut. We were rather worked up, and a ripping Major was here, and we sang on till late. It was a wonderful day. We calculated that we had talked to an average of 1,000 men each.

The next report in the *Bath and Wilts Chronicle* of 11th September 1915 shows that, although less frantic than the last few days, Charlie continues to lead a busy and exciting life.

> Sunday 22nd August, 1915. Today has been a great Sunday - rather more so, as there has been a spice of adventure about it. The Germans have been favouring us with a lot of shelling the last three days, every village and all the billets and woods. So today there was vigilant watching for warplanes and much effort to get well covered. All my regiments were 'out' *(of the trenches)* except one, so I had three parade services, taking two regiments together ...

> I had fixed a service this evening close to X-. When I arrived I found one company assembled and lying prone to the ground. A Bosche plane was just overhead. We discussed what should be done. The other companies had been stopped on account of the 'plane. Something had to be done quickly, as they were shelling even then, a part only a quarter of a mile to one side. An idea occurred to me. A hop garden was near, so, as soon as the 'plane had passed, we all scooted to the hops and stood in the lines. Soon the other companies marched up, one just in time for the sermon, and took their places almost as in pews. Two more Bosches came over, but, of course, they could see nothing as the hops are in full leaf. The troops nearly filled the garden and the singing sounded far better than in the open. Also the place was easy to speak in; in fact, it made an excellent church.

> Monday 23rd August, 1915. Yesterday I took back to his billet on the back of the motor bike *(Lt. Armstrong R.A.M.C., attached D.L.I.)*, one of the doctors who had come to our place to see V-, who has unfortunately hurt his back. He got off close to his bivouac *(in the woods at A30)* and we both talked to the Colonel for a bit. A few minutes later *(Lt. Armstrong)* was killed by a shell! I did not hear of it until this morning and have just had the sad duty of arranging for his funeral. He was one of the very best and was so gentle with the wounded. He was the man I worked most with on that terrible night in the advanced ambulance that I described not long ago.

Alas! all looted pianos have been called in and ours, being the only one for which permission was obtained, was the first one pounced upon and it has gone!

Sunday 29th August, 1915 ... I have had no evening service having just received word, from O.C. of the battery I was due at, that the service is off. I expect they have been suddenly called out. It is just as well because the weather has broken and it is streaming with rain and very cold and we could hardly have held it as there is no cover at all there. I am now sitting in my 'British warm' and rubber boots to try and keep warm. There is no window to this apartment and we have to keep the door open for the purpose of light. Our 'Zoo' here is getting rather interesting. The four horses come and clamour for bread and even walk in at the door, poking their lovely noses right up to the table. It's no good driving them away, they only snort and run round and back again. Then two ancient ducks stand nearly all day looking in at the door asking for scraps, coming over the threshold when we throw something to them. Lastly we caught a young pheasant and kept him until someone else bagged it.

Tuesday 31st August, 1915. I had rather an exciting time when I rode into the ambulance for a funeral, and then had to go with another Chaplain to visit certain of my Brigade. We went in an ambulance part of the way and walked the rest. Just short of Z- the ambulance stopped at a signal and we saw and heard shrapnel bursting over the road right in front. That meant a wait of half an hour, so we dropped off the ambulance and cut across the fields at an angle. It was well we had not gone on, as several more big chaps came most beautifully placed over the road. One burst about 100 yards away. None came any nearer so we walked on and paid our visits without further molestation, only the terrific noise of our own guns all round, which apparently were doing most of the punishing that day.

The brigade front line now ran 200 yards south of the Velorenhoek road to 400 yards north west of Wieltje. Charlie's walk would therefore have been across the fields between the Ypres - St. Jean Road and the Ypres-Potyze Road. His destination was St. Jean or possibly Potyze. Continuing in the *Bath and Wilts Chronicle* he writes,

Wednesday 1st September, 1915. Unfortunately we are to be moved again. We are really in the area of another Division, not our own, and they require the farm themselves. I have been running round trying to find another billet, but fear there is none, and we shall have to draw tents, though we may get one room in some cottage where we can have a fire.

Saturday, 4th September, 1915. We are moved and at the present moment are crowded with all our goods into one single room in which we must sleep and eat and have our being! The move was conducted with great éclat and considerable difficulty; the amount we have accumulated is perfectly awful, and the roads are beyond words. Our tents haven't come, so we shall have to get on as best we can until they do.

I had a regular steeple-chase of a ride to J- today, a place some considerable distance back. It was raining, as usual, and the roads were mostly cobblestoned and of the very worst I've struck yet. Where they were not cobbled they were broken into deep holes full of mud. Such rides become adventures! On the return journey the sun came out and it was more pleasant - only my gear wire got rusted and I couldn't change, so had to come back all the way on the low. Tomorrow I shall have to travel the same road again after an early Celebration at Divisional Headquarters at 7.30 *(Vlamertinghe Château)*. We are much nearer in than before, but quite as safe. Our big guns shake the whole house.

Will some layman say a few suitable words as to the weather? It has been raining and bitterly cold for days now. Poor V- had to go up to the trenches last night. He arrived back about 1 a.m. very wet and cold. The motor-bike has proved itself today more of a treasure than ever. I had to go up to the trenches after breakfast through drenching rain and wind and cold, over roads that could only be associated with nightmare. I could only ride at all on the pavement and got too near the edge - a slide slip into the mud was the result. The motor traffic all sympathised and gave me room, but the others evidently did not realise the troubles of a cyclist. It was no sooner clear of the streets of *(Ypres)* than the beastly shells whipped over behind me and made big holes right in the middle of the road. The dug-outs and trenches were in an awful state and what the poor chaps suffer on these occasions passes expression. I took the funeral in the pitiless rain and the Germans were kind enough to be silent during the ceremony.

Sunday 5th September, 1915. Today I'm basking in the sun, the clouds having at last rolled away. I have had a somewhat strenuous day so far. The early service was all right, as there is a metal road all the way to Divisional Headquarters *(Vlamertinghe Château),* though even that is a sea of mud two inches deep. Had breakfast there with the General and his staff, came back and got ready for my longer run. It was pouring as I again started, and by this time the whole bike was in such a state of slime that the belt wouldn't grip, and I could not get her off. So that meant the dirty business of cutting a bit out - not so bad with these rubber belts as it used to be with the old leather ones. She went all right then and I slipped and wriggled and plunged and bumped for about 12 miles through traffic so heavy that bobbies are needed to control it at many points. Had the service at rather a nice farm (everything inches deep in mud) in a barn with a piano. Holy Communion followed in the house. It was a fine old building surrounded by a double moat. I had lunch with the (Artillery) Brigade Headquarters in a village near, and it was so nice to see all the ordinary life going on and hear the church bells ringing. The people all in their Sunday clothes and all so still and peaceful. Got back safely, and am just going to have tea, and then one more service.

Monday 6th September, 1915. Have just been up to the trenches, and quite enjoyed the trip. No shell came anywhere near me, and the roads were nearly dry or paved all the way, and the weather was, and is now, glorious. Everyone was drying and very cheerful. Our guns were pegging away gaily, but there was only an occasional reply. I had to bury three men, and afterwards visited some other people. Incidentally I found a group of about 30 pioneers of my Brigade who have been working in *(Ypres)* for months and never had a service or a visit from a chaplain. So I am going there tomorrow morning. Just off to have tea with some gunners, not officers, but some non-coms, most delightful chaps, who want to show me their dug-out ...

Last night I dined with a regiment - not mine - as the guest of the O.C., a man I have seen much of here and like tremendously. We had a splendid band playing all the time, and the usual toasts. It was a special night to commemorate their coming out a year ago, but of all the original officers who came with them only one is left.

In the October issue of *St. Luke's Magazine,* Rev. Chisholm (Chizzy), the curate, writes:

There is no 'Letter from the Vicar' this month. I am glad, however, to report that he is well, but extremely busy. In a letter I have just received, the Vicar writes: 'I have had a very nerve-shaking time lately, doing the whole brigade for just a month, and have been very frequently up to the firing line. Today I was up for nearly six hours, and had a great deal of hiding in dug-outs and dodging out to take funerals.' There is just a possibility of the Vicar getting three or four days' leave of absence about the end of October. We must hope that he may succeed in this. Perhaps we may have him for our Patronal Festival on October 17th; but we must wait and see.

It was announced last month, the Bishop of the Diocese has promised to preach at St. Luke's on October 17th, in the morning, and we look forward to his visit with eagerness and delight.

Charlie's pips and whistle.

8 - Return to the Front

'Wipers' - a watercolour by Lt. Col. Buchanen-Dunlop, Leicestershire Regiment.

9. The Final Days

By October 1915, Charlie had not written anything for the newspapers for over a month. His early reports had shown an almost boyish excitement at encountering the new experiences of war, but after nearly six months, his pastoral duties had become a repetitive routine of horror. Originally it had been expected that the war would be over within a few months and that the Vicar would have been back in his Bath parish by now, but the confrontation ground relentlessly on.

Charlie was due a few days leave and all at St. Luke's hoped he would be home in time for the patronal festival service. With this in mind, Charlie wrote to Zoe.

2nd D.L.I.
W.I.B.
6th Div.

11/10/15
My Darling,

Again - if it be not forgotten - this letter will be posted in England. This time it is Wheeler who is going on leave.

I will not say more now but will add, if I can, more details as to my leave, before this goes.

Had a grand day yesterday *(Sunday)*. H.C. *(Holy Communion)* at S-, then a tremendous parade service of the - in the woods, the biggest crowd from one regt. I have yet had. Then a service in - with 2 comps *(companies)* of *(Westminsters,)* a London terri. regt. and we simply took possession of a small theatre and had such a perfect service. H.C. followed with 60. I used a table in front of the stage!

Later. Don't know yet whether I shall get off this week. Wheeler is off in a few mins. If I know before he goes I shall add 'yes' or 'no'. Yes meaning Friday and most likely afternoon. No means it is put off for a bit. I shall put it on the envelope.

Much love
Yours
DADS

The letter was posted in England at 11.30 on 13th October, and written on the back of the envelope, 'Still Uncertain'.

9 - The Final Days

Two days later his leave had been confirmed and Charlie wrote to his niece, Miss Ivy Gollmick.

> 2nd Durham Lt. Inf.
> W.I.B.
> 6th Div.
>
> 13/10/15
> My dear and honoured niece,
>
> You are right and wrong. I did wonder why I was so honoured by being called by my right name by you but I did not think it cheek.
>
> Many thanks for the composite letter and please thank Mums for hers.
>
> I am let off for 5 days and shall race home. I start tomorrow (Thurs.) and ride down to a hospital at - to see a man who is rather bad and then on to - from where if I can persuade the authorities that I'm not a spy I shall be allowed to sail to Albion. A'll be on shore, allbion well, towards the end of the week, probably Saturday. However I don't think I shall have time to see anybody as I shall race to Bath to stay over Sunday.
>
> There is a lion in the path of all this joy as I have to go tonight to the trenches to bury 8 men! However, that is my usual nightly job and has occurred about 3 times a week for getting on for 5 months so I mustn't grumble. It's always an adventure. The nights are pitch dark now and we are not allowed any light and the roads are shelled and full of transport. It ain't no picnic! You would be interested in our camp and we have very good fun. We are all (4) Cambridge men, the other 3 are much younger than I and call me Daddy and mock me and have no respect for my grey hairs. However I can still tackle any of them separately and administer that corporal punishment which was so frivolously omitted in their youth.
>
> Much love to you all
> your doddering old
> Uncle Charlie

That evening Charlie set off for his nightly vigil in the trenches to bury those eight men. Excited at the prospect of tomorrow, he set off with his leave documents in his pocket. His parting comment to his fellow chaplain was 'Remember, whatever happens tonight is best'. The story is continued in part of a letter from the officer commanding 18th Field Ambulance, published in the *Keenes Bath Journal*, 6th November 1915.

> It was just before 9 p.m. on *(Wednesday)* 13th October that he turned in at our

billet and asked me to take him up to one of our regimental aid posts to bury a soldier. He was in his usual cheery mood and I was delighted to have him for the sake of his good company. There had been a heavy bombardment to the south and a few shells were passing over and around our village. He got on the front of the front car with me, and said that he would like to sit on the left side. He was accustomed to sit in the middle between me and the driver, but after a few minutes he said that he would sit on the floor with his feet on the left step, obviously to give me more room, kindly soul that he was, and so we went on with him leaning against my knees. He talked to me about wireless telegraphy and X-ray apparatus that he had repaired or worked at the base, and about my work which he said was divine. I wondered indeed what he thought his own work was. A few shells dropped some distance away, but otherwise things were quiet. Just after we had got into the ruined town *(Ypres)* which you know; and as he was turning round to talk to me a shell burst to the right and in front of us. Immediately I asked if anybody was hit, and both he and the driver said 'No' and I told them to get off and take cover. I found all three in the front of the second car, 15 yards behind were wounded. On getting into the cellar of the nearest house, Mr. Doudney said he was bruised in the right side, and the driver, who had been sitting on my right was obviously wounded in the thigh.

I first examined Mr. Doudney, although he strongly protested saying I should examine the driver first, and found a small wound but to my grief I could see that it was serious. Incessant shelling continued in our immediate vicinity and he begged me to go on and call for him on our way back. He asked me this time and time again, but two of our cars were out of action and I could not make him believe that in any case we were better where we were. Corporal Wilkinson and Private Spedding got a stretcher for him and gave him morphia of which he had a supply in his pocket. He was very comfortable, and I believe almost happy, or he would have been if he could have persuaded me to get away the men. At last things quietened, and I got him into a car which had come up. The last words that I heard him say to his driver, Ganley, who that night drove on the road three times under shell fire, 'Go as hard as you like driver, don't mind me'.

At my request he was sent on immediately from our dressing station to the clearing station behind, whilst I went on my way to the aid posts.

Charlie was taken to No. 10 Casualty Clearing Hospital, which was just east of the village of Abeele, south west of Poperinghe, where he was attended by the Surgeon General. The officer of the 18th Field Ambulance continues,

... but it was of no avail and with him I know there left us the bravest and kindest of gentlemen, a good, self sacrificing Padre, a true friend, and the most open and honest man it has ever been my lot to meet. He was borne to the grave only a few hundred yards from the field where I first saw his serious yet smiling face, by those stretcher bearers who had carried him wounded to the ambulance

9 - The Final Days

and he was buried with a beautiful sun breaking through the Flanders mist and our heavy guns booming in the distance, and only a stone's throw away from that railway which, as he told me after he was wounded, should have carried him home the following day. I could tell you many things about him, how at the battle of Hooge, when the wounded were coming in faster than we could clear them, he took off his coat, acted as a dresser of wounds under me, and worked until he nearly dropped with fatigue, and always with stimulating cheerfulness.

Cannon Macnutt, vicar of St. Matthew's, Surbiton, ministered to Charlie in his last hours and paid the following tribute.

We did so hope that he would pull through, and everything that skill could do was done. When it became apparent that he was passing, the Archdeacon *(Southwell of Lewis)*, the sister *(Thorold)* and I knelt down and commended his spirit to God *(9 p.m. Saturday, 16th October 1915)*, and gave thanks for his life and ministry, and especially for his splendid service over here. The end came very quietly and peacefully, and as he was passing we repeated the words. 'Blessed are the dead that die in the Lord, from henceforth, yea, saith the Spirit, they rest from their labours, and their works do follow them.' There in the marquee, in the dim lamp-light, he passed into perfect peace to receive his Master's 'Well done, good and faithful servant, enter thou into the joy of thy Lord', the other side. I could hear the guns roaring in the distance and tried to picture the peace into which he had gone out of this scene here of pain and death. During Sunday his body lay in a coffin in the mortuary tent covered with the Union Jack, and in the evening Captain G.E.L. Poulden, R.E. *(Charlie's brother-in-law)*, who had hurried up on receiving a wire from London telling him that the Vicar was dangerously wounded, but only arrived in time for the funeral ... On Monday *(18th October)* we met there with some of the officers of his Division, the Major commanding his Ambulance, and the doctor officers from it, a bearer party of the men who had carried him when wounded from the house where they sheltered to the ambulance car, the Senior Chaplain of the 6th Division, five or six of his fellow chaplains, and some of the officers of the Casualty Clearing Hospital. We had the full funeral service, at the request of Captain Poulden. The senior chaplain took the opening sentences and read the lesson, and the Archdeacon as chaplain of the hospital, took the committal. It was a beautiful autumn morning and all was peace except the roaring of the guns and we spoke all afternoon of what he had done and been here to so many men ...

In his death they were not divided. His two last longings, when the splinter gangrened and the operation failed, to commune with his wife, to commune with his God.

Extracted from *Keenes Bath Journal*, 30th October 1915:

- but he sank rapidly at the last, and when he was asked for a message to send to his dear ones he could only whisper 'My love'. At the last, speech was beyond him and all he could do was just to smile on his friends, who among them would never forget his smile; and they could well understand how that smile uttered his faith, hope and affection more eloquently than any spoken word.

The grave of the Rev. Charles Edmund Doudney - photographed in 1919 (right) and again in 1992 (below). Lijssenthoek British Military Cemetery, near Poperinghe, Belgium. Grave No.31. Plot I Row A.

9 - The Final Days

By 1918, the little cemetery attached to No. 10 Casualty Clearing Hospital had become the second largest within the Ypres Salient, containing some ten thousand graves, and is now known as Lijssenthoek British Military Cemetary. Charles Edmund Doudney is buried in grave number 31 of plot 1, row A. All is beautiful, tended by faithful Belgian gardeners under the administration of the War Graves Commission. Bordering the cemetery to the north is a new roadway which has been built on the site of the old railway track, the one that would have taken Charlie home on leave.

◊ ◊ ◊ ◊ ◊

The Vicar, due to go on leave the day after he received his wound, was eagerly awaited at home. The sad news arrived in his place, soon reaching the local papers. The following extracts are taken from the *Bath Chronicle*, Monday 18th October, 1915.

> ... Imagine the sorrow felt throughout Bath and especially in the parish when the news that the Rev. Charles Edmund Doudney had succumbed to wounds received in Flanders ... It was on Thursday night *(14th October)* that Mrs. Zoe Doudney received the first intimation that her husband had been wounded. It came in a telegram from a brother chaplain *(the Rev. J.C. Kinnear)* saying that Mr. Doudney was wounded slightly on Wednesday. Then on Friday followed a wire from the War Office stating that Mr. Doudney had been dangerously wounded in the abdomen, and was in a casualty hospital at the base. It also stated his condition was such that no one could be allowed to see him ... On Saturday morning *(from the Rev. J.C. Kinnear)* ... came a letter to St. Luke's Vicarage which explained how Mr. Doudney had been injured ... The writer afterwards visited Mr. Doudney in the hospital and found him fairly cheerful ... an operation was performed; but the writer seemed quite hopeful that he would make good progress. On Saturday evening came news that Mr. Doudney was worse and the bulletin posted at the Vicarage on Sunday morning made many apprehensive.
>
> Sunday 17th October, 1915, was the Festival of St. Luke's. Because of the serious news, the musical service arranged for the afternoon had been postponed, and in the morning special prayers were offered for the Vicar ... For the fourth year in succession Dr. Kennion - Bishop of Bath and Wells - attended the patronal festival. He tried to make his sermon hopeful ... 'Pray for him and do your best to further his work' ... Shortly before the evening service a War Office telegram was received regretting that Rev. C. E. Doudney had died of his wounds at 9 p.m. on Saturday 16th October, 1915.
>
> ... To warn the congregation, the service bell was tolled slowly. The hymns and the remainder of the service were hastily changed and re-arranged and the 'Nunc Dimittis' (Now lettest thou thy servant depart in Peace) was moved to the end. It

had been the intention of the late Vicar to preach at this service, but it fell to the lot of a retired clergyman, Canon Lamb ... to read the telegram to the congregation: no regular member of the church would have trusted himself to read it without breaking down. 'It was with great difficulty that clergy and choir overcome by their feelings, were able to carry through.'

Not alone in the Parish of St. Luke's but throughout every Parish in the city; not alone in the Anglican community but equally in non-conformist circles an overwhelming sense of loss was felt to the religious life of Bath. The appalling losses of brave men in this appalling war, so terribly frequent in their sequence, have, perhaps, rather dulled the public sense of due appreciation of the value of gallant lives laid down on the battle fields of Europe. When lives are sacrificed in hundreds of thousands the edge of public conception of the value of individual lives is apt to become blunted. Yet there are tidings of individual losses which stir within the public generally poignant feelings of deep sorrow and regret ...

Zoe went to London to stay for a few days with her sister Sashie, Mrs. Ashton Bullock. As if she had not enough to bear, it was found that two of the children had contracted scarlet fever. On 21st October, Zoe wrote an open letter to all her friends in the parish.

10 Albion Street,
Hyde Park West.

Oct. 21.1915.

Dear Ones,

Let me first say - that I think there is not the slightest risk of infection. The children were isolated the moment the trained nurse came on Saturday and directly I had handed everything over to her. I changed all my clothes, and when I came up here on Sunday by the midnight train I brought nothing that had been in contact with them and this is absolutely fresh paper from the stores, and as the various doctors all said that as the rash only appeared on Baby on Fri. and on Essie on Sat - there would be scarcely any risk if any at all. Of course they said it would be criminal to go over to France in to a Hospital where men were lying wounded, which I know of course ... He had one of the finest surgeons in the world to overlook him - Sir Anthony Boulby - & the operation for extracting the piece of shrapnel (which pierced only one layer of the bowel) was performed by a brilliant Scotch surgeon ... On Friday he was going on as well as could be expected and that went on until Saturday, when he became suddenly worse at about 6.30 p.m. & he passed into Everlasting Life at 9 p.m.

A proper memorial service conducted by the Bishop will be held on Sunday morning at St. Luke's - I hope God will give me strength to go ...

9 - The Final Days

A worker at the daughter church of St. Philip's, Odd Down, writes an appreciation of the late vicar in the following extract from the *Bath and Wilts Chronicle* of 26th October, 1915.

> - then the news arrived that he had been slightly wounded, news which we did not take seriously, almost the reverse. We all felt that he himself would be proud of a scar received on active service for his King and Country ...
>
> For we not only lose a Vicar but a friend, a guide, a leader, who was intensely interested in this part of his parish, and to whose influence, work and energy Odd Down owes so much. Never before as during this short (all too short) time of about eight years, has so much been done, socially and religiously, for those who needed shepherding ...
>
> Our splendid institute stands today as a memorial to his untiring effort, also our church which has been almost entirely renewed. To this we might add the acquisition of land for, and the re-building of the Day Schools, the building of a new house for the schoolmaster out of his own private funds; and so we might go on ... Generous he was almost to a failing, no wonder therefore, that he achieved so much during his Vicariat.

Three weeks later, a meeting was convened at the Bath Guildhall in order to discuss funding a memorial to the late vicar. According to the Bishop, Mr. Doudney was the first beneficed clergyman to fall in the war and, if he had lived, he might have become a Prebendary of Wells. It was decided that the focus of the memorial fund would be to pay off the debt of some £3,000 which was still outstanding on the three building projects instigated by the late vicar. These included the completion of the church, the enlargement of the schools and the erection of the parochial institute at Odd Down. Each of these three buildings now bear a commemorative tablet dedicated to the work of Charles Doudney's life.

When a successor to fill the now-vacant clerical position was considered, thought turned naturally to the Rev. H. W. Doudney, the late vicar's brother. Herbert Doudney, however, was hesitant to follow in Charlie's shadow. Throughout his life, Herbert had followed his brother from school to college, from college to curacy, from England to Australia and back again to England. Also, as Rector of Shellingford in Berkshire, he was receiving £400 a year, whereas St. Luke's was only valued at around £330. In all, the job must have offered few attractions. In the end, however, he accepted as another of God's commands the invitation to be Vicar of St. Luke's, an appointment well received by the parish. Herbert was to remain at St. Luke's until June 1921, at which time he returned to Australia with his wife and family, and took over a parish in Melbourne.

Meanwhile, Zoe had been left homeless and nearly penniless, with three young children to bring up. Apart from her war pension, which amounted to about £80 per annum, she had only two very small investments left to her by her grandparents, which brought in about £200 a year. Also, due to the scarlet fever outbreak which started on 15th October 1915, it wasn't until January 1916 that the family moved out of the Vicarage and took rooms down in the centre of Bath. After a time they moved to Old Headington, near Oxford, and rented an old cottage for £25 per year. Zoe somehow managed to keep a maid, Edie Porter, at 10/- a week plus her uniform.

During the early 1920s the family moved from place to place, including St. Minver, North Cornwall, Clevedon and Hampstead. Zoe's situation continued to be fraught with financial problems. Apart from occasional help from her brother-in-law, Ashton Bullock, money continued to be scarce, certainly at least until all her children were old enough to earn livings.

Zoe lived until 1958, when she died at Beckenham in Kent at the age of 81.

CHARLES EDMUND DOUDNEY

OBITUARIES AND LETTERS OF SYMPATHY

Within five days of Charlie's death, Zoe had received over 200 letters of condolence. They ranged from the formal telegram received from Their Majesties to letters from private soldiers, parishioners and friends. These alone stand as a tribute to the life of Charles Edmund Doudney.

Telegram to Zoe from Their Majesties, King George V and Queen Mary:

O.H.M.S Buckingham Palace.

19th October, 1915.

The King and Queen deeply regret the loss you and the Army have sustained by the death of your Husband in the Service of his Country.

Their Majesties truly sympathise with you in your sorrow.

Keeper of the Privy Purse.

Letter from the Chaplain General to the Forces:

War Office,

20th October 1915.

My Dear Mrs. Doudney,

These few lines are just to express my deep sympathy with you in the great loss that you have sustained.

Your dear Husband, beloved by all who knew him, has been the intermediate service, of which this life is only the beginning, and given quick promotion.

I shall never forget the Bishop of Bath and Wells' remark, when your Husband was appointed. He said, 'You have one of the best Chaplains in the Army in ......'

Believe me,

Yours sincerely,

J. Taylor Smith

Obituaries and Letters of Sympathy

Letter from the Major General commanding 6th Division:

Head Quarters,
6th Division,

20th October, 1915.

Dear Mrs. Doudney,

I hope you will excuse my writing to tell you how deeply I and my staff sympathise with you in the death of your husband whilst serving with my Division. On all hands I hear nothing but praise of his unselfish hard work and of his popularity with officers and men. We all feel we have lost a friend and a good man. I fear words can be of little use to you now, but I felt I must write to offer our sympathy and to tell you of our regret.

Yours sincerely,

W. N. Congreve. Major General.

Letter from the Senior Chaplain, 6th Division:

17th October, 1915.

Dear Mrs. Doudney,

A telegram from Archdeacon Southwell has just reached me giving me the - to me and to all who knew and loved him - sad news that God has taken to himself the soul of your dear husband. I know that dear Doudney would not have you sorrow over much for him, for he is at rest. A truer and more loyal colleague no man ever could wish for. His whole heart was in his work, and he would give himself no rest. If WE had learned to love and value him so much after our too short acquaintance with him - how great must be the loss to YOU and to his congregation of whom he frequently spoke to me.

God who spared not His own Dear Son for the sake of others, has called upon you to make the Great Sacrifice.

Dear Doudney passed away last night (Saturday) at 9 o'clock.

May God bless and strengthen and be with you now and always.

I am, Yours sincerely,

Tudor Moreton

A second letter from the Senior Chaplain, sent after the funeral:

18th October, 1915.

Dear Mrs. Doudney,

We laid to rest at 9.15 this morning all that was mortal to your good and dear husband in the little cemetery attached to No. 10 Casualty Clearing Station situated by the side of the railway between Abeele and Poperinghe ...

The service was taken by Archdeacon Southwell, Canon Macnutt, and myself.

Dear Doudney, I am sure, had a prevision, as, just as he was leaving to go up to Ypres before receiving his wound, he turned to the other Chaplains and said 'Remember: if anything happens it is for the best'.

He was buried on St. Luke's Day.

I am sending back your letter which arrived today. I was able to see and have a good talk with Capt. Poulden *(Charlie's brother-in-law)*. I am writing to the Bishop of Bath and Wells.

I am,

Sincerely yours,

Tudor Moreton. Chaplains' Farm.

The Bath and Wilts. Chronicle, 25th October 1915, reproduced the comments given by the Rev. Tudor Moreton, Senior Chaplain, to the Forces of the 6th Division.

I cannot express to you the sense of loss that I and all the Chaplains associated with him in the work in the 6th Division experience in his departure from our midst. To me, he was a loyal and trusted colleague, upon whose judgment I could always rely. To the other younger Chaplains he was as an elder brother, yet ever with the heart of a child. Always ready to undertake the lion's share of the work; I blamed myself at times for expecting so much of him; he never spared himself in the execution of it. His wide and varied experience, his kind and sympathetic nature, his tact in dealing with all sorts and conditions of men, made him an invaluable help to me. He had the love and respect of both officers and men with whom he came in contact. I had recommended him for mention in dispatches and the Military Cross for his good work. Of course that lies with the higher authorities whether or no they will give effect to my recommendation.

Obituaries and Letters of Sympathy

Letter from the pall-bearers:

20th October 1915.

Dear Mrs. Doudney,

We, the undersigned, beg to offer you our deepest sympathy and condolence with regard to your recent bereavement.

In our capacity as ambulance orderlies, we were with Mr. Doudney at the time he was wounded and we would like you to know that he bore his wound with wonderful fortitude, considering the seriousness of the injury.

After the shelling had somewhat subsided, we put him into the ambulance, and he remarked, 'Don't mind me lads, go on as fast as you like'. We mention this incident to show that even in his hour of trial his consideration for others did not fail.

We attended the funeral as pall-bearers, with the exception of Pte. Birch, who was slightly wounded by the same shell, and is now home on leave.

We voice the regret of the whole of the ambulance on losing a much-loved Chaplain.

The news must have been a great shock to you, but please be comforted with the knowledge that Mr. Doudney met his death whilst performing a great and noble duty.

We are,

Yours sincerely;

L. Corp Wilkinson,
Pte. R. Mooney.
   " E. Spedding.
   " T. Birch

18th Field Ambulance,
B.E.F.

Obituaries and Letters of Sympathy

Letter from the Military Police:

1089. Cpl. R.W.R. Bond,
Military Police,
Att. 11th Kings Liverpool Regt., B.E.F.

21st October 1915.

Dear Madam,

We the members of the Military Police who are stationed at the place where your dear husband was wounded, and since died of his wounds, tender our deepest sympathy to you and your family in your great loss. Your dear husband was the means of getting a party of us ready for Confirmation for which we owe an allegiance to our dead comrade. He is greatly missed among us all - a brave and plucky gentleman. We will do our best to get to your dear husband's resting place, and do our best to make it up properly. While I am writing these few lines I must thank you for the copies of the C.F.N. which I distribute among my comrades, who find a very healthy bit of literature very acceptable in this awful place. Again tendering our deepest sympathy to you and family in your sad bereavement.

Believe me, Madam,
I am, Yours sincerely,

W.R.W. Bond

Three letters from colleagues known through the No. 8 General Hospital, Rouen:

No. 8 General Hospital,
Rouen.

20th October, 1915.

Dear Mrs. Doudney,

As officer commanding No.8 General Hospital, I enclose an expression of the very great sorrow your husband's death has caused us.

Yours very sincerely,

C. B. Lawson.

Obituaries and Letters of Sympathy

No. 8 General Hospital, Rouen.

7th November, 1915.

Dear Mrs. Doudney,

You will excuse me writing you, for what I am going to ask of you as a favour. It was a great blow to us at No. 8 here to hear of the sad news of your dear husband's death from wounds. I will always remember him for the great interest he took in my work in the Bacteriologist laboratories here. Even he was interested in all the microbes I could exhibit under the microscope.

How he used to cheer us all up here with his ever increasing games. So much did I admire him that it would be a great honour to a person otherwise a friend of his to have a snapshot of him just as a reminder of him in after years. You can take it from me that it would be cherished. You will excuse me asking this from you, if it is not too much.

Asking you to accept my sincere sympathy in your bereavement, and that from one who admired our Padre so much.

I am, Yours sincerely,

John L. Annan,
Lieut. R.A.M.C. Bacteriologist.

FRANCE - To Mrs. C.E. Doudney,

30th October, 1915.

Dear Madam,

I cannot give expression on your sad bereavement. I first met Mr. Doudney at Rouen Hospital. I had the honour to be X-rayed by him, and he greatly cheered me. He will be greatly missed by all of us. He was loved by every one that came in contact with him. I had great hopes of seeing him. Last week we received a letter from him asking if we were not too far away, so that he could pay us a visit.

Dear Madam, Mr. Doudney was a grand man, and we have lost one of the best.

Yours sincerely,

A. C. Cairncross.
(D. Coy. 3rd K.R.R.C., Rhodesian Platoon.)

Obituaries and Letters of Sympathy

Letters from fellow chaplains at the front:

Headquarters,
14th Division.

18th October, 1915.

Dear Mrs. Doudney,

Please forgive me for intruding in your grief at this moment, for nothing I can say in sympathy can soften the blow to you and your children, but I have lost the best man friend I have ever had, in your husband, and as we stood by the grave this morning in the cold October fog it seemed as if some thing was wrong with things. He was so splendid a Chaplain, and I know of no one so universally beloved by officers and men. I have learned a great deal about his work at St. Luke's for we spoke with open hearts together, and to know that all his fine work was cut off when so many years lay before him of usefulness and power, it seems wrong. But then I saw back to his patient old smile that always seemed to buck one up. 'It's all part of God's plan' he would say, and even on Saturday morning when I saw him, the same smile shone through his agony, and I knew that things were right. It may comfort you to know that always his thoughts were for others. Even when he was wounded he didn't want to be a bother to anyone, whereas tommies and everybody were only too glad to do anything for him at any time. We all think of you to-day with deep sympathy and may God smooth out the sorrow with His own hand.

Yours very sincerely,

John C. Kinnear (Chaplain)

18th October, 1915.

Dear Mrs. Doudney,

As one who had the very deepest affection for your husband may I express to you my sincerest sympathy for you and his children in this time of great sorrow. I cannot tell you what a help his cheery and loving nature has been to me personally - and I am sure there are scores of men out here to-day who would say exactly the same thing. Here, in our Chaplains' Mess, he was 'Daddy' - and now things can never be the same again. If it is not asking too much I should like something to remember him by however small - but please do not trouble about it NOW - and some day I should so much like to copy the two small sketches he

Obituaries and Letters of Sympathy

enclosed in one of his letters to you.

We shall pray that you may realise to the full that 'underneath are the everlasting Arms'.

Yours sincerely,

Frederic Northop (Chaplain)

3rd Bn. Rifle Brigade, B.E.F.

21st October, 1915.

Dear Mrs. Doudney,

Will you let me intrude on your sorrow with a few words about your husband. He has been such a father to us younger chaplains in the 6th Division during the last three months and at the time he was as young in spirit as any of us. It was always a pleasure to me who lived with a Brigade to ride round and see him, especially at the Padre's billet and we had great fun there whether in fast and furious theological discussion or in games or chaff - the gaiety of it all springing out of a great unity in the Spirit. I know, also, from conversations with stray officers how he was endearing himself to the troops he was serving.

I saw him on the day of the evening on which he was hit - he said as we parted that he would come over and see me (for my Brigade has moved to another Division). I went also and saw him as he lay in Hospital at Poperinghe. It was on the Friday morning after the operation on Thursday night. He was a good deal changed and very drowsy with morphia. He knew me though, and pressed my hand v. especially, and called me Gigas as he used to do owing to my height. I told him that he had all our love and prayers, and he said 'I know I have'. And so we parted, I hardly expecting to see him again. My Brigade moved and when I got over again on Monday morning I heard of his death. I stood by his grave (I was too late for the funeral) and said truly fraternal prayers for him to our Common Brother and Lord, and asked for his prayers.

So he has passed on - laying down - losing his life, yet surely finding in the losing. Yours - ours is the loss. May unbroken confidence in the Love of God sustain you.

Yours sincerely,

N. S. Talbot (Chaplain)

c/o 1st Leicesters,
16th Inf. Bde. B.E.F.

19th October, 1915.

Dear Mrs. Doudney,

It is difficult for us to try and express the very deep sympathy we feel for you and your children in your awful loss. I can assure you that you have been in our thoughts and prayers these days. We all learned to love your dear husband, and it was a very great shock to me to learn when I returned from 'leave' last Sunday, that I should not see him again on this earth.

There is no need for me to say anything more at present, but I feel that I have lost one of the most loveable, and delightful, friends that I have ever had in life. So naturally my whole heart goes out in sympathy to the one who has lost SUCH a husband and to the dear children who have lost SUCH a Daddy.

That God bless you and yours and grant him eternal rest and peace will always be my prayer.

Yours faithfully,

S. M. Wheeler (Chaplain)
(Sunny Jim)

Extract from the *Bath and Wilts. Chronicle,* 25th October 1915. The Right Rev. Dr. Harmer, Bishop of Rochester, previously Bishop of Adelaide (on hearing of Charlie's death):

Of all the clergy who were drawn out from England for service in the Diocese of Adelaide during my time, no one made a deeper impression or exercised a wider influence for good. His manly character, with his varied gifts, enforced the spiritual lessons which he knew so well how to deliver. He won his way to the hearts of all by the charm and the force of his personality. I sympathise very much with the sad loss which the Diocese of Bath and Wells has sustained. To me it is a great personal loss, for I counted Charles Doudney as one of my closest friends.

Keenes Bath Journal, 30th October, 1915, the Ven. Archdeacon of Bath, Preb. Fish:

... He enjoyed to an unwonted degree the confidence of clergymen and laymen alike. That was partly accounted for by the breadth of his sympathies and the varieties of his interests. No person, except perhaps Charles Kingsley, ever touched life at so many points. He was keenly interested in all the manly intellectual pursuits; and to that width of sympathy in things human, he brought a most astonishing cheeriness of heart and manner. No doubt that buoyancy of spirit was largely inherent; but I suspect that it was developed by his experiences in those remote Australian settlements. At any rate he never entered the most sedate assemblies without seeming to bring with him a breath of that free, open and unconventional breeziness ... That optimism, that hopeful outlook on the universe never failed. During his last leave, when he came up to see me, he told me of his work at the front and its dangers. But seeing how deeply I was impressed with the perils to which he was so shortly returning, he said: 'My dear Archdeacon, don't you worry about me', and he went on to say what I know he also said to someone else - 'Don't pray for my safety, but pray rather that I may be given the physical courage to do my duty under fire'. And then he just leapt on his cycle, and was off, looking back however to throw me a smile whose radiancy will brighten my heart to my dying day ...

... And now he is gone. Is he? I recall one memorable evening I passed in his study. He first tuned the receiver of what is wrongly called wireless telegraphy, and then handed it to me, and told me to listen to the calls all over England and from the North Sea and even from Germany. Then he took the receiver himself, noted the message, decoded it and told me what they were saying. You will remember what use he made in the pulpit of that fascinating hobby of his. Those lectures which he called parables of science now seem to us to have been almost prophetic. He showed us how it was all a picture of how we can communicate with the unseen God, and our unseen loved ones, if only our spirits were in tune with theirs. He has passed into the unseen, but by prayer and communion of spirit ... we can still be in touch with him and he with us ... No he is not gone. It is only his bodily presence that has withdrawn from his earthly sphere of work. God removed the workman but carried on the work ...

Extract from the *Bath and Wilts. Chronicle,* 25th October 1915, the Rev. A. Chisholm, Curate of St. Luke's:

It is impossible at present to realise what the loss of our dear Vicar means to us, individually and as a congregation. To me personally he was everything, truest of friends, kindest of Vicars. To us as a congregation he was the very centre of our life. And we are stunned by the blow. No one but himself could have kept together and moulded into one a congregation so diverse and of such differing opinions as our own. But by his wonderful personality his broad mindedness, his sympathy, his deep spirituality, he achieved the seemingly impossible. 'You are so united at St. Luke's' has been remarked to me frequently during the past six months and that blessing we owe to him who has been taken from us. The letters which have come from the front in a regular stream from officers, chaplains and men alike, all testify to the wonderful influence he exercised out there. Such letters do not surprise us who knew him. They state just what we expected

Obituaries and Letters of Sympathy

to hear about him and we should have been surprised had we not received them.

An anecdote revealing Charlie's characteristic pastoral enthusiasm; source not given, typed from Edith Doudney's Album:

Just about a year ago in an avenue in Mr. Doudney's parish I chanced one day upon the late Vicar. He was pushing a heavily laden hand-barrow whereon was a great variety of articles. At my greeting, he halted and in response to confessedly surprised enquiry concerning the business on hand, cheerily informed me that he was on a collecting expedition gathering in blankets and other comforts 'for the boys at the Front'. Aiding him in this labour of love were several girl guides who, collecting promised articles, dumped them on the aforesaid barrow, and I was persuaded that as the load got heavier the Vicar's heart grew lighter. It was, I think, the most inspiring incident in ministerial work I have ever happened upon. Such a man was it who, sacrificing all, now rests in a soldier's grave in France, leaving behind him the fragrant memory of one who was, if I may be forgiven the colloquialism, 'the best of good fellows'.

The War Office (A.G.10)
27, Pilgrim Street,
London, E.C.4
16th May 1923

Madam,

I am directed to transmit to you the accompanying "1914-15 Star, British War & Victory Medals" which would have been conferred upon The Reverend C. E. Doudney, had he lived, in memory of his services with the British Forces during the Great War.

In forwarding the Decorations I am commanded by the King to assure you of His Majesty's high appreciation of the services rendered.

I am to request that you will be so good as to acknowledge the receipt of the Decorations on the attached form.

I am Madam,
Your obedient Servant,

Mrs C. E. Doudney.

R. Whigham
Adjutant General

INDEX

Page numbers in bold typeface denote illustrations.

A

Abeele, 173.
Aborigine, 25, 29, **45**
Adelaide, 25, 46, 58, 59, 189,
- Bishop of, see 'Harmer',
- Rifle Club, **58**.
- University eight, 58
Ainslie, Brigadier-General, H.S.,129, 155.
Annan, Lt. John (R.A.M.C.), 115, 186.
Armentières, 123.
Armstrong, Lt. (R.A.M.C.), 166.
Army Service Corps, 99,124.
Asquith, Prime Minister, 89.
Athletes Volunteer Force, **103**, 104.
Austria, 91-92.
Australia, South, 25-60.
Austro-Serbian War, 85, 87, 89.
Automobile Association, 86, 87.

B

Bacteriology, 115, 186.
Barcowie, 36, 42-45.
Bath and West Chronicle, 78.
Bath and Wilts Chronicle, 107-150, 159-169, 178, 183, 189, 190.
Bath Chronicle, 25, 78, 81, 85, 87-105, 176.
Bath Journal, 151, 153.
Bath and Wells - Bishop of, see 'Dr. Kennion'.
Bath Volunteers, 103, 104.
Belgian refugees, 99, 100-105.
Belgian troops, 123, 146.
Birch Pte. (R.A.M.C.), 184.
Bisley, 58, 67.
Boisguillaume, 108.

Bond, Cpl. R.W.R (Military Police), 185.
Boulby, Sir Anthony (Surgeon), 177
Boy Scouts, 157.
Brigade, 18th Inf., 8, 123, 124, 126, 140, 147, 155, 160, 167.
Buchanen-Dunlop, Lt. Col., 158, 170.
Bullock, Ashton **19**, 21, **22**, **23**, 94-97, 179, Back Cover.
Bullock, Mrs. ('Sashie'), see 'Poulden, Esther'.
Byfield, The misses, 101.

C

Cambridge Volunteers, 13, **14**.
Canadian, 109, 113-115.
Canal (Bank), 127, 133, 134, 145, 147.
Caincross, A.P. (D. Coy, 3rd K.R.R.C. Rhodesian Platoon), 186.
Carlisle, Bishop of, 13.
Casualty Clearing Station, (No. 10), See hospitals.
Censor, see Macnaughton, Lt.
Chadwick, Miss Connie, 67, 101, **150**, 157.
Chaplains, Army, 154, 155.
Chaplain-General, see Taylor Smith, Bishop.
Chisolm, Rev. A. ('Chizzy'), 66, **150**, 157, 169, 190.
Christchurch, N. Adelaide, 58.
Church Lads Brigade, **157**.
Church Times, 25.
Clarke, Lt. Col. J.L.J., 129.
Clayton, Rev. Tubby, 2, 7, 8, 145.
Cloth Hall, **132**, **141**, 143.
Commonwealth, 52.
Congreve, Major Gen. W.H., V.C., 126, 127, 135, 140, 147, 168, 182.

Coronation Medal-1902, **58**.
Corps Alpine, 98.
Corpus Christi Coll., Cambridge, 13, **16**.
Coutoue, Château de, 126.

D

Defence Rifle Club
- Port Augusta, 57-58.
- Wilmington, 57.
De Grey, Nigel, 82.
Division, 6th, 8, 123, 126, **165**, 166, 168.
Division, 14th, 187.
Doudney, Alfred Cecil, 13, **14**.
Doudney, Rev. Charles Edmund, **2**.
- Birth, 13.
- Education, 13, **14-16**.
- Curacy, 13, 21, **17**, **22**, **23**.
- Missionary work, South Australia, 25-60.
- Courtship, 46-50.
- Rector, Port Augusta, 50-58, **50**.
- Married, 50.
- Chaplain to the Commonwealth Troops (South Australia), 58.
- Acting Curate, Christchurch (North Adelaide), 58, **58**.
- Rector of St. George's Church, Gawler, 58-60.
- Vicar of St. Luke's, Bath, 63-82, **64-66**, **69**.
- Trip to India, 72-78.
- European trip (July-Sept. 1914), 85-102.
- Home Front, 103-105.
-Chaplain to the Forces, 107-178, **106**, **150**.
- Grave, **175**.
- Memorial fund, 178.
- Obituraies, 181-192.

193

Index

Doudney, Rev. David Alfred (1811-1893), 12, **15**.
Doudney, Rev. David Alfred (1837-1912), 13, **14**, **15**, 72.
Doudney, Désirée Gawler ('Ba'-Mrs. Peter Warcup), 9, 72, 101, 177.
Doudney, Edith Mary (Mrs. Victor Gollmick), 8, **14**, 141, 191.
Doudney, Esther Eirene (Mrs. W. Scaife), 50, **51**, 60, 63, **65**, **67**, **71**, 79, 80, 177.
Doudney, Rev. Herbert, **14**, 39, 67, 70, **71**, 72, 80, 101, **150**, 178.
Doudney, Joy Poulden (Mrs. Kenneth Horne), 9, 59, 63, **65, 68, 69,** 72, 111, 112, 116-122, 162.
Doudney, Noelle Mary, 59, 63.
Doudney, Raymond Pelly, **14**, 67, 70, **71**, 72, 86, 103, 104, **150**.
Durham Light Infantry, 2nd Battalion, 123, 129, 145, 160, 166.

E

East Yorkshire Regiment, 1st Battalion, 123, 129, 130, 140, 160, 164, 166.
Eirene (Mission to seaman ship), 78.
Electricity, 72.

F

Field Ambulance, 18th, 8, 125, 126, 129, 137, 138, 139, **139**, 155, 160, **161**, 172, 173, 184, see also 'Hop Store'.
Formidable, H.M.T.S., **20**, 21, 70.
France, 87-89, 97-100.
French, Archdeacon, 52-56.
Fry, Elizabeth, 13.
Fry, Georgina (Mrs. David Alfred Doudney), 13, **14**.

Fylton - nr. Bristol, 20.

G

Ganley, Driver, 173.
Gas, 109, 123.
Gawler, Katherine (Mrs. Edward Poulden), **20**, 21, 46-48.
Gawler, Lt. Col. George (Second Governor of South Australia), 21, 59.
Gawler, Aunt Jane, 47, 49, 52.
Gawler (South Australia), 58, 59.
Germany, 89, 90.
German Cavalry, 100.
Gollmick, Mrs Victor, see Doudney, Edith Mary.
Gollmick, Miss Ivy (Daughter of Edith Doudney), 9, 172.
Girl Guides, 67, 101, 157, 191.
Gospel Magazine, 12.
Gregory, Mr., 86.

H

Harding, Mr. Herbert, 97.
Harding, Mrs., **65**.
Harmer, The Right Rev. Dr. (Bishop of Rochester, previously Bishop of Adelaide), 13, 21, 189.
Hastings Grammar School, 13.
Hatford, Berks, 72.
Hell Fire Corner, 159.
Homfray, Frank, **19**, 47, 60.
Homfray, Mrs. F., see 'Poulden, Mary'.
Hooge, 160.
Hooge, Battle of (Chapter 6), 174.
Hop Store, 8, 129, 130, 139, **139**, 140, 145, 146, 155, 160, **163**.
Hop Store Cemetery, **163**.
Hospitals
- Mineral Water, 102.
- Royal United, 102.
- No.8 Base, Rouen, Ch.4, 185, 186.
- No.10, Casualty Clearing, 173-176, 183.
- Barts. (St. Bartholomew's), 21.
- Ship, 72-78.
Hummocks, The, 30.
Hussars, 20th, 99.

I

Industrial Training Ship for Homeless and Destitute Boys, **20**, 21.
Italian mobilization of troops, 97.

J

Jew, 113.

K

Keenes Bath Journal, 154, 172, 174, 189.
Kennedy, Studdert, 7, 8.
Kennion, Dr. (Bishop of Bath and Wells), 82, 105, 176, 178, 181.
Kinnear, Rev. J.C. (Chaplain), 145, 149, 150, 176, 187.
King's Liverpool Reg't., 11th, 185.
King George V & Queen Mary, 181.
K.R.R.C., 3rd (Rhodesian Platoon), 186.
Kurhaus Hotel, Terasp, 85, 93-96.

L

Lamb, Canon, 177.
Lawson, C.B. (R.A.M.C.), 185.
Leicestershire Regiment, 158, 170, 189.
Life Guards, 1st., 114.
Liquid Fire, 160.
Lijssenthoek - British Military Cemetery, 174, **175**, 176.

Index

London Rifle Brigade, 114.
La Louie Convent, **126**.
La Louie Château, 126.
Lundy Island, 78.
Lyons, 98, 99.

M

Macnutt, Canon F.B. 6, 174, 183.
Macnaughton, Lt., R.A.M.C., 110, 111, 116-122.
Maple Copse, 160, **161**.
Medic, S.S. **61**, **62**, 63.
Methodist, School, 60.
Military Police, 185.
Mooney, Pte. R. (R.A.M.C.), 184.
Moreton, Tudor (Senior Chaplain, 6th Division), 182, 183.
Motor Machine Gun Corps, 145, 146, 156, **156**.
Mount Remarkable, 25.
Mourmelon (French Flying Centre), 88.

N

Naval Intelligence - 40 O.B., 82.
Nonconformist, 155.
Northop, Frederick (Chaplain), 187, 188.
Nurses - Army, 74, 77, 108, 113.

O

Odd Down, 64, 66, 67, 178.
Ore, 13.
Orroroo Mission, **24**, 25, 27, 39.

P

Paris, 99.

Penge, 21.
Plaint, Mr., **16**.
Plassey, H.M.T., 72-78, **73**, **74**, 108.
Plumer, General Sir H., 164.
Poperinghe, 134, 145, **158**.
- Railway Station, 144.
Port Augusta, 26, 39, 50, 52, 56, 57.
Porter, Edie, 179.
Port Germain, 52, 55, 56.
Potyze, Château, 8, 130, **136**, 137, 138, 147, 167.
Poulden, Capt. Edward, R.N., **19**, 20, **20**, 46-49, 70.
Poulden, Edward (Son of Luther), 9, 83.
Poulden, Esther ('Sashie'-Mrs. Ashton Bullock), **19**, 21, **22**, **23**, 46, 93-97, 151, 177.
Poulden, George Edward (Luther), Capt. Royal Engineers, **19**, 124, 174.
Poulden, Joanna ('Zoe'- Mrs. Charles Doudney), 9.
- Birth, **19**, 21.
- Courtship, **22**, **23**, 46-50.
- Marriage, 50.
- Port Augusta, **50**, **51**, 50-58.
- Gawler, 58-60.
- Bath, 63-72, **64**, **65**.
- European trip (July/Sept. 1914), 85-102, **150**.
- Letter from the Front, 171.
- Widowed, 176-179.
Poulden, Lydia (Arly), **19**, 47, 48, **70**.
Poulden, Mary (Mrs. Frank Homfray), **19**, 47, 48, 52, 56, 59, 60, 85, 88, 93, 95, 96.
Poulden, Rhoda (Popsy), **19**.
Preston King, Dr. and Mrs., 86, 151.
Provost Marshal, 140, 146.

Q

Queen's Westminster Rifles, T.A., 123, 133, 134, 160, 171.

R

R.A.M.C., see Field Ambulance (18th).
Ramparts, 160.
Ridley Hall, 13.
Rochester, Bishop of, see 'Harmer'.
Roman Catholic, 76, 122, 147, 155.
- Women's League, 102.
Rouen, see Base Hospital.
Royal Engineers, 99, 124.
Rush Hill School, 66, 178.

S

St. Augustine's, Port Augusta, **50**.
St. George's, Gawler, 58.
St. Jean, 147, **148**, 149, 164, 167.
St. James's, Carlisle, 13.
St. John the Evangelist, Penge, 13, 21.
St. Luke's, Bedminster, Bristol, 13.
St. Luke's South Lynecombe, Bath, 7, 63-72, **80**, 151, 178-179.
- Coronation Fete, 67, **68**.
- Foundation stone, 65, **66**.
- Rebuilding, **64**, **65**.
- Vicarage, **63**.
St. Matthew's Surbiton, 6, 174.
St. Philip's Odd Down 153, 178.
Samedan, 95-97.
Sanctuary Wood, 160.
- Cemetery, 160.
Satty, Mr. A.R., 66.
Serbia, 85, 87.
Shaw, Rev. Vernon, 66.
Shellingford, Berkshire, 178.
Sherwood Foresters, 2nd Battalion (Notts./Derby Regiment), 123, 126, 140, 147, 160, 166.

195

Index

Smith, Pte. Thomas, 103.
Smyly, Rev. W., 13, **17**.
Somersetshire County Volunteer Regiment, 2nd Bn., **103**, 104.
Somersetshire Regiment, 4th, 105.
Spedding, Pte. E. (R.A.M.C.), 173, 184.
Southwell (Archdeacon of Lewis), 174, 183.
Spencer Gulf, 26, 53-56.
Stanwix, 13, **14**.
Suicide Corner, see 'Hell Fire Corner'.
Switzerland, 90, 92-97.
- Troop mobilization, 96-97.

T

Talbot, Gilbert Lt., 7, 8, 145, 159, 160.
Talbot House, 7, 8, 145, 160.
Talbot, Neville (Chaplain), 8, 129, 145, 159, 160, 188.
Tarcoola, 26, 57, 58.
Taylor-Smith, Bishop (Chaplain-General), 7, 105, 107, 181.
Tennyson, Lord (Governor of South Australia), 52.
Territorials, 101.
Thorold, Sister, 174.
Toc H, 7, 145.
Troopship to India, 72-78.

V

V- (Chaplain), 126, 127, 129, 130, 133-135, 140, 143, 146, 147, 166, 168.
Velorenhoek Road, 167.
Vlamertinghe, 8, 129, **134**, 135, **139**, see also Hop Store.
- Château, **165**, 166, 168.

W

Waller, E.H.M., **16**.
Warrimo, 30.
War declared, 93, 94.
Waterford Cathedral, 13.
Wesleyan, 135.
West, Rev. Arthur, 30, 39, 85, 87, 89, 94-97.
West, Miss, 85, 87, 89, 94, 95 97.
West Yorkshire Regiment, 1st Battalion, 123, 126, 140, 160.
Wheeler, Rev. S.M. (Chaplain), 171, 189.
White Comrade, The, 152.
Wieltje, 147, 167.
Wilkinson, Corporal (R.A.M.C.), 173, 184.
Wippehoek, 125.
Wireless telegraphy, 78-83, **79**, **81**, 190.
Woodbine Willy, 7.

X

X-ray plant, 109, 110.

Y

Y.M.C.A., 122, 154.
Ypres, 123, 126, 127, 130, 132, **132**, 133, 140, 143, 146, 150, 154, 164, **170**, 173.
- 2nd Battle of, 123.
- Cathedral, 130, **132**, 133, **141**, **142**, 143, 154, Front cover.
Yanyarrie, 48.
Yarrowie, 31, 32.
Yatina, 32-34.

Z

Zouave Wood, 160.